Refiguring
ENGLISH
STUDIES

Refiguring English Stu~ ___ ___ ___ ___ ___ scholarship on English studies as a discipline, a profession, and a vocation. To that end, the series publishes historical work that considers the ways in which English studies has constructed itself and its objects of study; investigations of the relationships among its constituent parts as conceived in both disciplinary and institutional terms; and examinations of the role the discipline has played or should play in the larger society and public policy. In addition, the series seeks to feature studies that, by their form or focus, challenge our notions about how the written "work" of English can or should be done and to feature writings that represent the professional lives of the discipline's members in both traditional and nontraditional settings. The series also includes scholarship that considers the discipline's possible futures or that draws upon work in other disciplines to shed light on developments in English studies.

Volumes in the Series

Laurie Grobman, *Multicultural Hybridity: Transforming American Literary Scholarship and Pedagogy* (2007)

Bruce McComiskey, editor, *English Studies: An Introduction to the Discipline(s)* (2006)

Ray Misson and Wendy Morgan, *Critical Literacy and the Aesthetic: Transforming the English Classroom* (2006)

Linda S. Bergmann and Edith M. Baker, editors, *Composition and/ or Literature: The End(s) of Education* (2006)

Shari J. Stenberg, *Professing and Pedagogy: Learning the Teaching of English* (2005)

Robert P. Yagelski and Scott A. Leonard, editors, *The Relevance of English: Teaching That Matters in Students' Lives* (2002)

Chris W. Gallagher, *Radical Departures: Composition and Progressive Pedagogy* (2002)

Derek Owens, *Composition and Sustainability: Teaching for a Threatened Generation* (2001)

Amy Lee, *Composing Critical Pedagogies: Teaching Writing as Revision* (2000)

Anne J. Herrington and Marcia Curtis, *Persons in Process: Four Stories of Writing and Personal Development in College* (2000)

Charles M. Anderson and Marian M. MacCurdy, editors, *Writing and Healing: Toward an Informed Practice* (2000)

Stephen Parks, *Class Politics: The Movement for the Students' Right to Their Own Language* (2000)

Stephen M. North, with Barbara A. Chepaitis, David Coogan, Lâle Davidson, Ron MacLean, Cindy L. Parrish, Jonathan Post, and Beth Weatherby, *Refiguring the Ph.D. in English Studies: Writing, Doctoral Education, and the Fusion-Based Curriculum* (2000)

Bruce Horner and Min-Zhan Lu, *Representing the "Other": Basic Writers and the Teaching of Basic Writing* (1999)

Michael Blitz and C. Mark Hurlbert, *Letters for the Living: Teaching Writing in a Violent Age* (1998)

Jane Maher, *Mina P. Shaughnessy: Her Life and Work* (1997)

Robin Varnum, *Fencing with Words: A History of Writing Instruction at Amherst College during the Era of Theodore Baird, 1938–1966* (1996)

James A. Berlin, *Rhetorics, Poetics, and Cultures: Refiguring College English Studies* (1996)

Jed Rasula, *The American Poetry Wax Museum: Reality Effects, 1940–1990* (1995)

David B. Downing, editor, *Changing Classroom Practices: Resources for Literary and Cultural Studies* (1994)

Deranging English/Education

Teacher Inquiry, Literary Studies,
and Hybrid Visions of "English" for
21st Century Schools

JOHN A. STAUNTON
Eastern Michigan University

National Council of Teachers of English
1111 W. Kenyon Road, Urbana, Illinois 61801-1096

Staff Editor: Bonny Graham
Production Editor: JAS Group
Interior Design: Jenny Jensen Greenleaf
Cover Design: Quemadura

NCTE Stock Number: 10836

It is the policy of NCTE in its journals and other publications to provide a forum for the open discussion of ideas concerning the content and the teaching of English and the language arts. Publicity accorded to any particular point of view does not imply endorsement by the Executive Committee, the Board of Directors, or the membership at large, except in announcements of policy, where such endorsement is clearly specified.

Every effort has been made to provide current URLs and email addresses, but because of the rapidly changing nature of the Web, some sites and addresses may no longer be accessible.

Library of Congress Cataloging-in-Publication Data

Staunton, John A., 1969–
    Deranging English/education : teacher inquiry, literary studies, and hybrid visions of English for 21st century schools / John A. Staunton.
        p. cm. — (Refiguring English studies)
    Includes bibliographical references and index.
    ISBN 978-0-8141-1083-6 (pbk.)
    1. English philology—Study and teaching (Higher)—United States. 2. English literature—Study and teaching (Higher)—United States. 3. Language and culture—United States. 4. Culture—Study and teaching. I. Title.
    PE68 .U5S73 2008
    420.71'173—dc22
                                                            2008016235

For Melissa and Jack, my lovely derangers

. . . pues si conociera, como debo, esto mismo no escribiera
[. . . for if I knew all I should, I would not write.]

—Sor Juana Inés de la Cruz,
La Repuesta a Sor Filotea (1691)

CONTENTS

Permission Acknowledgments

Merman image from *Harper's New Monthly Magazine* reprinted courtesy of Cornell University Library, Making of America Digital Collection.

Excerpt from "Diving into the Wreck." Copyright © by Adrienne Rich. Copyright © 1973 by W. W. Norton & Company, Inc., from THE FACT OF A DOORFRAME: SELECTED POEMS 1950–2001 by Adrienne Rich. Used by permission of the author and W. W. Norton & Company, Inc.

Images of "View on the Ohio," "Education of Nature," and "The Verb 'To Love'—They Love" from *Ladies' Repository* courtesy of University of Michigan, Making of America Digital Collection.

"The Red Wheelbarrow" by William Carlos Williams, from COLLECTED POEMS: 1909–1939, VOLUME 1, copyright © 1938 by New Directions Publishing Corp. Reprinted by permission of New Directions Publishing Corp.

"Stopping by Woods on a Snowy Evening" and excerpt from "The Ax-Helve" from THE POETRY OF ROBERT FROST edited by Edward Connery Lathem. Copyright 1923, 1969 by Henry Holt and Company. Copyright 1951 by Robert Frost. Reprinted by permission of Henry Holt and Company. LLC.

James Wright, "Lying in a Hammock at William Duffy's Farm in Pine Island, Minnesota," from *Collected Poems*, © 1971 by James Wright, and published by Wesleyan University Press. Used by permission.

Permission Acknowledgments

"Harlem (2)", from THE COLLECTED POEMS OF
LANGSTON HUGHES by Langston Hughes, edited by Arnold
Rampersad with David Roessel, Associate Editor, copyright ©
1994 by The Estate of Langston Hughes. Used by permission
of Alfred A. Knopf, a division of Random House, Inc.

Jacopo Zucchi's "The Coral Fishers" reprinted courtesy of the
Superintendency Photo Archive of Artistic and Ethnoanthro-
pological Heritage and the Polo Museum of the City of Rome.

"Thirteen Ways of Looking at a Blackbird", from THE COL-
LECTED POEMS OF WALLACE STEVENS by Wallace
Stevens, copyright 1954 by Wallace Stevens and renewed 1982
by Holly Stevens. Used by permission of Alfred A. Knopf, a
division of Random House, Inc.

ACKNOWLEDGMENTS

The division between the fields of English and Education I draw attention to with my title is an often subtle institutional and discursive border; it can nonetheless profoundly circumscribe the work that teachers and researchers on both sides of that line see as their domain. The spring of 2000 saw a decisive shift in my thinking about what "English" as discipline and practice was for, and what the conversation about *teaching* English might become among English and education faculty. The book before you traces the history of what happened once I crossed the threshold of my own practice and began an inquiry along the borders of those institutional domains, investigating in each of the chapters the possibilities of seeing that relationship between English and Education from what I call throughout the book a *deranged* perspective. As I explain in Chapter 1, I use the term to evoke the physical, geographical, and dispositional unsettlings that occur when we range beyond our traditionally defined fields of study. Such life-altering transformations can also reorient us to our driving beliefs, bring us to new insights, and be endlessly joyful and entertaining. It is in this spirit that I want to acknowledge those who have been my partners, mentors, and collaborators on that deranged inquiry.

Mary Beth Hines has been there since the beginning of my professional transformation, when I was roaming the halls of Indiana University's School of Education looking for someone to help me frame and pursue the questions I had about putting English and education into dialogue. She directed my graduate capstone project, which eventually threaded its way through much of Chapter 1, conclusion, and early chapters of this book, and worked with me over the course of years and across several states to refine my thinking and keep pushing at the edges of my inquiry. She also invited me to join an ongoing conversation among local teachers of English who were interested in looking at their classrooms and practice from an inquiry and social justice perspective. This group, the Indiana English Teachers Collaborative (ETC), has vitally shaped my thinking about how classroom teachers can influence the field of English at local, state, and national levels.

Also at Indiana University, Joan Pong Linton and Peter Cowan offered close reading throughout the initial project and sage advice about the book when it was still mostly a proposal. Jerry Harste and the folks at the NCTE Reading Initiative profoundly shaped my approach to teaching literacy and, of course, introduced me to *transmediations*. Luise McCarty first introduced me to Dewey and sparked a renewed interest in art and aesthetics that is evident throughout these chapters. In their friendship, Janet Johnson and Tasha Laman helped me maintain my sense of humor during my return to graduate school, and through their own research helped me to think differently about qualitative research and classroom discourse. A 2004 Everett Helm Fellowship from IU's Lilly Library supported some of the research on regional authors and the history of education that appears here.

Through my association with the ETC, I was fortunate to participate in a nationwide teacher-research project organized by Peg Graham, Bob Fecho, and Sally Hudson-Ross of the University of Georgia. Funded by an Arthur Vining Davis grant, these three outstanding leaders in English Education initiated the PorTRAIT (Practitioner or Teacher Researchers As Inquiring Travelers) Project of cross-site visitations among teacher researchers in different networks and supported the collaborative work described in Chapter 2. To them and to Gloria Reeves, Leslie Pratt, Bonnie Tipaldi, and Joanne Wisniewski, the teachers who opened their classrooms and practice to me at this early stage in my professional transition, I offer my deep thanks. They continue to influence my teaching and research. The Western Massachusetts Writing Project graciously supplemented our already generous support from the AVD grant to give us time and space to write together at the Five Colleges retreat house in Amherst, Massachusetts, in the summer of 2002.

Since coming to the University of North Carolina at Charlotte in 2003, I've had the distinct privilege of having two remarkable partners and collaborators in my teaching and research. Many of the engagements and activities described in this book first saw light in the classrooms where we taught together. Lil Brannon has been a constant mentor and friend, offering advice and critique throughout the process of writing and researching the book. Sally Griffin has been the ideal co-teacher each summer during our Open Institute of the UNC Charlotte Writing Project. Her unflagging enthusiasm for teaching English and classroom research are an inspiration and model for me and for our students. I would also like to thank my students in my literature and teacher education classes over the years, especially those who appear in the pages that follow: Lynn Abbott-McLeod, Derek Borchardt, Mark Buzzee, Lindsay Cobb, Jamey Evans, Justin Hessburg, Lindsay Houser, Erin Kerns, Ashley Matson, Ron Shook, Lisa Simmerson, and Caleb Sinclair. The College of Arts and Sciences at UNC Charlotte offered a key semester research leave through the Schley R. Lyons Junior Faculty Reassignment of Duties Program in fall 2006, and a Frances Lumsden Gywnn Award in 2006–2007 in support of this book.

This book was completed while I was on leave from UNC Charlotte and teaching at Eastern Michigan University, where my wife had just begun her own tenure-track journey. Eastern has been a fitting and reorienting derangement to my thinking about the prospects for English/Education. I'd like to thank Doug Baker, Craig Dionne, Cathy Fleischer, Andrea Kaston-Tange, Rebecca Sipe, and Bill Tucker in particular for their encouragement and support in the crucial last months of the writing. Most of all I thank my wife Melissa Jones, who has been my partner in derangement these many years—even as she completed a dissertation of her own, moved to and from three different states, and shared in the daily astonishments of being parents to Jack. Her love, support, and keen criticism throughout this long process has constantly shown me the regenerative excitement of teaching, research, and writing—and the joys of discovering what it is all for.

Deranging English/Education

*People wish to be settled; only as far as they are unsettled
is there any hope for them.*

RALPH WALDO EMERSON, "Circles" (1841)

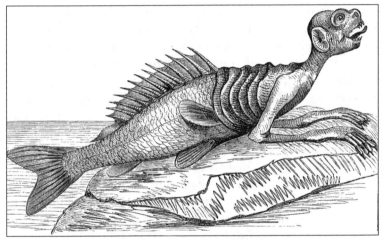

FIGURE **1.1.** *Merman (From a specimen in Agassiz's Museum)*, Harper's New
Monthly Magazine *(1869)*

The Hybrid Creature of the English Educator

This is the place.
And I am here, the mermaid whose dark hair
streams black, the merman in his armored body
We circle silently
about the wreck
we dive into the hold.
I am she: I am he

ADRIENNE RICH, "DIVING INTO THE WRECK" (1973)

For some time now I have been deranged: personally, professionally, and pedagogically. Despite the pervasiveness of the condition in my life as a teacher and scholar, it has proved to be a rather benign affliction; unsettling, certainly, but not altogether unwelcome. The image above (Figure 1.1) captures for me something of the unwieldy hybridity of English/Education and the unusual spaces English educators like myself inhabit in yoking together the diverging discourses of literary studies and teacher education. This book is an exploration into what can happen at the site of contact between those discourses, that is, at the cleaving of English and education—represented throughout the text as *English/Education*—to transform our teaching lives.

I am drawn to the term *deranging* and this notion of hybridity in light of the constantly evolving state of English as discipline and practice in the twenty-first century. The capacity to signal both physical and psychological movement and displacement, especially out of zones of comfort, joins nicely with the new knowledges called for by the current educational climate; this is an age of global Englishes, expanding canons, high-stakes assessment, and ubiquitous talk of "teacher accountability." But the word *derangement* also evokes the ways in which the notion of remapping the *terrain* of English and education—not to mention simply living the life of a preservice English teacher or professor of English education—can itself be frustrating and disorienting. In one sense, the chapters here are reports from the field, moments of practice, inquiry, and discovery on the contested borders of English/Education. They follow two roughly contemporaneous trajectories: one tracing the life cycle of the profession from English teacher candidate to teacher educator; the other marked by the more recursive path of my own transition from a professor of American literature to an English teacher educator. That second path influences the form of the present chapter and those that follow by highlighting the deranged aspects of acquiring and living a hybrid life in the current educational climate. And so, a caution: readers accustomed to more traditional linear narratives of teacher-research may find themselves a bit deranged or unsettled by this discursive approach. I've tried to offer periodic reminders and signposts along the way to help reorient you. But I am also trying quite deliberately to disrupt some prevailing ways of thinking about what should happen on and around the borders of English/Education. My hope is that the process of derangement I am both describing and employing might offer new ways of seeing what happens when we dive together into the hold of English/Education.

The strangely compelling figure above, embodying the derangement of the field, is at once a beacon to and admonition against what we might become as English educators. The caption to this image indicates that it is a "Merman (*From a specimen in Agassiz's Museum*)." Etymologically it carries a balance of its being (*man*) and its environment or field of action (*mer*, sea). Of course it looks like a fusion of two creatures—half man, half fish. Drawing upon our memory of other texts, we might surmise that like its close and far more familiar relation the mermaid, the merman seems to be of that species of creature whose songs and stories enticed unwitting sailors to their doom. But this *particular* merman signifies more than just a dangerously seductive hybridity, for as a "specimen in *Agassiz's* museum"— as opposed to, say, P. T. Barnum's contemporary American Museum—it is also potentially an artifact of scientific knowledge and understanding. Louis Agassiz was one of the most important scientific figures of his day, and he was a particularly influential mediator, as both a teacher and a public intellectual, of scientific discoveries for the larger public. His inquiry-based approach to teaching and learning remains a powerful model for innovative and learner-centered practice. And following Agassiz's famous injunction to his student studying the physiology of a fish, we must "look, look, look" (qtd. in Tierney 12) again at the merman if we are to discover what it means. In highlighting some of its other literary, cultural, and textual dimensions of meaning-making, I want to invite consideration of the merman as a sign of what can happen when the domains of literary studies and literacy education come together as English/Education. In this chapter I will be working specifically with examples from my own area of literary studies—the nineteenth-century literary mode of American regionalism, which offers a counter narrative to the canonical history of American literature. In this parallel account, regionalism is especially useful for thinking about English education today.

I came to the merman somewhat accidentally while doing archival research on the nineteenth-century writer Alice Cary, who developed her regionalist aesthetic in a range of popular and literary journals to which she was a prolific contributor from the late 1840s until her death in 1871. This long and embedded history within the instructional and discursive apparatus of literary and literacy production of her time makes Cary's work, and regionalist literature more generally, an ideal site to begin a refiguration of the place of American literature in the teaching of English and of English teachers. In its history and in its thematic focus, regionalism allows us to see differently, but also to see *with difference* those who might otherwise be ignored, overlooked, or viewed as exotic anomalies from a more dominant, nationalist perspective. It is not so much a literature *about* place as it is immersed in questions *of* place and placement, providing a useful critical model to think through the twenty-first-century challenges to teaching English in America.

The picture of the merman appears at the end of an article in a series by Cornell physiologist and biologist Burt Wilder in the December 1869 issue of *Harper's New Monthly Magazine.* Immediately below it sits one of Alice Cary's later poems, "A Passing Wish" (31) in which the poet momentarily envisions herself as a "Gipsy girl," free to range across the boundaries and borders of class, gender, and sexuality (see Appendix 1.1). Telling her "restless conscience, / Be still; you are no more mine" (53–55), Cary imagines exchanging her life of responsibility and artistic confinement "for the life of a Gipsy! / A strong-armed, barefoot girl; . . . So gloriously free" (1–2, 10). Cary's appropriation of the exotic to explore alternative subjectivities is certainly problematic, especially in light of her own regionalist aesthetic discussed below. But the poem also reinforces the merman's visual rhetoric, suggesting a similar liberating, evolutionary movement out of a placid past into a new way of being in the world, not without its difficulties—as we see the merman apparently gasping for breath in the unfamiliar air—but perhaps just as "gloriously free." Yet the proximity of the image troubles the poem's transformative musings, turning exotic subjectivity into monstrous spectacle. The readerly effect of this juxtaposition then unsettles—deranges—the possibility of a separate reading of either, calling instead for an intra- and intertextual encounter that must eventually move beyond the page and out into the experiences of readers.

What begins as a curious coincidence of pairings acquires a heightened significance through the accretion of images and themes. During the run of Wilder's series in consecutive *Harper's* issues from November 1869 through February 1870, for instance, we see a story and several poems by Cary; but in the editor's literary and scientific records in these issues, we also see commentary on the latest "Philosophy of Teaching" (December 1869, 143), scientific discoveries about optics and vision ("New Revelations of the Spectroscope" [December 1869, 144–45]), curiosities of evolution in "Man and the Monkey" (December 1869, 148–50), and even a brief review of an autobiography by "the Prince of Humbugs," P. T. Barnum (January 1870, 296–97), himself a friend of Alice and Phoebe Cary. Rather comically, the story immediately following both the merman and Cary's poem is "The Fisherman's Daughter" by Mary N. Prescott (December 1869, 32–37). Indeed, the cumulative effect of such a deranged encounter importantly reveals *Harper's* and other post–Civil War magazines turning repeatedly to images of hybridity or the exotic to address questions of national, regional, and racial identity. In a striking parallel to our own cultural moment, we witness through this deranged perspective an acute preoccupation with the problem of educating a growing and increasingly more diverse population to become productive American citizens in an age of scientific and technological transformation.

Just before Wilder's conclusion to this part of his series, he moves from a discussion of buoyancy and the capacity for swimming among mammals to a digression about "those fabled creatures the Mermen and the Mermaids, which figure largely in the Northern legends" (December 1869, 30). He turns finally to the aquatic abilities of humans, "Man alone, the head and the chief of animals, is lost without immediate exercise of a quality which education alone can make to take the place of instinct—presence of mind" (31). Wilder, of course, deploys the image and the digression to reinforce the authority of science and the scientific habits of mind that allow us to see through such entertaining hoaxes as the merman. Yet the merman figure itself seems to resist Wilder's taxonomic gesture. As I look again and again at the image perched incongruously above Cary's wistful poem of escape, I am brought to a surprising thought: how like the life of an English teacher (or even better, an English teacher *educator*), whose siren call summons students to sweet doom. See if this sounds familiar: Here we sit, comfortably ensconced in our universities, waiting for naïve young English majors whom we can ship off to graduate programs in literary studies; or perhaps we wait for preservice teachers to seduce to our progressive pedagogies, only to set them up for rough sailing when they have to go out in search of the "real world." Out There, they will land in places where they have to "teach the test," plod through curricular units on "the short story" or "the poem," and plow through worksheets, thesis statements, and five-paragraph essays, all while preparing their own students (in the language of many state departments of education) to chart their own "pathways to success"—but not before passing a battery of tests, and of course leaving no child behind.

Perhaps I have overstated the case a bit. And eventually, I want to resist that first reading of the figure. As dexterous as it may be, it doesn't really engage the materiality of the figure as "scientific artifact" or "textual event." But for now I offer it as a very powerful image of what the double vision of English/Education can be for teachers and students. One perspective captures the view from outside the academy, which often restricts or collapses the capacity of English/Education, ossifying it through "scientifically based" federal mandates into a discrete set of literacy skills and practices. The other, coming from within the practice of English/Education, itself unsettles efforts to establish a fixed way of becoming English educators, and imagines an identity seen as if from the inside of its changing context—a transformation of vision that has important implications for the practice of literacy and teaching.

Imagining English/Education

Perhaps more than any other group of student, not excluding PhDs, preservice English teachers are a continuing responsibility, to the university, to their teachers, and to themselves. No other group has a greater impact on the hardest question of all: How will the knowledge, abilities, and canons of judgment that make what we call English exist and do their work in the culture and politics of our country? (Flannery et al. 61)

In 1999 the Teacher Education Project (commissioned in 1993) of the Modern Language Association (MLA) issued an extensive self-study of model programs that acknowledged the importance of integrating teacher preparation into departments of language and literary studies. *Preparing a Nation's Teachers: Models for English and Foreign Language Programs* argues for language and literature faculty to "take a self-conscious role in the education of students who will teach our subjects in secondary schools" (Gray 1). In the quote above, one of the model English education programs goes even further, putting the future of the field in the hands of preservice English teachers. In relocating power over the field to the classroom, it repositions the discourse about English to the very act of teaching the discipline. Despite the importance of these graduates on the practice of the curriculum, on the changing discourse of twenty-first-century literacy, and on public understanding of our field, "teaching" is typically characterized by English faculty as the *least* desirable and prestigious career option for our majors. Our tacit instruction to and rhetoric about future English teachers reinforces the institutional and epistemological divisions between English and education. And yet as James Marshall claims elsewhere in the MLA report, "all teaching is about teaching" and "every class that enrolls teachers is a class in teacher preparation" (380–81). Such a proposition means that we in English studies are already deeply implicated in English/ Education. Not to recognize our influence on future English teachers doesn't just trouble the project of teacher preparation, it jeopardizes the very future of English studies, leaving all English teachers adrift in an ever-changing educational environment.

In his 1897 essay "My Pedagogic Creed," John Dewey makes the provocative claim that "the image is the great instrument of instruction" (436), and what learners get out of any subject presented to them is simply the configuration of images that they themselves form with regard to it. In its *Guidelines for the Preparation of Teachers of English Language Arts* (1996), the Conference on English Education (CEE) of the National Council of Teachers of English (NCTE) echoes the observations of Dewey and the MLA report, putting image- or meaning-making practice at the fore of English teacher education. CEE has been a crucial advocate for innovative and substantive preparation of English teachers, and its guidelines significantly advise teacher education programs to provide opportunities for English teacher candidates to construct their own unique working versions of what English/language arts teachers in the real world might be, to become "makers of their own teacher selves" (42). Since 1996 a host of articles by researchers and classroom teachers in *English Education*, *Research in the Teaching of English*, and *English Journal* have examined the process of developing teacher identities among preservice and inservice teachers. At the center of this identity formation, according to this literature and echoed year-in and year-out by CEE position statements and in reports from MLA model teacher education programs, is the construction of viable collaborative networks between all those involved in teacher preparation. But as Peg Graham et al. remind us, the reach of the field ranges beyond our individual domains (126), and the figure of the future "English educator" becomes a sort of wayfarer moving constantly among community schoolrooms, colleges of education, and colleges of arts and sciences.

CEE updated its guidelines further with its July 2006 call for "Reconstructing English Education for the 21ˢᵗ Century." This new document highlights even more explicitly the necessity of *teacher-research* for the future of English, noting that "the field of English Education is built upon knowledge gained from systematic and multimodal inquiry into the teaching and learning of English" ("What Is English Education?"). But despite the promise of this scholarship to shape the training and practice of classroom teachers through teacher education programs, and despite the earnest rhetoric of both the MLA Teacher Education Project and the many NCTE and CEE initiatives aimed at bridging differences, the divisions between faculty of English departments and colleges of education remain wide. We can't seem to fashion a viable image of English/Education at work. The current "trouble with English," as Alan Luke notes in his article of the same name, lies in recognizing that the challenge facing teacher education, the curriculum, and school reform is *not* to find, standardize, and implement the one true method, but for teachers to develop flexible repertoires of field-, discourse-, and text-specific pedagogies, suited to particular textual artifacts, technologies, social and linguistic/interactional outcomes, and adaptable for students of different cultural and linguistic backgrounds. (90)

My attempt to bring the double vision of English/Education into some sort of harmony involves just such a process of configuration. Part of the account begins with a way of seeing my experience, and that of other English and education faculty, as illustrative of the challenges in teaching and learning English. I have been a faculty member in colleges and departments of education and departments of English; at home in each, I have also seen each made strange by the assumptions of the other. I have collaborated as both teacher and researcher in the classrooms of middle and secondary school teachers, and I've joined my own teacher candidates and English majors in pursuing teacher- and classroom research. These experiences have offered me a perspective that imagines how the image of the merman, or the "Gipsy girl" and other characters from American regionalist texts, might operate theoretically and pedagogically to overcome the divisions of English/Education and to prepare future English teachers.

Teacher-Research, or Looking at English/Education from Within

(1) Pedagogy is a knowledge-making activity that involves the interplay of visions and practices; (2) pedagogy is dependent on learners and is remade with each encounter, as the students and teachers change; (3) pedagogy cannot be finished; we cannot "finally" learn to teach. (Stenberg xviii)

In many ways, for me these questions come out of the same impulse that Dewey recognized about learning over a century ago and that New Literacy Studies and theorists of multiliteracies such as Luke have articulated more recently. And they require the interplay of visions that Stenberg cites above. As a teacher educator, writing teacher, and specialist in American literature at a large state university with a site of the National Writing Project, I regularly find myself positioned at the intersection of multiple disciplines and discourses that come together to prepare future English teachers. Literary studies, critical pedagogy, literacy and learning theory—not to mention state and national performance and learning standards—each has its own (and sometimes competing) design on the field of English/Education. But fashioning an integrated and interdisciplinary union of these fields can, I believe, be powerfully transformative, enabling teacher candidates and teacher educators to become critically reflective practitioners; that is, teachers who make their own teaching of literature and writing an object of sustained inquiry and research. Weaving these threads together is akin to the pedagogy of multiliteracies, in which the "process of shaping emergent meaning involves re-presentation and recontextualization" and in which "meaning makers remake themselves," reconstructing and renegotiating their identities through a transformation of "Available Designs" (Cope and Kalantzis 22–23).

The web of meaning that results, however, is not a union without considerable costs and risks to one's own security, comfort, and stability. One need only recall the fate of another mythological figure, the spinner Arachne, to know that re-presenting and recontextualizing "official" or "authorized" stories can be dangerous. Appropriately, Arachne herself (or spiders and other weavers) recurs throughout the work of nineteenth-century women regionalist writers, figuring their work as a tireless, necessary, and of course potentially futile challenge to the dominant cultural narrative. Rose Terry Cooke's poem "Arachne" (appearing above a chapter of Henry James's *Portrait of a Lady* in the *Atlantic Monthly*, March 1881) is a typical example, in which the poet parallels the spider's spinning of "Her home, her bed, her nets for food, / All from that inward store" (5–6) to her own creative work, though she knows that "heartless hands / [may likely] Sweep all that hard-earned web away" (25–26). As Nancy Miller has argued, "arachnologies" such as Cooke's are crucial sites for exploring discursive fields, and emerge from a sort of hybrid interpretive act, simultaneously "a poetics of the *underread* and a practice of 'overreading'" (83). This critical perspective is certainly pedagogical in Stenberg's sense of the "interplay of visions and practices." For the sake of deranging the curriculum of English/Education—especially in light of regionalism's re-visioning of the literary canon and the value of local knowledges about teaching and learning—it is an apt metaphor. The methodology regionalism adopts to interrogate the assumptions of the dominant, national culture is very much like the *emic* approach taken by qualitative researchers and teacher-researchers. Rather than coming from the outside to look *in* or *at* students and student work, teacher-researchers speak from the perspective of participants critical of their own practice, participants whose inquiries emerge "from that inward store" to take a disciplined look *around* them to see what is going on.

In the spring of 2000, I was a visiting professor of American literature at a small liberal arts college in the Midwest, where a number of the English majors were also seeking certification as secondary English teachers. I had become increasingly puzzled and frustrated by the inability of students and faculty alike (myself included) to put literary studies and teacher education into what seemed like an authentic dialogue; yet I had no idea at the time what a more satisfying conversation might look like, or who would do most of the talking. A shift came, however, when I discovered the Indiana English Teachers Collaborative (ETC), a cohort of likeminded English teachers and faculty involved in a regional school-university partnership, which had been featured in the MLA Teacher Education Project report.

The teacher-research network of ETC has offered me an ongoing immersion in teacher-research that has become a model for what I encourage my own students to do in my pedagogy courses. They look at their classrooms from the inside, but they also cross borders of practice to investigate the classrooms of critical friends/co-inquirers. "Diving into the wreck" of each other's classrooms and practices, they then use what they've learned through their reflection and observation to find ways to meet the needs of all literacy learners. Chapter 2, "A Collaboration of 'Perfect Economy': Carrying Teacher-Research Across

Country in Williams's 'The Red Wheelbarrow,'" provides an examination of the sustained inquiry among classroom teachers that
has inspired this collaborative approach in my own research
courses, and which establishes the inquiry frame of mind that
allowed for the subsequent discoveries and investigations of the
other chapters. Since this initial collaboration, I have spent hun-
dreds of hours in secondary classrooms and with classroom teachers, thinking and talking about the teaching of writing and
literature. Although our own pedagogy is arguably the most public
and visible enactment of our research pursuits, as Judith Fetterley
recently argued in "Teaching and 'My Work,'" this is not work
that often "counts" professionally for English faculty. Stenberg
likewise cautions that pedagogy and teacher-research need to go
beyond a facile sharing of methods to be seen as praxis-oriented
endeavors within a theory-practice dialectic. Such work "is reflective of . . . [the] specific, embodied location and the contexts"
teacher-researchers work within (52). For me, this embodied work
brought both personal and professional transformations. I began a second doctoral program (in language education), became
part of a long-term collaborative inquiry among teacher-researchers from six established national networks (see Fecho, Graham,
and Hudson-Ross), and began to test in my own classrooms the
possibilities of deranging the curriculum. When, as part of a collaborative network, I traveled to classrooms in western Massachusetts, Philadelphia, and Indianapolis to work with other
teacher-researchers, I was moving along this dialectical axis. My
first forays into teacher-research were not solitary pursuits, but
were connected to other teachers interested in the intersection of
student writing, the teaching of literature, and classroom ethos.
Although I had been teaching for more than five years, teaching
and classroom learning now became for me part of a new curriculum in an "apprenticeship of observation." I began to see
signs and designs for making meaning of teaching and learning,
and I began to turn them to my own configurations. I have continued this process of *transmediation* in my current work with
undergraduate majors, teacher candidates, and graduate students
in English education, as I try to convince students of the value of
inquiry to generate literate lives.

Sideshadowing English/Education Pedagogy

> How is it that as a well-read English major, I have never heard of these authors? How did they "disappear" from the canon? And how have they managed to get "re-appeared"?
>
> STUDENT IN AMERICAN WOMEN WRITERS CLASS *(September 2005)*

But this is only part of the story, only one way of seeing from the deranged perspective of the merman. For me, arriving safely on the shores of teacher education didn't mean abandoning the ship of English studies altogether. This story of coming to English/ Education from literary studies—particularly exchanging a study of the ethics of American regionalism for an inquiry into *teaching* regionalist literature—is linked to another, related set of teaching moments and images mapping my trajectory from regionalism to teacher-research. In the context of Cary and regionalism, the merman has a very particular resonance, for regionalism disrupts traditional ways of seeing literature and history. It invites a shift in perspective about what it means to be American, to be a reader, and to be a writer, through a series of narrative and stylistic moves fostering a readerly refiguration of ethical dilemmas faced by the overlooked of society (who Fetterley and Pryse call the "out of place"). By showing us alternative visions of what it can mean to be located or placed as a certain kind of American or reader or writer, regionalism constructs what Gary Saul Morson would describe as a "sideshadowing" perspective, one that "projects— from the 'side'—the shadow of an alternative present. It allows us to see what might have been and therefore changes our view of what is" (11). The work of teacher-researchers more generally adopts a similar perspective on the "region" of classroom teaching, moving from local accounts of practice out into the larger field. That process, according to Fecho, Graham, and Hudson-Ross, is both recursive and often unsettling, for it frequently challenges the very enterprise of English education in the schools. And it forces teacher-researchers to come to terms with "'the wobble'" of classroom inquiry, a vertiginous state "of uncertainty that lies between and among figured worlds" (175). The classroom inquiries of Chapters 3, 4, and 5 attempt to describe the promise of finding our pedagogy along that uncertain line between the figured instructional worlds of English and education. The derangement of classroom practice through such inquiry offers a sideshadowing pedagogical perspective on the questions always at stake for teachers of English at secondary and post-secondary levels: What is English for? Who is it for? And, given our responses to these questions, how should we proceed with our own research, writing, and teaching?

The continuing need for that shift was made glaringly present for me in the student query heading this section. At the time, the questions raised by my student, from a split graduate/upper-level undergraduate course in American women writers, sparked a lively discussion about the nature of literary history, the politics of aesthetic criticism and evaluation, and the institutional structure of the academy. But as we talked, this host of women writers seemed alternately to appear and disappear; they were not yet coherent images in our understanding of American literary history so much as they were entertainments in an academic game of now you see them, now you don't. As I listened to my students, I tried to construct an image of what they were really grappling with. Who or what is behind this "disappearing act"? What sort of—and whose—sleight of hand is at work here?

The pedagogical challenge of teaching in a way that will help students and future teachers recast their images of American history and literature is in part the methodological question behind Dewey's claim about the image as the instrument of instruction: What is the image or set of images I want or need to use to elicit such a reconfiguration? This question was part of the design for the American literature courses described in Chapter 4. There again, the sideshadowing perspective of regionalism and historical transmediation, making visible the overlooked and outcast, offers pedagogical models. When students encounter a series of competing or complementary images, the "disappearing" of authors is understood not only as a historical process, but also as something that is not inevitable. Students thus may begin to refigure a complex past. But for the instructor and student engaged in academic discourse about issues of teaching the canon and revisioning the literary and cultural history of America, the question remains: How can students re-vision their understanding in ways that will not simply mirror back to those in power their own cherished assumptions (however high-minded)? Students must find ways to construct a coherent image that is held together by their own experiences, inquiries, and meaning-making systems.

Cary's Sideshadowing Perspective on the *Ladies' Repository*

> I believe that for these sketches I may challenge of competent witnesses at least this testimony, that the circumstances have a natural and probable air which should induce their reception as honest relations unless there is conclusive evidence against them. Having this merit, they may perhaps interest if they do not instruct readers who have regarded the farming class as essentially different and inferior, and entitled only to that peculiar praise they are accustomed to receive in the resolutions of political conventions.
>
> ALICE CARY, *Preface to* Clovernook *(1852, vii)*

In the first issue of *The Ladies' Repository, and Gatherings of the West*, an engraving appeared, titled "View on the Ohio" (Figure 1.2), which offers a visual demonstration of the way regionalism can help us consider how to proceed amid the placement and displacement of "English" in America. The journal was a mid-twentieth-century Ohio magazine, which by the 1850s would become virtually synonymous with the name Alice Cary (much to the chagrin of its editors). The pastoral perspective of this frontispiece, the editor's commentary on it, and the two essays that follow it, "Reading" and "Female Education," frame the aesthetic, ethical, and educational horizons of the magazine. This first issue of January 1841 no doubt helped to shape the moral and artistic imagination of twenty-one-year-old Alice Cary, as she set out to develop her own vision of life in the Midwest.

The engraving provides a view from the Kentucky side of the river three miles below Cincinnati. In the editor's estimation, the piece "is thought to be correct, presenting in just and striking shades the principle graces of this charming scene" and "the peculiar features of our Ohio scenery" ("View" 1). The aesthetic vision the editor applauds is one of selective verisimilitude, which

FIGURE 1.2. *"View on the Ohio,"* Ladies' Repository *(1841)*

speaks to a familiar—and familial—audience, but only of a certain authorized kind. This idyllic view is one that keeps the regional and local subject a distant spot on the horizon, and reinscribes privileged sites of white male viewing. The engraving captures the estate of Thomas Yeatman, a major figure in the social and political life of Cincinnati—not Cary's "farming class." But what we do not see here, for instance, are those whose labor has allowed the Yeatman estate to command this view. Cary's work in later volumes of the same magazine refuses to allow the inclusion of "correct" local and familiar details to portray regional subjects as objects of ridicule or oversight. Instead, through a recurring narrator who knows her subjects as friend, neighbor, and often family member, Cary fashions both story and teller as an "honest relation," whose insider's perspective can expose those community structures that establish and threaten regional identity—particularly the familial and social bonds that alternately stifle and enable individuals to live "out of place."

Using one of Cary's stories from this journal, I want to offer a more explicit reading of how English/Education can move from literary studies to questions of practice. The story anticipates Cary's ethical reminder of the "orphaned" status of us all, and shows how social institutions such as the school are implicated in the ethical project of the region. The reading I am suggesting attempts to draw out the pedagogy of that project and to consider the implications for today's educational institutions, especially university English/Education programs. Published in the March 1851 issue of *Ladies' Repository*, "Peter Harris" is the tale of a boy deliberately orphaned by his parents. The sketch relates the boy's abandonment by his father, his forced relocation to his relations' home, and his subsequent (and rather rapid) death there. The plot, in fact, is little more than this brief outline of what happens to a child quite literally left behind.

What gives the story its force is the focus on character and the restrained voice of Cary's narrator, which underscore the utter hopelessness of a boy whose only crime is to have had the effrontery, after he has been abandoned by his father, to confess that he would like a great many things in life. The boy's relations laugh at this desire and quickly put it in check. For example, the aunt, "a pious woman" (as the narrator remarks in an aside), immediately questions Peter on his arrival in a manner that already includes her expected answers, eliminating any volition and agency from his responses. "You would like to be grateful," she says, and then elaborates the meaning of this word for the boy: "You must feel as if the consecration of all your energies to your uncle and me could never repay us." In the aunt, Cary presents a version of the morally self-satisfied reader of the magazine. Ruled by the desire to maintain propriety rather than foster charity, such a "religious" woman, the narrator reveals, must *know* that she will be obeyed. So she quickly continues her interrogation about Peter's gratitude: "You will feel so, will you not?" (103). Harboring more directive than inquiry or dialogue, the question *inquiry + dialogue* is designed to ensure the knowledge and power only of the one who asks it.

Cary's narrator here encourages us to identify not with the *monologic* monologic voice of propriety, but with the perspective of the overlooked. It is a critical narrative pedagogy. Accordingly, the narrator informs us that "Peter was quite at a loss. He knew no more than he knew what grateful was, what his energies were, or how to consecrate them to his uncle and her; but he said he would

* *critical narrative*
pedagogy
↳ *ID w/ overlooked*

try." The indirect discourse forces us to give voice internally to Peter, thereby making his condition in some sense ours. Not surprisingly, then, Peter's answer seems humble and reasonable, especially for one newly deserted by his own father in a strange town. But the aunt's rejoinder comes with all the conviction and violence of the absolutist: "There must be no *try* about it. You must do it, or be whipped everyday, till you do" (103). Given this reception from the community, Peter's rapid decline and death as a result of the neglect of his family and his teachers is hardly surprising.

What *is* surprising in the story is the extent to which Cary delineates the patterns of abuse that terrorize the young boy. A scene in school is especially troubling, and the passage is worth quoting at length:

> The master, a tall, dark-faced man, called him [Peter] to his desk, and asked him the following questions:
> "You come to this school to be taught the rudiments of an English education, I suppose?"
> Peter knew he came to be taught something, and tremblingly answered, "Yes, sir."
> "'Yes, sir, if you please,'" said the teacher; and Peter said, "Yes, sir, if you please."
> "Where do you live?"
> "At Uncle Jason's, if you please."
> "Why, boy, you must be a numskull. You must say 'if you please,' if it's appropriate. What is your name?"
> "Peter Harris, if you please, if it's appropriate."
> "The boy is a blockhead!" said the master; and boys and girls, putting their books before their faces, joined in a general titter.
> "Come, come! That will do!" said the master, looking over the school, and frowning with great severity. Then taking a limber switch from his desk, and shaking it over the head of Peter, in a menacing manner, he told him, that all the scholars got whipped who did not mind and study their lessons. He then told him to go to his seat, and study his book.
> This seat was a high, wooden bench, without any back; and Peter found sitting there, for four hours at once, very tiresome, especially as he did not know *a* from *b*, and, consequently, could not study. After a while, he was called to say his lesson, but not

knowing [a single] one of the letters, was made to stand on a
high stool for ten minutes, and all the children were required to
point their fingers at him, the master laying his watch on the
desk, to see the time. At its expiration, he was sent back to his
seat, and told to see if he could study *now*; but he could not
study any better than before; and when the boys went out to
play, he was "kept in." (104)

By her casual recounting of its apparent ordinariness and of the
systematic way in which the children themselves become
complicit—first with their tittering, then with their pointing—in
the ostracism of Peter, Cary makes the abuse here and at the
home of his aunt and uncle present and frighteningly real. She
also demonstrates how that abuse is inscribed institutionally and
pedagogically. Beginning with Peter's father, who, as he gives up
on Peter to seek his fortunes farther west, informs the boy that
he will amount to nothing, Peter's life is filled with those who
delight in administering verbal and physical torture.

To indicate that this abuse comes from the very systems that
Ladies' Repository says should care for children—the extended
family and the school (Peter does not live long enough to see the
church)—is a particularly daring narrative move for Cary to make
in a magazine claiming to uphold those institutions. Cary's story
challenges the presumption of the magazine to be, in its words,
an organ for imparting piety and developing ethical wisdom solely
because of its institutional affiliation or its stated intent to provide its readers only moral bits. Such moral theorizing is dangerously circumscribed and not without its own rendering within
the pages of the magazine itself. The fate of Peter Harris—at the   *Huck*
hands of just such readers of moral magazines as the aunt and   *Finn*
the schoolmaster—presents a clear challenge to the very journal
that publishes the story. The story suggests that if this magazine
is truly to be a pedagogical tool for social justice, it must be prepared to direct its critical gaze inward, to see whether its literary
renderings of the good, moral, and just life have managed to
become written on the hearts and can be read in the actions of
both its editors and readers.

Troubling English/Education

Often my brightest students are told by certain members of the
English Department that they are too bright to become teachers.
(Foster 261)

The thematized framing of ethics, social justice, and regionalist
difference in these texts certainly envisions new ways of viewing
American literary and cultural history. But I would argue that it
also suggests ways to investigate how difference and the ethics of
teaching are worked out in real classrooms, where we attempt to
teach "the rudiments of an English education." It is this link that
enables literary studies, and regionalism in particular, to inform
the work of teacher education in ways requiring us to see past
our own areas of comfort and specialty. Recognizing such a connection has been the crucial component in my beginning to derange the curriculum of English education, a claim that I found
myself presenting at a job talk to a roomful of English department colleagues in the spring of 2003. What happened when I
read the above passage from "Peter Harris" surprised me: as literate and literary "English" people, we shared a moment of laughter at Peter's expense. There was something simultaneously so
ridiculous and so painfully true and current about the scenario
that it brought the presentation momentarily to a pause. Yet here
was something that could not be laughed away, or passed along
to our colleagues in education, or disappeared into the pious rhetoric of federal mandates. We had somehow become complicit in
the very thing that we thought we could avoid having to consider—the practice of the English teacher in the face of students
in need (fictional or real). It was, as we say, a teachable moment,
one that became an occasion to talk further, during the interview
and subsequently as a new colleague, about what it is we do
when we are teaching English.

But there is something about that moment of laughter at the
expense of Peter Harris that still lurks in the shadows of my practice and acts as a grim reminder of how easy it is for an encounter with literature to turn into a platitude about the value of
looking at one's own practice and of learning to respect the needs
of all students. It reveals an uneasy tension at the juncture of

English and education masked by a simple celebration of hybridity. Just as Cary's critique of *Ladies' Repository* relies upon the status she has acquired through that magazine's own project of literacy and reform, my own critique of English and education rested upon my ability to establish a certain esprit de corps with my future colleagues. On the one hand, the moment of laughter I shared with them was a moment to show that I was someone who could translate between the two worlds of English and education; it was a well-designed gambit to *perform* the "teaching moment" of catching us all out in order to reorient our sympathies to the needs of all learners, enabling us each to give lip service to the ideals of teaching that every department mission statement claims as its own. On the other hand, it was a chance to show that really I was still one of them, someone who might make an interesting and entertaining reading of literature, but who would protect English from the "blockheads" that the college of education might send our way.

The second interpretation leaves us with a grotesque image of a roomful of English teachers laughing at a Peter Harris-like student who just has no clue. And it's all the more unsettling for me to acknowledge that it was also a genuine moment, despite the motives I've ascribed to myself in constructing it as a textual event for my colleagues. But I think this is also the same impulse that makes us keenly aware of what is potentially *lost* when we bring English and education together. It's the feeling I get when I hear young men and women gush about the love for children that has made them want to *be* English teachers, yet they claim to hate reading and writing. I cringe because, frankly, that love is simply not enough. Unless they also have a genuine interest in pursuing the hard questions that literature poses—about the meaning of life, death, love, and even teaching and schooling—then really, I want to tell them, they ought to find another major and leave those kids alone. And a mere love for literature—particularly as experienced in traditional college-level classrooms—as Pamela Grossman observes in *The Making of a Teacher*, is itself poor preparation for the exigencies of secondary-school English teaching. But as Robert Yagelski and other English educators have argued recently, we likewise "need to abandon the idea that our primary task is to prepare English teachers for contemporary classrooms" (Yagelski, "Stasis and Change" 268). English/Education, of course, is not just about the teaching of children or the teaching of literature. Instead of clinging stubbornly to a fetishized notion of the literary or of teaching, it may be time for us to acknowledge that both college and secondary English need to change radically at the curricular and pedagogical levels if either is to succeed or even survive.

As mediators of literacy and culture, English teachers are in the implicitly ethical position of "norming" for students the ways in which language and literacy matter in America. We can help students raise the same sorts of questions about what it means to be American that regionalism does; together we can examine what is at stake in privileging certain views of literacy and learning. But *any* curriculum of American literature questions what it means to be American (here, now, in the past, in the future), what it means to be literate, and how literature can both promote and constrain visions of literacy and identity. The image of the schoolmaster in "Peter Harris" casts one way of being a teacher, though certainly not one we would encourage our students to emulate. The teacher-researchers I've worked with have shown me another way of thinking about how best to acquire "pedagogical content knowledge," as Grossman calls it—that is, knowledge about how best to teach *x* text to *y* group of students. But teacher-research networks like ETC also do more, seeking through sustained inquiry into each other's practice to foster the sort of professional and praxis-oriented communities that Yagelski argues are necessary for English education "to prepare students to engage in the messy and uncertain process" of building just and sustainable communities ("Stasis and Change" 268). Critical inquiry into our own practice (not just as English educators, but as English faculty) through teacher-research *can* provide the corrective lens on that connection among texts, teaching, and action. But there is no guarantee that it will make things better for us, or for our students. And this is what I'm left with in that moment of laughter: an uneasy sense that, in the face of continuing pressure from those outside our fields to standardize curriculum and notions of literacy, English/Education is a potentially empty hybrid, an elaborate fantasy of bridging disciplines that ultimately changes nothing, producing neither effective teaching nor genuine inquiry into literature or classrooms. At its worst, it's not even a device for containing and maintaining the status quo of either discipline; it becomes simply a way of shuttling students back and forth across campus until they graduate, never having had to think about why they want to be English teachers or English majors in the first place.

The Future Praxis of English/Education: Opportunities and Obstacles

> *Praxis* is really a theory about theories, in fact, a way of explaining how theories are derived, made workable and necessarily alter. Engagement in *praxis*, then, is crucial for teachers as they attempt to nurture the literacies of their students in the English classroom, to experience, to understand experience, and to use understanding to change and improve experience. It requires both the time to speculate, explore, and theorize and the ability to apply reflection to action. (Roskelly 289)

In its July 2006 call for "Reconstructing English Education for the 21st Century," CEE has identified several ways English educators and colleges of education can think differently about how they each construct the discipline and practice of "English." Some of these alternatives we have known about for some time through the MLA Teacher Education Project. While the deranged perspective on English/Education I have been arguing for here, and that I extend throughout the following chapters, shares much with the proposals, I want to offer a brief wish list of specific practices that English departments themselves might adopt to take the lead in reshaping the field. These practices require us to think about how we want students' encounters with "English" to matter in our classrooms and research (see Appendixes 1.2 and 1.3).

Teacher-research directs its critical lens on these encounters, and English departments in particular can certainly do more to foster a climate for faculty to pursue classroom inquiry. Reflective practice emerges from our ability to name the meaning-making moments in teaching and learning. In place of the often ceremonial and rote format of yearly colleague evaluations, I would like to see English faculty take a page from the practice of national board certified teachers and even our own teacher candidates: audio- or videotape what happens in our classrooms; examine it as data; and describe and critique what teaching and learning look like. Even if this sort of investigation were to happen only once in every review cycle, it would transform the weight of teaching for us and for our students.

This sort of inquiry also makes acts of learning more available to our students. We can point to what and how they know and understand. Helping students become aware of their own learning and make connections between their textual encounters and lives outside our classes is another step we can take. As I describe in Chapter 5, my teacher candidates investigate their own literacy histories as well as their students' multiple literacies to acquire the materials for their own inquiries about teaching English. In my own literature courses, I ask students to find a historical or contemporary text, or to produce an original artifact in a separate sign system (a transmediation) that captures their understanding of a particular reading. I call these extensions (with apologies to Roland Barthes) *Image-Music-Text*. Each transmediation comes with a brief written rationale in which students make text-to-text, -self, and -world connections. The result has been a productive pairing of historical and contemporary, high and popular cultural texts, and trans- and interdisciplinary links (see Appendix 1.4).

The movements outside the field from *within* the field of English that students take in these transmediations and "literacy digs" point to the productive possibilities of getting outside our departments, physically and metaphorically. Far too many accounts of English/Education in the past cite the institutional and theoretical divisions between English and education faculty. Having lived and worked on both sides of that institutional divide, I know firsthand that our colleagues across campus and in the schools have perspectives on English/Education that we need to know about; and they need to know about our understanding of the field too. The best place to see these understandings in practice is in each other's classrooms.

Several obstacles lie in the path of these new trajectories, however, and departments and faculty both need to be aware of the tensions and challenges that are embedded in their current practices. The first is workload. Until institutional rhetoric about teaching matches tenure policies and procedures, many of these shifts I am proposing will come at the cost of individual faculty. For instance, when I traveled to the classrooms of my teachers, I gained important insights about their work and the changing nature of English. But the hundred hours and thousand miles I put in during that semester were relegated to a single line under "service" on my annual review. The second obstacle comes with shifting power in the classroom. Perhaps the greatest challenge for students, and the most difficult work for teachers, is for us to help them reconceive the nature and function of schooling as something *they* create through their experiences. This requires trust in students and student willingness to assume responsibility for learning. Of course, statements that equate learning with a consumer transaction and a college education with the purchase of disposable goods (such as the Secretary of Education's recent Commission on the Future of Higher Education report) do not help matters. The third tension is related to this educational discourse. The expectations we create for preservice English teachers and English majors need to be similarly high, but students, too, need to commit themselves to excellence in the field if we are to see real change in English/Education. Part of changing the discourse is to put teaching and learning at the center of inquiry in English.

Repulsions, Reversions, and the Return of English/ Education

> Those fabled creatures the Mermen and the Mermaids, which figure largely in the Northern legends are very respectfully treated by Pontoppidan [in his 1755 *Natural History of Norway*], who reports that one merman "sang an unmusical song" in a strange tongue, but that another individual "swore in very good Danish." They were generally represented as half fish and half man or woman, and never as hideous or even ugly. But the *real* mermaids, the "genuine humbugs," if the expression is allowable, are *always* repulsive, even when, as in the case of the Japanese specimen featured [here] . . . the union of the fish's tail with a wooden head and chest can scarcely be detected. (Wilder 30; emphasis added)

I want to end by returning to the intersection of the illustrated merman, scientific method, and the ethical and cultural work of education. I wish to bring these various images back together into a single, deranged, but cautiously hopeful vision. The history of this particular merman offers another reading of the figure and provides a caution against an uncritical interpretation of such depictions of hybridity. As I noted earlier, the illustration is labeled as being a representation of a specimen from Agassiz's Museum, the Museum of Comparative Zoology at Harvard. Purported to have been recovered by sailors in Japan, it is in fact a rather fanciful hoax: a fish's tail attached to a carved wooden head and chest. What then is it designed to do as an artifact of scientific knowledge and learning in the 1860s? Agassiz's own pedagogical skill in recasting seemingly complex biological theories was especially significant in terms of his position concerning the great evolution debates of the mid-nineteenth century as they applied to an understanding of human difference. In this context, as Louis Menand has noted in *The Metaphysical Club*, Agassiz was a polygenist, which means that he believed in the separate creation of the races. In fact, each race was seen as a different species altogether, which "had been endowed with different attributes and unequal aptitudes from the start" (104).

For Agassiz, the Museum of Comparative Zoology was a place to gather specimens that would, among other things, validate the view of polygenism, demonstrating that species of all kinds and across different continents were in fact unique to their places, and that whatever hybrid species existed were either clever hoaxes or else so repugnant as to be undesirable. The cultural and educational work the museum did, in other words, was to amass a canon of artifacts that would foster an either/or thinking about evolution and other beings, and ultimately to support the hypothesis of polygenism. It is, I suggest, the same sort of either/or thinking that occludes the ethical dimensions of pedagogical content knowledge, separating theory and practice in the lives of our preservice teachers, and alienating English and education faculty from each other. This kind of thinking erodes the work of regionalist and popular authors from American literary history; and under the guise of scientific, aesthetic, or literary objectivity, it confines our approach to considering curriculum, literacy, and literary studies to a very narrow range of research, texts, and practices.

We see a disturbing example of this dichotomy at work, revealing the way false images and constructions can acquire the authority of scientific "truth," in Agassiz's counsel to Samuel Gridley Howe about policies for dealing with a large freed black population during the Civil War, as described below. It is a prescient example of ideology under the guise of scientific practice stacking the deck to legitimize one's political and cultural position. It should invite us to look critically at the purging of qualitative studies of teaching and learning from research databases, and the de facto exclusion of such studies from federal grant programs in education. A prominent abolitionist and educational reformer, Howe was appointed by Abraham Lincoln to head the American Freedmen's Inquiry Commission in 1863, the year the Emancipation Proclamation went into effect. It is striking to see Howe's anxious concern for the future racial character of the country in his query to Agassiz. According to Menand, Dr. Howe

> wrote to Agassiz to ask whether, in his opinion as a scientist, "the African race, represented by less than two million blacks, & a little more than two million mulattoes . . . will be a persistent race in this country; or, will it be absorbed, diluted, & finally effaced by the white race, numbering twenty four millions." (114)

The four letters Agassiz posted back to Howe in a single week register his considerable alarm at the prospect of racial mixing; his increasing obsession with hybridity as deviance is notable, as he "believed that racial interbreeding would be a biological catastrophe, on grounds that hybrids were defective and sterile" (114). And he concluded with the stern monition to the government "'to put every possible obstacle to the crossing of the races, and the increase of half-breeds'" (qtd. in Menand 114). Agassiz abhorred slavery, but we see in his response a reversion to racialized scientific understanding in the face of troubling political and social restructuring. To acknowledge a common humanity with an African living in America—to recognize, in Cary's phrase, that he might share an "orphaned" status—would demand an ethical obligation to envision and act for a much different kind of social justice than that found in Agassiz's scientific truth.

In this light, the merman viewed as the siren of English/Education is, as I suggested earlier, ultimately a contrivance, a dangerous distraction that serves other ends—to keep us focused on false dichotomies instead of on the people and the work immediately before us. Yet it is not simply an image to be used to spark this truth and then be ignored. When we recognize the deliberate and clearly racialized distortions of the figure and the ends they are designed to serve, we come to see that perhaps the merman is calling out to a ship that *needs* to be wrecked. Since 1999 MLA has known that English and education faculties must work together in the preparation of teachers. Both MLA and NCTE have known, too, that the *ways of knowing* common to our disciplines do not follow prescribed or normative processes that can easily accede to federal mandates or standardized outcomes. And yet, nearly a decade later, the separation remains—education faculty and English faculty each having "learned content" (to borrow a phrase from another of Cary's stories) to navigate the same waters without a sense of where the other is going. Under the current educational and political climate, it is naïve for either faculty to imagine that things can or should stay as they are. Powerful forces outside the academy *and* the classroom have already decided what the rudiments of an English education should be. For the sake of our own classrooms, our students, and the continuing relevance of our work, it's time for English/Education to start talking back and to decide for itself what sort of creatures we will be.

A Collaboration of "Perfect Economy": Carrying Teacher-Research Across Country in Williams's "The Red Wheelbarrow"

(WITH GLORIA REEVES AND JOANNE WISNIEWSKI)

*A poem is a small (or large) machine made out of words[;]
. . . there can be no part that is redundant. Poetry is a
machine . . . pruned to a perfect economy. As in all ma-
chines its movement is intrinsic, undulant, a physical more
than a literary character.*

> WILLIAM CARLOS WILLIAMS, *Selected Essays* (1969)

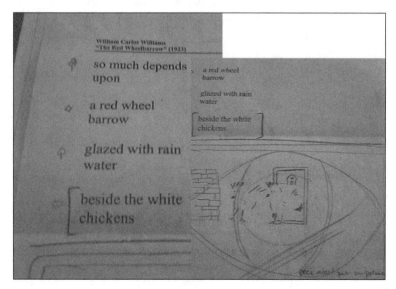

FIGURE **2.1.** *Red Wheelbarrow Transmediation (July 2006)*

T he image above (Figure 2.1) was produced on July 14, 2006, during a writing engagement I conducted at the Open Institute of the University of North Carolina at Charlotte Writing Project, but it carries a much longer history of writing, teaching, and collaboration. On this particular day, I invited participants to make a pictorial representation of their experience or understanding of Williams's poem, and then in small groups (determined by the suit of the card each selected from the deck I fanned out before them) to visually sketch their understanding of a chosen two-line stanza (see Appendix 2). The sketch above is my own and displays something of my meager talents as an artist, but it also attempts to capture something of the history embedded in my use of the poem to think about the teaching of writing and the teaching of writing teachers. And so the drawing "quotes" several images from more accomplished artists, first-time readers of the poem, and several teachers I joined in a collaborative teacher-research inquiry in the summer of 2000.

The outline of the eye, for instance, is borrowed from René Magritte's *Le Faux Mirror* (1928). The caption invokes the famous line from his painting *La Trahison des Images* (1929), "Ceci n'est pas une pipe" (This is not a pipe): "this is not a poem . . ." [about white chickens]. The brick wall, the barn in the distance, the chickens themselves, and the frame through which they walk (or perhaps strut) are all lifted from my memory of student writers encountering this poem for the first time. This range of references and meaning-making techniques helps trace what Stephen Kucer calls the "literacy event" of a text and allows me to fashion both an individual and a dialogic understanding of the poem's meaning. Such events, Kucer notes, are social acts, and "the meaning and language that are built and used are always framed by the social identity . . . of the individual and the social context in which the language is being employed" (5–6).

What is important to me about this act of transmediation, and what I think is of interest for English teachers, is not just that I have successfully constructed meaning from disparate sources (though I have) or that I have a satisfactory interpretation of the poem (which I now do). What is of particular personal significance is the collaborative and negotiated meaning that emerges from those disparate strands of significance; and that is part of the derangement of the field and our practice for which I argue throughout this book. This assemblage of images succinctly captures the history of my first encounter with those sources as part of a critical exploration as a teacher and researcher, for the student images came not just from my own students, but from the students of teachers I met at the very beginning of my transition from English to English education. It is their innovative classroom pedagogy and commitment to teacher-research and reflective practice I want to highlight here.

The collaboration into teacher-research described in this chapter began by chance, coincidence, and a willingness to follow someone else's hunch that interesting things may happen when teachers step outside their own domains and take a look across the thresholds into others' classrooms. Cross-site visitations and collaborations among teachers from several teacher-researcher networks was the vision of the PorTRAIT (Practitioner or Teacher Researcher as Inquiring Traveler) Project, funded by a grant from the Arthur Vining Davis Foundations, and proposed by teacher-researchers at the University of Georgia. The history of the grant and how it brought together teacher-researchers from several National Writing Project sites, Breadloaf, and university-school partnerships from Indiana and Georgia, as well as an overview of its impact on several teachers, has been described at length elsewhere (see Fecho, Graham, and Hudson-Ross). So what I offer here is a personalized account of how one such collaboration began modestly—as a one-year, cross-country adventure into the classrooms of fellow teacher-researchers—and took on a life of its own beyond our small group of teachers.

When our small collaborative first came together as a group in Athens, Georgia, in the summer of 2000, we cast a glance into the year ahead, trying to imagine how our individual classroom inquiries might move our conversations toward intrinsic questions about what is at stake in thinking about teaching and writing. We were seeking out—we now realize—a collaboration of perfect economy. We didn't want to waste our own or each other's time or impinge upon others' teaching space—though the project envisioned just such disruptions of our teaching sanctums as crucial for our own questions. None of us had met before traveling to Athens, and although we considered ourselves to be thoughtful and reflective about what we did in our classrooms, it's fair to say that we were essentially novices to teacher-research, trying to find and frame the questions that we had about our teaching and our students' learning. We all had our own teaching lives to consider, and they were very different lives. We wanted to capitalize on our range of students and grade levels, but not to pull each other needlessly outside the crucial local contexts of our work with students. At the time, for instance, I was shifting my career track from a professor of English to a new field I felt passionate about, English education; that was the beginning of the deranged trajectory that would bring me to this book. The shift required me to adopt a sometimes awkward working hybrid identity as both faculty and graduate student since I taught writing for international graduate students at Indiana University, some of whom were also my peers in the language education doctoral program. My partners in research came from a variety of backgrounds with multiple points of contact as classroom teachers, students, and researchers: Joanne Wisniewski, a veteran of the Western Massachusetts Writing Project, was a middle school language arts teacher for the second time after several years outside of education in an administrative position for a nonprofit; Leslie Rutkowsky was in the early years of her teaching career and taught English to suburban high schoolers outside Philadelphia, but she was also completing graduate work for a master's at the University of Pennsylvania; and Gloria Reeves, an adjunct instructor in Indianapolis working with urban college students in a basic writing course, was also a recent participant in the Indiana Teachers of Writing (ITW) Writing Project.

In a very pragmatic sense, then, William Carlos Williams's short poem "The Red Wheelbarrow" was for us a choice well suited to our interest in writing and literature: something that might appeal to college students without being too difficult for seventh graders; something short enough to insert into our already crowded curricula, and yet substantial enough to elicit rich student response from a range of cultural, generational, and linguistic backgrounds. But before I create the impression that this was a necessary choice of text integral to our cross-site discoveries, let me confess that it was also a rather arbitrary, perhaps even desperate, choice made literally minutes before we left Georgia at the end of that first meeting. Any number of poems might have worked just as well. Where—or who—the suggestion for the poem came from remains a mystery, lost to the moment of our first official meeting under our provisional moniker, PorTRAIT Writing/Curriculum Group. By the end of our cross-site visits a year later, and after seeing the kind of student responses generated throughout the first stages of collaborative research, however, we had come to appreciate the poem's descriptive capacity and its potential to foster engaged, provocative approaches to writing and representing the world around us. More important, we had come to see, in our writing about each other's classrooms, images of what writing pedagogy might be in our own classrooms. Our descriptive, research-focused acts created possibilities and scenarios for changing or resisting the scripts of our prior practice. In an attempt to capture something of that praxis-oriented energy and enthusiasm, we refigured our collaborative identity as the *DeScriptophiles.*

To invoke Williams's words heading this chapter, "The Red Wheelbarrow" was both the instrument of our collaborative inquiry and the metaphor for what we have since discovered about writing, thinking, and teaching over the course of a two-year collaboration. Those sixteen words became the vehicle for multiple cross-site observations, and they initiated a vital movement in our own dispositions and conceptions about teaching. Such possibilities for educational growth are, I believe, intrinsic to the images we create (and use) for teaching and learning. That is not to say that the meaning of such images is ever static, or that the impulse of our practice has been to fix (for us and for our students) a single way of being in the classroom. Indeed, throughout this collaboration each new view of the student artifacts and reflections on our lessons produced new questions, for us individually and for the group project. The collective range of student responses and teacher engagements has pulled us and our students away from a focus on the "accuracy" of representations, interpretations, and student compositions. What's more, our collaboration has confronted us with a similar range of images and interpretations about our own teaching and visions of student learning. These share some features for all of us, but each of these images is always also a personal *refiguration* in Ricoeur's sense, an active construction of meaning to shape our own lives and teaching situations.

Just as the poem contains layers of meaning, the research project itself had multiple layers and pathways that could be traveled or blazed. The current picture I'd like to offer emerges from this recursive collaborative process, revealing teachers from grade school to grad school stepping beyond their own classrooms, deranging their practice, to become critical listeners and observers but also *interpreters* of each other's practice. By joining and sharing in the local conversations and concerns of our colleagues, we helped each other envision vivid and growing images of successful practice that we could take back into the frameworks of our local settings.

Lucky Links and Critical Reflections

The confluence of settings and choice of engagements ended up being what teachers call a "lucky link," for it has been inexhaustible in its ability to help us generate new meanings and understandings about our own teaching practices. The first round of cross-site visitations, for instance, sparked initial conversations between Joanne, Gloria, Leslie, and me that began to generate a momentum of their own. The teacher reflections and visitor observations below offer an account of that first stage of the process, in which our physical displacements pointed us toward pedagogical movements; they witness the intersection of key insights, moments, and classroom acts. Although not every teaching reflection has an accompanying written visitor observation, the reflective narratives follow the chronology of the *poem in practice* and the general sequence of cross-site visits.[1] In this way, I hope to highlight not just the alternate perspectives of a particular day of teaching, but also the accretive power of the collaboration to create for the teaching of the poem *in multiple classrooms* an expansive capacity to meet students at the point of meaning-making. To this end I have attached additional commentary to the initial reflections and observations that invites further re-visioning of "what happened." The collection of classroom scenes as a whole shows a number of instances in which a particular strand of student interest or teacher practice in one attempt later threads its way through other attempts—acquiring pattern and more definite design with someone else. Though our interpretations of the engagements and our understanding of the poem vary, central to these interchanges is an appreciation for the value of alternate perspectives on meaning-making. The observations cumulatively create a sideshadowing perspective (see Morson; Welch) of classroom practice, offering not just alternative accounts of what was, but suggesting paths for what future practice might be.

In the late summer of 2001, when we met again in Athens, we were a slightly smaller group, though Leslie's wedding plans didn't prevent her from sending electronic dispatches about her own teaching of the poem and reflections on my classroom. Still, the attrition that affected the entire PorTRAIT Project created another fortuitous connection for our group. As Joanne, Gloria, and I were drafting an early account of the project, we acquired a vital critical listener, Bonnie Tipaldi. A writing instructor at Springfield Technical Community College (STCC), Bonnie was a Western Massachusetts Writing Project colleague of Joanne's and a stray member of the newly defunct PorTRAIT Literature Group. As reader, critic, and listener, Bonnie helped us transform the project from a story about "what I saw in my fellow teacher's classroom on a grant-funded site visit" to a developing and growing narrative about the value of teacher-research networks in English education. Through the many drafts and feedback sessions for our writing, there began to emerge confirmation that the discoveries gleaned from our early partnerships might foster more wide-reaching options for teaching literature and writing for the profession. What's more, as we solidified the story of our collaboration, we also started to envision new directions for our own teaching and research. Having a critical listener outside the original collaboration and site visits helped us shift our horizons of meaning—from composing a simple report of the PorTRAIT Writing/Curriculum Group to producing something from the DeScriptophiles that might just speak to the profession of English education at large.

Then, in the summer of 2002, Gloria, Joanne, and I met Bonnie at the Five Colleges center in Amherst, Massachusetts, to set about writing a collaborative reflection on our experience. With Bonnie acting as our writing coach and critic, the three of us began to think more seriously about where the conversation/collaboration/confrontation among our classrooms would take us. Drawing from her own expertise as a writing instructor at STCC, Bonnie invited us to use the Williams poem to help us draw and write our understanding of the collaboration and what it might mean for others. "During this collaboration," she prompted, "so much depended upon . . . what?" With Bonnie as conductor, we composed some of the alternating reflections of the next section. I've further orchestrated that account here, re-inserting fragments of Leslie's participation in the poem in practice, and I've added three brief reflective interludes to highlight further the key shifts in our inquiry. In February 2004, the three of us met again in Athens to compose the updated accounts of our collaboration and our current teaching, research, and practice. In our accounts, we take a brief "backshadowing" glance that turns our inquiry back to our individual contexts, viewing our present situations in the light of our past collaboration and all that still depends upon it; but we also suggest a range of viable trajectories for our continuing practice, and we hope for the role of collaborative teacher-research in the profession.

Finding the Music of the Classroom (Eight Variations on a Deranged Theme)

Overture

The facts of our collaboration are these: The idea for using William Carlos Williams's poem "The Red Wheelbarrow" in different ways at our different grade levels emerged collaboratively. Joanne, Leslie, Gloria, and I used the poem (with considerable success) in middle school, high school, undergraduate, and graduate classes. We visited each other's classrooms and wrote our observations, then shared our impressions of those experiences. But on their own, such "facts" say very little about the process of discovery and the embedded contexts that gave meaning to these events and teaching acts. In an essay on the writing process as discovery, Bob Tierney invokes Louis Agassiz's famous assertion that "facts are stupid things . . . until brought into connection with some general law" (12) to chart his own transformation as a science teacher, from presenter of facts to facilitator of learning. Despite my own reservations about Agassiz in the context of American history noted in Chapter 1, I share with Tierney an interest in Agassiz's injunction to "look, look, look" again (qtd. in Tierney 12) at any object or phenomenon we hope to understand. Although we are less interested in asserting a general law about teaching writing or teaching Williams's "The Red Wheelbarrow" in particular, the accounts here follow the advice to see and see again what it is that happens when teachers and students encounter the same piece of literature in multiple and diverse contexts.

I used the poem as a *thesis-generator* in two different sections of an academic writing class designed primarily for international graduate students in the school of education at Indiana University, Bloomington. In one section, students were asked to finish the sentence, "In order to do/understand _____X_____, *so much depends upon . . .* " In the second section, students were asked to finish the sentence in a similar fashion, but in reference to an essay focusing on the differences between expert and novice teachers. Both sections of students were encouraged to follow the structure of the poem and to attempt a similar level of concreteness in imagery. Gloria introduced the poem activity in a college composition class at an urban university, as a vehicle for the study of descriptive scene building in student prose. Students were also asked to finish the sentence "So much depends . . . " in relation to their understanding of successful strategies for writing. Joanne similarly asked her seventh-grade students to consider the imagery of the poem and their own writing of poetic sentences through transmediating their understanding of the poem into visual texts (Shorte, Harste, with Burke). Leslie used the poem in a ninth-grade humanities English class to introduce "weight of words" in sentences. As her students began to find their own voice in their writing, simply committing words to get an essay or composition finished wasn't enough. They became fascinated with "why things are the way they are" in writing, and Leslie mobilized the poem to open inquiry into how words inscribe meaning, and how, in the service of meaning-making, "much" hangs upon the placement of words and things with respect to each other.

In the descriptions and reflections that follow, I want to draw particular attention to the moments of realization and understanding about what meaning-making looked like in our classrooms—for us, our students, and our visiting collaborators. Our views as teacher-researchers are located and figured by our own memory and position within the classroom and pedagogical space. The perspectives we offer as observers of each other's classrooms are no less positioned, and they are not meant either to contradict or to necessarily "authorize" the teacher's view. Rather, what I hope will become clear, through the juxtaposition of views and the year-long chronicle of the poem in practice, is that the sites of teaching, learning, and knowing in our classrooms are always moving, subject to negotiation and perspective, and often lie somewhere amid the conversation and confrontation of our classrooms. This particular refiguration begins and ends with my own classroom, and the movements are thus orchestrated in part by those opening and closing scenes as they have shaped my own understanding and practice. My colleagues' stories might begin elsewhere in their own histories as teachers and researchers. To allow those alternate views to create a sideshadowing perspective on the larger collaboration, I've also included their end reflections on *this* version of events to help highlight some of the ongoing tensions between individual achievement and community building in classroom practice as well as the effect that regional differences have on teaching. Even with those variations, our experience underscores the vital importance of the shift that occurs when teachers become researchers: these connections and dislocations among professionals and within individual praxis become visible, objects available for reflection and critique.

First Movement

GENERATING FOCUS WITH THE THESIS-MAKING MACHINE, VERSION X: JOHN'S GRADUATE WRITING CLASSROOM FOR INTERNATIONAL STUDENTS (INDIANA UNIVERSITY, BLOOMINGTON, OCTOBER 2000)

My first attempt at using Williams's poem to help generate thesis-type claims for larger research and inquiry was a mixed affair;

and the story of my two passes at the engagement with the same type of English for Academic Purposes (EAP) course ironically refigures the discussion about expert-novice teaching differences (see Livingston and Borko) with the second group. With the group in the fall class, I was an occasional instructor, interning with another professor so that I could take over responsibility for the course the following semester. I was also a new doctoral student in the same program as many students in the class, which made my standing somewhat ambiguous, both for me and for my peers/students. Prior to teaching the poem, I had sent an email to all the students in advance of our class meeting. I included the poem and an explanation of the activity I would pair it with, stressing that we would not really be concerned about the poem's meaning, but more with its form and use of imagery to create meaning. I invited questions via email about the poem or the activity and received none. In a presentation in a graduate seminar I was taking, I had recently used the poem with what I thought was great success to explicate the nuances of Dewey's philosophy of education in "My Pedagogic Creed," and so I looked forward to using the poem in this writing class to focus the construction of an inquiry project.

I should underscore here, though, that as an intern in the class I was not regularly part of the whole-class discussions on writing and the readings on how to conduct educational research. This context is important, considering that my past research training was in the humanities and involved archival work and interpretive approaches to text and textual meaning. At the time, the social science model of research writing was to me a kind of graceless reportage, layered over a statistical foundation. This EAP course was also the first classroom I had had in which a majority of the students were not native speakers of English. My role as intern generally brought me into the room for only the last forty-five to sixty minutes of a three-hour, weekly class in order to address specific writing questions and strategies. For this meeting, I had been given additional time by the course professor, so I had planned for an engagement of forty minutes prefaced by a brief five- to ten-minute demonstration of how to use the poem as a thesis-generator, with any remaining time devoted to individual and small-group conferencing about inquiry ideas. I had not anticipated that thesis-focused research was likely the least of their worries.

I think I ended up spending at least forty minutes, and perhaps an hour, on the demonstration alone before I felt any confidence that the students were ready to try some verse of their own. They had been working on doing interview papers and had been reading a dissertation from one of their colleagues about the difficulties experienced by international students when writing academic prose in the American academy. I thought that these two topics would be grounded in their own experience and would allow for drawing vivid pictures of their encounters with writing in English. That was the image of success for the engagement that I had in my mind, anyway. What happened instead was that I had students wondering what poetry had to do with educational research and writing research in the first place.

It was a good question and one I thought would be easy to answer—as I said, "Both involve the structuring of language for particular and specific rhetorical and hermeneutic effect; each is a doing of things with and through words."

No go.

Try again.

Silence. Smiles.

Some nods.

Try again.

It didn't help that the regular professor for the class entered halfway through one of my early explanations and (not unreasonably) asked for clarification herself, in a rather pointed way that suggested (so I felt at the time) that perhaps I didn't really know what I was doing or asking them to do, and that I should explain it again.

So, try again.

Eventually, some students started talking among themselves in their own language, and it became clear that some understood what I was asking them to do and were attempting to explain the activity to others. I decided then to let them work together, and I would work the room, fielding questions individually and from pairs, rather than in a whole-class discussion setting. This worked perfectly well, and the final images were quite evocative of what their lives in a new country were like—learning to drive, preparing a formal meal for a guest, advising a peer on how to approach a professor about a grade: these were the analogues the students offered at the end.

By then I was exhausted, but I realized that for the success of the engagement that day, so much depended not only on the prior interaction between student and teacher—especially on the perception of where authority and knowledge reside in the classroom—but also on the ability of students to become co-inquirers, alternately scaffolding each other's knowledge in the face of new ideas and situations. This was something I hadn't set out to discover; but by tracking events of the class, that is, by *living* classroom research, I began to get close to new ideas, ones I could investigate further, about how teachers and students learn in the second language and the EAP classroom.

Second Movement

FINDING METAPHORS: GLORIA'S OBSERVATION OF JOHN'S CLASS (OCTOBER 2000)

While visiting John's college class for international graduate students, I observed that John used a very professional approach with "The Red Wheelbarrow." Professionals in their own countries, these are graduate students pursuing their major fields of study at Indiana University at Bloomington. These are serious students.

John placed the poem on the overhead projector, read it aloud, and then began describing the activity. The students appeared puzzled. From the questions they asked John, I could tell they were trying to discern why they were doing this and how they could do it "right." John continued to re-explain the assignment, making it friendly to them by allowing them to work in small groups. He allowed them to converse in their native language to help each other understand the assignment.

It was obvious that with the cultural background, educational experience, and professional level of these students, creative assignments such as this were out of the ordinary. They were caught off guard until John chose the word *metaphor* to help explain the concept. The students immediately showed relief, some even delight, to relax into a figurative exercise that would engage them in a different way of thinking about language. They read their work aloud, no doubt feeling successful as students studying English.

When John used the word metaphor, the students were able to relate the assignment to a concept they recognized. Immediately, their home language words for metaphor were bandied about the room, smiles appeared, pens hit paper, and the students began reading their work aloud to one another. It took about twenty minutes for the class to allow integration of the red wheelbarrow activity into their past ideas of education. So much depends on the background of the students. In John's explanation of the assignment, he reacted to students and continued to vary the vocabulary and order of instructions until the students found the specific clue, familiar to them, that allowed their minds to pass from concrete areas of English usage to the softer space of Williams's poetry. So much depends on a teacher's persistence.

Reflective Interlude 1: John

What is immediately apparent in these two versions of the same literacy event is the weight attached to notions of expertise and success in the classroom. In her observations, Gloria ascribes much more "professional" demeanor to me and to my students than I had considered. At first this puzzled me, until I remembered that I almost always wore a tie and pressed shirt to teach. The reasons for doing so are perhaps linked to my own focus on feeling out of place and without a sense of legitimate authority in the classroom when I began teaching graduate students instead of the undergraduates to whom I was more accustomed. Elsewhere, the inside/outside differences in our two perspectives do not necessarily point to a truer or more reliable account as much as they suggest ways that another view locates and names "success" in the classroom differently.

Back in her own classroom a few months later, Gloria attempted to create a similar space for student expression, what she describes as an effort for the class to be able to look at "differences without feeling different." This concern for a classroom ethos of care and respect comes through in the rapport students have with each other and with Gloria. Here, her preoccupation also reinforces what she had identified as the success of my experience with the poem, that is, student experience matching teacher expectation. But where I had located my teaching failure in students trying to align their productions with what they *perceived* as my expectations, and viewed as my success those moments when students' own learning agendas frustrated my planning, Gloria highlights correctness and accuracy of representation among student productions. There is no anxiety on her part about being taken seriously. In fact, throughout Gloria's description there is a sense of affection for and protectiveness over her students. I offer her account of her own classroom here as another look at teacher-student-poem in the writing classroom. As you read her description of her students and classroom setting, consider how she places herself and locates the desires for student success. These positionings take on a different cast in Gloria's retrospective at the end of this chapter.

Third Movement

LOOKING AT DIFFERENCES WITHOUT FEELING DIFFERENT: GLORIA'S FIRST-YEAR COLLEGE WRITING CLASSROOM BUILDS SCENES FOR COMPOSITION AND CONVERSATION (INDIANA UNIVERSITY–PURDUE UNIVERSITY INDIANAPOLIS, DECEMBER 2000)

The day I brought the giant pack of crayons into the room, the students in my basic composition class sat up straight, then leaned forward attentively. One of the course goals set forth by the writing department is *oneness* or uniqueness. I had seen in my students a reluctance to include originality in their writing. I knew that these students, who chose to wear multiple piercings, tattoos, unnatural shapes and colors of hair, and eccentric clothing styles, had more oneness than they were incorporating into their classwork. In essays, they defined and discussed a topic but failed to relate their own involvement with the topic. They could dance around a topic with incredible agility. I encouraged students to include their previous experience and knowledge to engage the reader in a dialogue of shared ideas and thoughts as people from the same world, yet different and unique.

On several occasions we had discussed scene building as a tool for "showing" what we mean rather than just telling. For this activity students were asked to work in small groups, which they did, but they all remained unusually close together. Today there was an unusual amount of open, comfortable verbal interaction compared to other class days. I asked the students to identify scenes in the poem and represent them with crayon drawings, then gave them twenty minutes to work.

I chose to pull directly from the imagery of the red wheelbarrow poem to motivate the students, appealing to their creative side and multiple literacies. I wanted this lesson to help them draw from their bank of experience and value those experiences as something of interest to readers. At first the students were reluctant to create with crayons, as if they were being asked to bare their souls on paper. But the call of the crayon was too strong, and eventually the students' individuality became evident. One young woman drew chickens with four legs. Another drew pink and purple mountains, reminiscent of her home country, behind the wheelbarrow. Several Indiana natives drew cornstalks growing alongside the wheelbarrow. The students compared their drawings; they laughed and communicated on a level that differed from that of the first two months of class. The comfort level shifted as they took turns sharing stories about the time they gathered eggs from chickens or worked on Grandpa's farm. The experience of smelling the crayon wax, seeing the colors, and touching the familiar shape wrapped in tinted paper seemed to help ease the students into the literary world of the red wheelbarrow.

The students shared and recognized their artistic individuality and uniqueness, finding that most drawings showed something new, something they hadn't thought of before, or something that surprised them. An appreciation of their unique thoughts, ideas, and experiences helped the students understand the power they carry as writers. These students took our class to a place of understanding, where we looked at individual differences without feeling different. Regardless of racial, religious, or socioeconomic parameters, family orientation, or community membership, the students talked about the ways that people are unique rather than different. We didn't make judgments of "bad" or "good." The dynamics of this group caused the conversation to center on diversity within the framework of a classroom that united to work together and appreciated the thoughts and talents of each student.

Now, was this all the poem and the students could produce? Could data be produced on a more collegiate and cognitive level? Donald Graves uses a bucket metaphor to express this aspect of collecting pertinent data: "So much of gathering data is in knowing where to put your bucket in order to get worthwhile information" (155). In addition to the drawing exercise, I asked students to complete this statement: "[In relation to writing,] so much depends upon . . ." The result was a bucketful of imaginative and expressive written data.

A serious student with sharp wit wrote

> "So much depends"
> on writing
> street signs, books, magazines, newspapers, and four-
> lined poems that don't rhyme.

One of the quieter students in the class (up to this point) stayed late to complete a rap poem with admirable rhythm and rhyme:

> *So much depends upon . . .*
> Writing your name.
> Writing the essays is the
> *Name of the game.*
>
> My name is [. . .] and
> *I write enough*
> But rap is my thang
> *So don't get too tough.*
>
> *So much depends on writing*
> *To as far as book, novels, poems, essays, they all*
> *require reciting.*
> *You realize when your done you feel warm*
> *But in the beginning you have to think hard*
> *On whether you want it in open or closed-form.*

One student spent most of her time constructing a pen for the chickens. With pencil, she drew a six-sided figure showing detailed panels of chicken wire fencing. She then chose crayons for the colored background of rain, grass, and the magenta wheelbarrow (complete with brown stains on the inside). Perhaps unsure about how to draw a chicken, or wanting to see how well others did theirs, the artist quickly drew in the two confused-looking chickens before she handed in the paper.

This student had considered her process as she worked, thinking about the chickens as she prepared their context. How big should they be? What characteristics should they have to be believable? How should they look? How do I make them look real for the audience? Everyone here will see them when I draw them; how will my peers react? How do I want them to look?

All are good questions to ask in the composition process, for whether one is drawing or writing, context, audience, voice, and other elements of composition are crucial considerations.

Reflective Interlude 2: John

The opening focus on scene building that Gloria takes with her students is echoed throughout the ensuing movements. Though Gloria's college students bring to the poem academic and life experiences that differ from those Joanne's seventh graders draw from, both classrooms and teachers trace a similar meaning-making process based on transactional reading, prior knowledge, and scene and imagery building practice in student writing. Those emphases return later in the final movements of Leslie's and my classrooms.

Fourth Movement

"CLOSE YOUR EYES AND TELL ME WHAT YOU SEE": IMAGINING THE POETRY OF SENTENCES IN JOANNE'S SEVENTH-GRADE CLASSROOM (WEST SPRINGFIELD MIDDLE SCHOOL, MASSACHUSETTS, JANUARY 2001)

On the first day after Christmas break I introduced the genre of poetry. My students were very familiar with rhyming poems and even longer works like Alfred Noyes's "The Highwayman," which they had read in reading class. We started with the concept of imagery and notions of how a poem creates a picture in your mind. We stressed the transactional aspect of reading: the fact that all of your previous experience is also important in how you interpret the work.

Each student was asked to write one sentence, and being in New England in January, many focused on snow. Two examples were "The sun came out and melted my snowman" and "the snow falls on my backyard." Students were then instructed to insert "phrase breaks" and rewrite their sentence as a poem. For these two students, the resulting sentence poems became

The sun	Snow
Came out	falls
And	gentle and quiet
Melted	on my
My snowman	backyard

Just as the second student above removed "the" and inserted "gentle and quiet," several students added or deleted words for clarity of image and understanding. By the end of each class, every student had written one or more short poems.

On day two, I began with a review of one-sentence poems the students had revised for homework and then introduced William Carlos Williams as a famous poet. I told students that the poem we would consider was written in 1923, and that Williams was born in New Jersey and worked as a country doctor. Once they had discussed what this life experience could mean, I introduced the poem. I handed students a copy of the poem and asked them to draw what it meant to them. At first students weren't sure what to draw, and they needed some prompting to think about what they saw and how to begin. I didn't give out crayons or markers, but a few students did introduce color.

After a short time, we used their illustrations to begin a class discussion about the poem. Students focused on words or phrases they felt were important—"red wheelbarrow," "white chickens," "glazed with rain," and "so much depends upon." To draw the discussion to a close, I read a poem I had found on the Internet entitled "Ruminations on a Wheelbarrow." Some students recognized the word *ruminate* because it had been previously introduced as our school "word of the day" during morning announcements. Teachers at my school refer to happenings like this as "lucky links."

For my second class of the day, I presented the poem in similar fashion but instructed students to draw only one stanza. Each row was assigned a stanza, and students in rows two, three, and four began to draw almost immediately. The row with stanza one—"So much depends upon"—struggled because no pictures or images came readily to mind. One student came up with a plate of eggs and bacon; another drew an illustration of Atlas with the world on his shoulders; a third made a collage of the earth, people, a house for shelter, a truck for transportation, and a plate of food.

One student then came to the board and did a whole-class illustration. Students told her what to draw and where to put it on the board. We also introduced some colored chalk to add to the picture. Sometimes students agreed on what to put into the illustration but argued on placement and size; some felt size was equal to importance in the poem. Class ended with a picture on the board that represented the class consensus of what "The Red Wheelbarrow" meant to them.

For my third group of the day, I went back to the original lesson plan. As I look at the results from this group, I see much more detail in the pictures and wonder if this is because these students benefited from my own previous experience with teaching the poem, and the explanation of what I expected was clearer. After their drawings were done, I raised the screen that shielded the picture drawn by the previous class, and they were amazed by the similarities.

I certainly left that day with a sense of awe at how much could be learned from sixteen carefully chosen words. I made a note to myself that *parsimony* has a place in lesson planning and encouraging students to express themselves—because when given a platform, they will draw on their own resources. Interestingly enough, I had never used this poem with seventh graders before, but I look forward to using this lesson another year. It was a terrific springboard for discussion and became a reference point throughout the remainder of the school year. It was not uncommon to hear students say, "Close your eyes and tell me what you see" when they were looking for imagery in small group discussions.

Fifth Movement

FINDING THE BREAKS: JOHN'S OBSERVATION OF JOANNE'S CLASSROOM (JANUARY 2001)

I spent the first two days after winter break in Joanne's seventh-grade classroom. The first day Joanne introduced an excited but reluctant group of students—back in school too soon!—to a unit on poetry by asking them to write at the top of a sheet of paper a single sentence about something that happened to them over vacation. The directions were to write one sentence, find the breaks, write out the breaks, and use condensed language. (My own sentence, based on a Christmas Eve trauma with our dogs still fresh in my memory, was "The German Shepherd mauled the Chihuahua." The Chihuahua, by the way, is alive and well.) During the engagement Joanne talked with her students about what "finding the breaks" in their sentences meant. With a sentence of her own, she demonstrated how to isolate parts of the language. Students worked as a class and individually to try to construct a picture of the event related in the single sentence. Each break would become a separate line, and students could add information to the sentence. After that, students tried to enhance the detail and description of each line. (My sentence-poem became, "The monstrous / german shepherd / mauled the / feisty chihuahua / on grandma's / lap.")

This exercise allowed students to talk about their vacations, but it also helped set up the discussion of Williams's poem the next day. On that day, Joanne had the same basic engagement for her three English/language arts periods (fourth, sixth, and eighth periods): she would hand out a copy of "The Red Wheelbarrow" and ask students to draw their impressions or thoughts about the poem or its meaning on the sheet of paper. But during her conversations with me between each period, she might suddenly think of something new or slightly different to try. The result, then, was actually three related but entirely different lessons.

In fourth period, the class began with a brief review of homework, then announcements about upcoming homework and extra credit, and finally the engagement with Williams's poem. As Joanne handed out the poem on a sheet of paper with title and author at the top (below was the poem itself, separated from the title and author and the bottom two-thirds of the page, which were completely empty), she gave the history of Williams's life and work. After she read the poem aloud a few times, she asked for student responses, and with them, briefly linked to the language of the poem some of his biography as a Patterson, New Jersey, doctor serving some rural and poor communities. Then students were asked to draw the poem on the handout. Students shared their drawings, and it was clear that each chose to focus on a different aspect of the imagery, although they talked about the differences that they had inferred about the poem (many drew farm yards or barns, for instance; one added fog). This led to a brief discussion about the accuracy of representation—some students drew only what the poem explicitly mentioned (red wheelbarrow, white chickens, rain) whereas others drew extended scenes to provide a context to help explain why "so much depends upon" the rest. Joanne ended the engagement for this period by reading a tribute poem titled "Ruminations on a Wheelbarrow," which the students cited as having the school's word for the day—ruminate.

The sixth-period class began with students reading their own sentence-poems from the previous day. There were several interruptions and student comments (good natured and enthusiastic) before Joanne handed out the sheet with the Williams poem. This time she had each row of the class focus on a single stanza to draw. Joanne and I moved through the room consulting with the students, especially the row that had the first stanza. The class started a discussion about their individual row drawings, arriving at the observation that many had drawn "things people need." Then Joanne asked a student to draw on the chalkboard the things that each row had come up with. The result was a whole-class picture for the entire poem. The class ranked the poem as a 3 on a scale of 1–5. Joanne recalled for them that the poet Elizabeth Blackwell, whom they had studied, was often paid in food. So in this economy, William Carlos Williams might merit his two chickens for the poem, a student remarked, but not the whole farm. The period ended with students reversing the process of the day before and trying to turn the poem back into a sentence.

The eighth period had a teacher's aide. Again Joanne tweaked the introductions and instructions to the engagement. This time she asked students to "draw a picture of what you think the poem is about, and include something from each of the four stanzas." Here the students all read the same poem, but each drew a different picture. Joanne herself drew the whole-class picture on the chalkboard, as students called out details that they thought should be part of the image. In the process of this group composition, students added details and images that were not necessarily part of their original drawings.

Reflective Interlude 3: John

When looking at both accounts of the same two days, we see again the demurral of the teacher and a reluctance to claim authority drawn from an active and engaged reflection on her practice. Joanne's memories of the class dismiss or dilute her active reflection on her practice throughout the day, whereas my observations focus on the rich variety of student response across the day that both elicited and emerged from these teaching variations. But what stays with me about this experience is the nimble and confident way in which Joanne switched her plan. The overall objectives remained the same, but her delivery changed with each group of students. Joanne's brief contextualizing information about poem and author offered the necessary minimal information that everyday readers routinely expect when they look for a book to read (Blau 43), but she did not over-determine students' responses with such information. Instead, she allowed the lesson to take its own natural course in each of the different class periods. Joanne embodies here the very qualities of the expert teacher that my own students and I discussed some weeks later, when I introduced the poem to another group of international graduate students. And this willingness to let students lead the teacher and each other is further echoed in the scene from Leslie's classroom below. The scene and dialogue are transmediated from Leslie's electronic dispatch to the DeScriptophiles prior to our summer 2001 meeting in Athens, and from my own memory of her classroom on my visit in December 2000.

Sixth Movement

SCENES OF STUDENT-TEACHER DIALOGUE ABOUT THE GRAMMAR OF POETRY AND THE POETRY OF GRAMMAR, A FRAGMENT: LESLIE'S NINTH-GRADE HUMANITIES/ENGLISH CLASS (LOWER MERION HIGH SCHOOL, PENNSYLVANIA, MARCH 2001)

The scene: a suburban high school classroom. Students are seated at desks arranged in a crescent, roughly facing a chalkboard, which is covered by a screen, its contents hidden from view. The teacher, Leslie Rutkowsky, sits at a student desk within the semicircle. On this day in her writing class, Leslie has chosen to look at grammar holistically in relation to poetry. Grammar is an area that many of her students find particularly frustrating. Using the poem to help them look at issues of grammar, Leslie hopes the exercise will be different from most of their prior experiences with grammar. Later, students will report that it was "more fun." Leslie begins the engagement by asking students first to consider what they know about poetry, and then to consider the way in which "The Red Wheelbarrow" confronts that knowledge.

As students settle into the routine of classroom conversation, the teacher begins.

> LESLIE: What is poetry? How do we expect poetry to appear, sound, make us feel?
>
> STUDENT 1: Poems should rhyme—
>
> STUDENT 2: . . . be about flowers—
>
> STUDENT 3: . . . meadows—
>
> STUDENT 4: Robert Frost stuff . . .
>
> STUDENT 5: The form looks like a lot of lines in order, short sentences with descriptive words.

Leslie reveals "The Red Wheelbarrow," which has been hidden behind the screen covering the blackboard.

LESLIE: How does this poem fit our expectations?
STUDENT 1: This is *not* a poem.

Sounds of general agreement from students.

STUDENT 6: My three-year-old sister could write that!

A discussion of Williams's poem begins. The students wrestle intensively to locate the "hidden symbolism" of white chickens and rain water.

LESLIE: What images did William Carlos Williams create? Did he "show" rather than "tell"?
STUDENT 7: He showed us color, texture, where things were placed.

These ninth graders are trying to negotiate meaning on the level of the sentence—a very peculiar sentence by Williams.

LESLIE: How did the author make us think about how sentences are put together?

Murmurs. Shrugs.

LESLIE: What must all sentences have?
STUDENT: [*inaudible*]
LESLIE: Where are the subject and verb in this sentence?

Furrowed brows.

After parsing the sentence for parts of speech, Leslie explains to the class that "grammar is not about memorizing a list of words that are supposed to be adjectives or adverbs; instead it is about making sense of how specific words are used in a specific context to create a specific meaning."

The class makes a chart of how this sentence worked to make meaning, to create images, and to inspire the reader without making its complex structure known to the reader. "Here," Leslie later tells her colleagues in her graduate program at the University of Pennsylvania and passes along to her collaborators, the DeScriptophiles, "were the ways we found where the grammar rules didn't help us, but where figuring out the logic of the language did."

Students leave the classroom with profound questions about the nature of writing that pull at the fabric of their prior understanding, unraveling a newly found sense of what it might mean later when Leslie asks them in their compositions, "Why did you use this word here? What is it doing? What do you want it to do?"

Seventh Movement

GENERATING FOCUS WITH THE THESIS-MAKING MACHINE, VERSION Y: JOHN'S GRADUATE WRITING CLASSROOM FOR INTERNATIONAL STUDENTS (INDIANA UNIVERSITY, BLOOMINGTON, APRIL 2001)

The next time I used the poem—this time in the spring term—I had my own class, so I was the default authority figure in the room. But I also had worked throughout the semester to build a collaborative relationship with my diverse group of students, many of whom were accomplished professionals in their home countries before coming to the United States as graduate students. I did not want to become the sole dispenser of knowledge, so I encouraged ongoing negotiation about what our class could and should be in order for the students to become the writers they wanted to be. This work had gone on for almost an entire semester before I introduced Williams's poem.

I had the whole of a three-hour period to work with the students through the poem, the essays we had read, and their own writing. I planned to begin with the poem engagement, and then use it to move into a discussion of an article by Livingston and Borko, "Expert-Novice Differences in Teaching: A Cognitive Analysis and Implications for Teacher Education," which offers a fascinating reading of the differences between the two groups of teachers, considering teaching as both complex cognitive skill and improvisational performance. We would then finish with an open discussion about the place of research in practice. I hoped to have at least forty-five minutes left at the end of class to conference with students individually or in their writing groups.

Again I sent an email to the students prior to our meeting. I included several announcements about changes in the syllabus and schedule of assignments based on their midterm evaluations and our subsequent discussions as a class about their writing goals. I also let them know that a high school teacher from Pennsylvania (Leslie) would be joining us to see what our class was like. The fourth announcement concerned the readings for the session:

> Expert-novice teachers essay and William Carlos Williams poem (which we will use to generate some focus sentences in class). The poem is included below. It is short and imagistic. We will have time in class to talk about it on its own if you like.

The chief difference between this announcement and the one from the previous term is that it was embedded as part of the larger negotiations and announcements for the class. Also, I allowed for the possibility of an open discussion of the poem itself before using it as a thesis-generator.

About a third of the students in this group were from Turkey, and as we considered what the poem might mean, several students began to whisper and then talk quietly but excitedly across the classroom in Turkish. They seemed to be in agreement about something. Finally, I asked them what they were discussing, and one of them, a doctoral student in early childhood education, said that Williams's poem reminded him very much of a famous Turkish poet, Orhan Veli Kanik. He recited some lines in Turkish and then translated: "I buy old clothes. / I buy old clothes and cut them into stars . . ." and one of the other Turkish students finished the poem. This discussion helped us to talk about the use of concrete imagery if only through simple words such as red, rain, water, wheel, chicken, and so on.

From there we moved to the structure of Williams's poem (so much depends on X and Y linked by Z), and then we began to look at an essay that addresses the differences between expert and novice teachers. The prompt for generating poems from the students this time was, "In order to understand the relationship between expert and novice teaching/teachers, so much depends upon . . ." Students wrote in groups, listing things that marked each category. At first the lists included abstract phrases or educational jargon such as "pedagogical content knowledge," "where planning occurs," and "organization of the lesson." But as they talked within their groups, and as I moved from group to group to talk with students, the lists became simultaneously more imagistic/figurative and concrete, taking on the shape of the Williams poem. One group latched onto the image of orchestration and improvisation involved in the transition from novice to expert teaching, saying that "so much depends on the music of the classroom." Another group said that expert teachers pay attention to ordinary things and so can present them in new ways, or as they said, their practice proceeds "in a 'glazed' way." The class wound down with a sort of whole-class discussion about how teachers teach, and about how important poetry and the imagistic use of language can be in writing and literacy.

Eighth Movement

Relational Meaning and the Enabling Constraints of Language: Leslie's Observation of John's Class (April 2001)

Not only is it necessary for students to wrestle with context and syntax when they are studying poetry, but it's also necessary for them to wrestle with meaning. The students in John's graduate class wrestled with the language and context of "The Red Wheelbarrow." John's emphasis on close textual analysis led his class to understand this poem in a literary sense and, perhaps more important, to synthesize the complex relationships between objects and location, between student and teacher, between novice and expert.

The initial reactions of "this poem makes no sense" and "who would write a poem about chickens?" were expected, and were used as a means to discuss manipulation of language. For these students, the subtle uses of English grammar and diction were becoming a tool rather than a hindrance. Students commented that "using 'a red wheelbarrow' makes the ordinary seem unusual, specific, special." Students asked, "Why was 'wheel / barrow' broken into two lines? What is the *real* subject of this poem?" Yet the language conveyed more meaning than the sum of any individual words, and the students explored this idea of *rela-*

tional meaning to explode the meaning of the poem. As John and his class illuminated that these seemingly random words were working for a kind of unified meaning, the poem was seen as moving toward a specific image, an image that could only be understood through implicit signals between the signifier and the signified.

The students, obviously intense, high-achieving adults who craved a sense of mastery and understanding, now had the tools to use this poem to understand relational comparisons between novice and expert. Given the model

> In order to do / understand _____X_____
> X1: [write a successful paper based on an interview]
> X2: [understand the difficulties experienced by international students when writing academic prose in the American academy],
> So much depends upon . . .

students were asked to construct a model that illustrated the difference between novice and expert teachers. Students drew analogies to music: expert teachers could improvise, and novice teachers would read the music carefully. Students drew analogies to writing: expert teachers knew what kind of revision needed to be made, and novice teachers needed to be told what to change. "The Red Wheelbarrow" was not, then, the lesson. Instead, the poem was a way into a larger discussion about language—its power, its constraints—and a discussion about pedagogy—its relationships, its theoretical base.

The DeScriptophiles, Redux: "Where are we now? Who are we now?"

In February 2004, Joanne, Gloria, and I met for the last time as a group, looked back over the reflections of the last section, and considered what our collaboration and cross-site visitations had brought us to see about teaching and ourselves. It was a difficult process because it seemed to be a valediction to our work together as well as to the poem that had carried us across country numerous times. But as Leslie notes above in her reflective observation, in the end our experience was not a lesson about the poem, but about pedagogy and relational meaning. What strikes me still about these summations is the shared sense that asking questions together changed us each professionally and individually in ways that we are still discovering in our practice.

John

Although I have to confess I was never much of a Williams fan before our collaboration, his poem now figures regularly both in my classes on literary history and theory for English majors and in discussions of learning theory with classroom teachers. To explain the poem's new priority of place in my pedagogical practice, so much depends upon writing, teaching, and thinking about writing, teaching, and thinking. Or, put another way:

> So much depends
> Upon
>
>
> Writing, teaching,
> And thinking
>
>
> About writing, teaching
> And thinking

More important, though, has been my use of the artifacts of the DeScriptophiles collaboration to talk about the location and place of teacher-research in the lives of classroom teachers and teacher educators. The double reflective entries that Joanne and I made on her classroom engagement—something we each had been trained to do through our local teacher-research networks—have allowed me, for instance, to demonstrate for new practitioners interested in teacher-research how they might begin to think about different kinds of data as they adopt an inquiry perspective on their classrooms: peer observations, reflective field notes, student artifacts. I share with my students these episodes of teachers sharing their practice, and by offering examples of my own struggles with practice—and the views of collaborative witnesses on those attempts—I try to keep my choices as a teacher open to critique and discussion.

The danger always exists, of course, that these things will simply become reified as artifacts of practice rather than as living examples of ways of teaching and thinking about teaching, but no less is true of Williams's poem. If we are only interested in fixing its meaning so that it becomes a machine casting out identical interpretations or meanings, then its value to us as teachers has a limited shelf-life. But what I have discovered each time I use the poem, and each time I talk about how our group has collaborated in that use, is that the images of praxis we come to fashion continue to change. They are alive with the energy, challenges, and tensions of our current situations, and they continue to glimmer with both the possibilities and the dangers that always attend any convergence of difference.

Joanne

At the beginning of this project, I was a grade 7 language arts teacher in a traditional classroom in a very new middle school. Today both the school and I show some wear, but my teaching is noticeably different, and I attribute part of that to my PorTRAIT experience. In 2000 I wrote a proposal for my school principal about my ideal situation for teaching writing. I described a classroom where every student would have technology available and have *time* to work at writing—that writing was actually their sole purpose, and days weren't devoted to separate studies of vocabulary words and literature selections that "must be taught."

During the summer of 2001 I received a letter from the principal informing me that I was to be the teacher in a new writing lab that was being established. This meant I would have a classroom with twenty-two laptop computers and have students for ten-week terms, and that mine would be an enrichment writing class under the auspices of Unified Arts rather than being tied only to the English department. I would also be teaching grades 6, 7, and 8 instead of just one grade level. Because of this change, I reworked the topic of my master's project to be writing curriculum for a writing lab.

On the first day of each new term, I ask students to identify three topics they would like to write about. I also ask them to identify their best piece of writing to date, and I receive a variety of answers. Some recall a project done at a much earlier grade level, and many insist that they have never really written anything "good." When I ask how they know a piece of writing is good, they tell me about the grade it received or how it hung for weeks on the bulletin board or the refrigerator door at home, or how they worked harder on this than anything else they ever wrote. To those who can't identify a piece that they consider their best, I respond, "Good, that excites me because it could happen right here."

For our project with PorTRAIT, I took a very visual approach to Williams's poem and concentrated on imagery or on having students draw out the poem. I find today that this focus on imagery works in my writing lab because my students often need to see something to understand it. I've learned too that many students don't have an appreciation of literature from the past. So I work hard to find samples of stories and poems that are good writing but written by young teens, rather than rely on Poe and Dickinson for model work. When my students see higher-level vocabulary employed by their own age group, they work harder to improve the quality of their own writing. Literary devices like similes, personification, and imagery become quests rather than accidental happenings in student writing. Not all of these ventures are successful, but students become more selective in word choice and what they want to keep in a piece and where they need to edit and revise.

Once students have a piece of writing that they are proud of because they have worked and edited and revised it and moved up the writing process to publishing level, it's easier to encourage them to persevere when the going gets tough. I offer a venue for student publication that allows them to share their work with the school and community. My lab gives them flexibility to focus on writing pieces they want to write, rather than constantly laboring over assignments that *teachers* thought would be good to work on. It is definitely more exciting to help a student find his or her own voice on a topic of personal interest than to make up constant assignments that students do halfheartedly because they must.

I used to think that a good teacher came up with assignments that students could relate to. My collaboration with my PorTRAIT colleagues, in my group and in the other groups, has given me the courage to allow students many choices within the classroom; so I might have twenty-two students working on eight or ten or twenty-two different projects within the structure of the same class. I would have thought it impossible to teach this way if I hadn't had experiences in my own life that encouraged me to write about things I had a passion for. I truly feel that we get mediocre results from many student writers because they are simply going through the motions of writing on an assigned topic that they really don't care about and aren't invested in. My teacher training had me working hard to design lessons that would appeal to the majority of students in the classroom. Now my students work with me to design a project that they *want* to write about. For some, the work might be autobiographical, while for others it's fiction or fantasy, prose or poetry. Each student picks according to interest and ability level. I might have them look at a certain work as a model, but they have a wide range of choices.

After I have looked at samples of first drafts, I still teach mini-lessons at the beginning of class to address topics many students are struggling with. These take five to seven minutes at the beginning of class and address topics like dialogue, incorporating research into historical fiction, and annotated bibliography. I base my teaching on a coaching model, where a clinic on a certain skill might benefit the group, but most of the time I work at the laptop with individual students. My colleagues have seen improvements in student willingness to write in their classrooms, try new things, seek out the best word choice, and even embrace revision.

I strongly feel that teachers learn techniques that work in classrooms when they study what others are doing, or when they feel enabled to make changes in what they do. An experience like teacher-research or cross-visitation allows teachers to feel empowered to try new things in their own classrooms. Maybe even beyond that, it makes them try things more than once, because not everything works the first time or with every group of students. Much like my students who need to have that first successful writing experience, I need successful teaching experiences and colleagues I can turn to who will help me evaluate my practices to make writing a better learning experience for each student and all students who pass through my lab.

Gloria

Standing in my composition classroom, I witness the flourish of abandonment as students exit in a bustle of backpacks and notebooks. A pile of free-writes awaits my attention—not for grading, but for my feedback that will encourage students to think deeper and write even more freely next time. I shuffle the papers, perusing the first lines; a smile comes across my face.

Before being introduced to teacher-research, the end of each class left me puzzling over a lesson for the next class that would motivate students, first, to return to class, and second, to write more than one-half page of text. But now I look forward to reading the thoughts and ideas that will allow me to identify the writing needs, as well as the societal needs, of my students. I feel confident responding in a way that encourages critical thinking and values identity. Teaching is now a means of expanding my pedagogy along with the world of knowledge for students. Ways of identifying student needs and subsequent approaches now have a vitality that has changed both my outlook on teaching and my career path.

For instance, in the semester following my first experience with "The Red Wheelbarrow," instead of asking students to draw Williams's poem, I asked students to represent their own writing in a form of artwork. The results became part of a presentation I made on teacher-research at the 2002 NCTE Convention. I asked my students to represent one of their essays and also to represent their writing process, in an art form of their choice. The only stipulation on the art was that it fit in the classroom. Most students chose to represent their narrative rather than expository essays, writing an additional paper on the metaphoric connections between the writing process and the creation of the piece of art. Students had a choice between doing this assignment or writing an argument essay alone. All the students chose to do the art-related assignment.

The results were overwhelming. These writers created and explained metaphors for their writing process through clay sculptures, color computer graphics, poetry, photographs, paintings, videos, and even a woodblock print. In making the cognitive connections between their essay, their writing process, and their chosen form of art, students returned to their writing, reconsidering its conception. They thought about what the essay meant to them, and then designed a new medium to transport the message to viewers who were once readers. The enthusiasm for the project showed me how students appreciate the chance to create and show their uniqueness, even if the time and effort involved are greater than what would be required for the alternative assignment. As one student wrote in her reflection, "I had to shape and reshape the clay until it looked like I wanted it to. It was like the revising I did in my narrative to make it sound the way I meant it for the person reading it."

When I stepped outside my classroom to engage in teacher-research, I was challenged to assess my teaching. Looking back at my teaching before I had recognized myself as a teacher-researcher, I see that I sought out the areas in which students needed help. I mentioned these areas to other teachers occasionally, but there was never enough time to systematically look for answers. For years, all the business of teaching made me feel I had no time to focus on identifying my own teaching philosophy. It wasn't until I met my teacher-research team that I engaged in conversations about my own beliefs. Exchanging questions and brainstorming answers helped me begin to design my own definition of who I am as an educator. My colleagues shared experiences and expertise. They directed me to books, journals, and websites to fill gaps and formulate goal-oriented strategies that addressed both the strengths and the weak areas of my students.

In addition to the innovation and support, for me the collaborative project became a journey that took me from being a member of the adjunct faculty at Indiana University-Purdue University Indianapolis to being a doctoral candidate in language education at Indiana University. The larger PorTRAIT Project and affiliated groups offered an ongoing intensive seminar in teacher-research, creating opportunities for me to meet amazing educators, learn new perspectives on cutting-edge pedagogical philosophies, and receive mentoring from top teacher-researchers at levels ranging from elementary to college teacher training.

Before my involvement in teacher-research, I was a teacher who cared, who tried to identify problems, and who tried to solve them on my own. When I stepped outside my classroom and met teachers from different grade levels, school districts, and geographical cultures, I realized that my concerns were shared. And as we shared knowledge, skills, and possible solutions, I gained a great feeling of support in my efforts. We expanded our vision and, in so doing, learned more about each other, all students, and ourselves.

As I turn now to observe my own classroom, I see myself watching these college students and the meaning they produce. The time I spent with teacher-researchers has helped me see my present students in a new light. I can better imagine where they have been and what they have brought here with them. I feel better prepared to give them what they need to take with them when they leave my class. In speaking with and listening to teachers of other grade levels, I have heard the concerns of the teachers who want to prepare their students for success in college and in their futures. I can see students more clearly as individual learners. Engaging in inquiry as a teacher-researcher has improved my own critical thinking in terms of more effectively addressing the needs of students.

Even though I had always wondered and looked for answers within the class I was teaching, I now see that what we do can make an impact on the field of education if we share our knowledge, insight, findings, and conclusions. Teachers with experience and knowledge, like Joanne and John, share with "younger" teachers like Leslie and me. I feel as though I have been an observer of the process that has taken me from the seat behind my desk into a world of education that I could only imagine. I have confidence in myself as a teacher because I know the value of pedagogical principles and theory, and I have the support of others who can help me find more information when I need it. I have confidence in myself as a researcher because I know the questions will have answers if I continue to seek and become informed.

Conclusion: New Movements

As Gloria notes in her reflection, through our collaboration as the DeScriptophiles, we gained the opportunity to look up from our local settings and peer outside the windows of our classrooms to see what was going on around us. Then, we went beyond the window and found support, shared concerns, offered interpretations, and helped reconfigure what we thought we knew about each of our local situations. We were able to look back through our own classroom windows at ourselves, and see the changes occurring within us as collaborators and as teachers. Looking at her students now, for instance, Gloria sees in them the former students of Joanne and Leslie. She sees what the students themselves may not know. She sees the Russian girl in Joanne's classroom who knows too much English to go into ESL classes, but who carries serious language issues in what Pat Thomson calls her "virtual schoolbag" (1), the hidden literacies (both successes and challenges) that students carry into school but which do not always become visible to teachers.

The red wheelbarrow project reinforced for each of us not only the fact that "teachers constantly are trying to improve their practice" (Graham, et al. 6), but that transformation is a long and complicated and arduous process of personal and professional confrontation, conversation, and collaboration. When the DeScriptophiles regrouped in Athens after the first year of collaboration and cross-site visits, bringing data samples from all class activities, we were surprised and delighted at the variety of data generated. The poem was used as a grammar lesson, an artistic representation of literature, an exchange of ideas used as verbal restructuring, and as a lesson in valuing the originality, uniqueness, and previous knowledge within each student. We heard how Joanne's Russian immigrant students represented farms as they remembered them in Russia. We saw the lived experiences of Gloria's college students take shape in the background behind a wheelbarrow and chickens. I brought the peer responses of my international students, which showed metaphoric response as a deliberate cognitive process. In the words of one of those students, the poem itself is "an imagination switcher," drawing readers into further levels of understanding from the starting point of simple images. The student notes that "a child could write something like 'A red wheel barrow is beside white chickens,' but not necessarily, 'So much depends upon.' That phrase heralds a much more profound philosophical observation." Indeed, despite the poem's simplicity, each of our experiences with it has brought us to deeper levels of understanding about our writing, thinking, and teaching.

But our use of the poem in our classrooms also showed us things we could do *without* the poem. As Joanne notes in her reflection, an undue reverence for "great authors from the past" may perhaps impede students' own discoveries and inquiries in writing. She moves away from the poem itself as a model, seeking examples closer in theme and age to her students' own lives, and finds her students motivated to work harder and become more invested in their own writing. The process of teacher-research for her is itself an imagination switcher, leading to new pedagogies and inquiries into our practices. Continuing to look, look, look at her practice, Joanne makes the changes that take her and her students to new understandings about what is important in their writing. And then she keeps looking.

In many ways, we are not now the people we were when we began, though we certainly hold in our minds the vision of that first meeting in Georgia, when suddenly the image of a red wheelbarrow glazed with rain water beside the white chickens rather magically came into view. We have moved into different classrooms, schools, even different states since our collaboration began. And although we are in periodic contact still, we do not have the opportunity to visit each other regularly. Nor have all of us been present for each stage. Still, our experiences with Williams's poem across grades suggests that the individual personalities involved in the collaboration are in some ways less important than the convergence of some or all of them at key moments—in the terms of Williams's poem, it isn't so much the individual chickens, rain, or wheelbarrow on their own, but the fact that they are there *here* and *now* and in *this* way. Whatever we know or understand about the poem, whether we like it or not, is tied to an image of witnessing things in context and in contact. The image of that relationship has carried through each of our classrooms and is a thread that continues to run through the fabric of our new situations. And like the wheelbarrow, it carries with it so much of who we are and who we may become as professionals as it moves us ever along.

Note

1. Gloria visited John in October 2000 and then taught the poem herself in December 2000. John visited Leslie in December 2000 and Joanne in January 2001. Leslie taught the poem in March 2001 and visited John and Gloria in April 2001.

"Langston Shakespeare's 'Harlem 41'": Found Poetry, Found Pedagogy, and the Transpositions of Student/Teacher Inquiry

The woods have promises to

must think   Over my head,

year. darkens and comes on.

;now

. sleep. two pines, floats over

ne stopping   in Pine

t William   And miles

The woods have promises to[o]—
[I/you/he] must think over my head
Year darkens and comes on
Snow
I Sleep . . .
  JOHN STAUNTON, Frost-Wright Found Poem

Deranging Poetic Meaning: Deferment, Destruction, and Discovery

The woods are lovely, dark and deep.
But I have promises to keep,
And miles to go before I sleep,
And miles to go before I sleep.
  ROBERT FROST, "STOPPING BY
  WOODS ON A SNOWY EVENING"

In the spring of 2004 a young man, Ron Shook, was sitting in my office threatening to take a box cutter to Robert Frost's well-known poem "Stopping by Woods on a Snowy Evening." During the first-day introductions in my Writing about Literature course, Ron had identified himself as a senior non-major preparing for law school after graduation; he was also, he said, a professional magician. His box-cutter proposition certainly had a theatrical air to it, but he also seemed quite serious about destroying the poem. As an English professor—a presumed custodian of literary culture and tradition—perhaps I had an obligation to stop him, but I confess that I was intrigued by the prospect and spurred him on. It's an impulse perhaps countless English students (and even classroom teachers!) have had when faced with Frost or poetry in general. Recall the exchange between Leslie and her students in Chapter 2; in the minds of secondary and post-secondary students, the equation for poetic meaning too often runs thus: poetry = Robert Frost stuff. Underlying the expectation of encountering such "stuff"—no matter how "lovely, dark and deep" (13) the poetic language may be—is the knowing and jaded rejoinder: whose woods these are . . . yeah, yeah, we know. As Ron calmly described the textual assault that would ensue in his ideal encounter with the poem, an image of glinting metal striking through words I'd read countless times, as both student and teacher, suddenly became welcome. Like a mad version of the poem's own woodsman persona, Ron was proposing to lay waste to Frost's lovely woods and violently transliterate the "downy flakes" of verse into interpretive confetti.

I suppose I had only myself to blame. Out of my own frustration with the way that poetry happened and mattered in English classrooms, including my own, I had begun to seek ways to try something—anything—new. I wanted to move away from the either/or approach to teaching poetry that dominated my past experience as both a teacher and a student, an approach that treated poetry either as canonical museum pieces to unpack and repackage for students, or else as an expressivist outlet for students amid more "academic" writing. Both views seemed only to reinforce the notion of a language-use given to frustratingly gnomic pronouncements such as Keats's famous claim in "Ode on a Grecian Urn" about all we know on earth and all we need to know: "Beauty is Truth; truth, beauty" (49). But surely our experience as English teachers tells us that for our students, there's always something left out of such an equation. Put another way, and without taking away anything from Keats, there must be more to know on earth, about poetry, and about our students than *that*. And yet one can often feel that the proper stance as a reader of poetry is to shade one's eyes or to bow down in deference at the feet of versified truth. I think it's an attitude that makes it difficult to encourage much critical analysis of how poetry works, certainly that socially stigmatizes anyone who might actually want to write or read poetry in our classes. Moreover, it sets up an enormous obstacle to any invitations we make to our students to write about the beauty and capacity of poetic language to help us create *real-life* or *non*-poetic meaning.

What would happen, I wondered, if we could find a way to demystify—if only temporarily—the poems we taught in order to look more closely at the mechanisms that allow them to work their power over us? If a poem really is, as Williams claims in the epigraph to Chapter 2, "a machine made out of words," then how might we better understand its physical and not just literary character? And how might we use that understanding to throw a wrench into the pedagogical machine responsible for the state of poetry instruction? I should note that despite this interest in language and form, I wasn't simply trying to reinstall a New Critical approach to interpreting poetry. Rather, I was particularly curious about the capacity of language, as utterance or discourse, to carry meaning both in form and also in spite of form. To help my students and me get at those questions during a unit on poetry in my introductory literature course, I presented students at the beginning of the unit with several options they would be able to choose from for their end product. Each option would have to make some sort of claim about the making of poetic meaning, and it would need to engage directly at least two poems from the subsequent readings. But the options also offered a range of possible responses that I hoped would allow students flexibility in demonstrating their understanding. The first option took the form of a Dada-inspired destruction and reassemblage of the poems to determine whether language, once it's been wrested from its host poem (and authorial intent), can still yield poetry. The second option proposed a more conventional thesis-driven interpretive analysis of two or more poems—with the general thesis already provided: "all poetry is about the making of poetic meaning and the making of poetry." The final option invited students to write an original poem of their own in response to one of the poems they had read. Students would then write an interpretive analysis of both their own poem and the poem to which it was responding. In a class of twenty-one students, the choices were almost evenly split among the options.

I want to focus first on two students whose responses to the Dada/Found Poetry option offer a look at what happened when the class as a whole took up these invitations, and then I will extend that focus to trace what happened when those students and some of their peers became the teachers at a professional development conference for area English teachers. In choosing to focus on the responses to one option, of course I am not discounting the usefulness or impact of the other two. Indeed, students were equally insightful about poetry whichever option they chose, and this in itself is interesting. For where students might have struggled with the more conventional comparative analysis of two poems, they might find ways to be successful through another form. However, the violent disruption of poetic sense, and the impulse to make meaning foregrounded in option one, offer a convenient site from which to examine my own practice. Following this trajectory beyond the transition from poetry to pedagogy, I then want to offer a hybrid version of found poetry and response poetry to show some of the possibilities that emerge when teachers join student inquiries about literary meaning.

Fulfilling an Appetite for Destruction: Ron and Ashley

> The Beautiful and the True in art do not exist; what interests me is the intensity of a personality transposed directly, clearly into the work.
>
> TRISTAN TZARA, *"Lecture on Dada"* (1922, 248)

The Dada option for my students emerged out of my own inquiry about poetry, and it was also, as I told them in class after they returned from spring break to begin the unit on poetry, a bit of a lark on my part when I placed it on the assignment sheet. I wasn't sure that they'd be able to tell anything about how one makes sense of poetry, as reader or teacher. But I had also just returned from a writing retreat in Athens in which my collaborators, Joanne and Gloria, and I had produced the first full report and reflection of our experience. Poetry, derangement, and teaching were all still very much on my mind, and so I shared with my students my own sense of confusion, trying not to make the disclosure seem like just a performance of teacherly wonder. This question about language had for some time been my own nagging question about poetic meaning, I told my students, and I'd welcome some help figuring a way out of the confusion. The procedure for this option was fairly simple:

> The Dada/Found Poetry Option (do each of the steps below):
>
> A. Take two or more poems from the available selections and cut them into pieces. Then put the pieces into a bowl and draw them out one by one, placing them in order on a separate sheet of paper as you do.
>
> B. What have you created? (Is it a poem? Why or why not? If so, how does it become a poem? If not, what would have to happen for it to become a "real" poem?)
>
> C. What is the meaning of the product you have created in A?

Despite making this the first option, I didn't want to restrict students from pursuing other options more suited to their own queries, so I tried to enlist support for each. Frankly, I didn't expect many students to elect this option at all—not that I didn't think it would be interesting for them to pursue, but it seemed to involve a rather tedious process of destruction and reassembly. Still, in trying to downplay this option, I was no doubt also playing it up as something that might be what I would like to see. What's more, my explanation likely also suggested few demands upon students at first; they didn't need to already "get" poetry to slice up a poem. If they had middle school or high school teachers who kept abreast of the latest *Voices from the Middle* or

English Journal, they might even have had teachers deploying the strategy of found poetry to isolate thematic and figurative emphasis within novel passages. Or they might have already done just this sort of thing with a box of magnetic poetry tiles on their dorm refrigerators. What was perhaps different from those other experiences was that here, they'd be working with famous poets and academically authorized verses; whatever poetry they might find would be from among the ruins of already poeticized language.

Ron's plan, then, wasn't just destruction for its own sake. Rather, he was working within my own expectations to use a little iconoclastic slashing in the name of bringing intellectual clarity and relief to his frustrated attempts to make sense of the poem and poetry at large. Admitting that he had selected this Dada option because it had at first seemed to be the least taxing given his schedule, he was now struggling with what had become for him an interesting dilemma. He couldn't unmoor the individual lines of his two poems, Frost's "Stopping by Woods" and James Wright's "Lying in a Hammock at William Duffy's Farm in Pine Island, Minnesota," from their previous meanings. The new lines made *too much sense* already and too easily. The problem was that Ron didn't think this discovery was all that interesting: since he had only cut up each poem at the line-level, every line would hold its original meaning. He needed to do more violence to the poems than he thought I had suggested, and he wanted to make sure it was okay with me. In fact, I hadn't considered how students would or should cut up their poems, and it wasn't until Ron's meeting with me that I realized not only that he was entirely serious about the box cutter, but that this very step in the process was a crucial one in which the seemingly random act of destruction was in fact quite deliberate. To draw an analogy to the teacher-researcher stance of Chapter 2, this step calls attention to the very participatory status of the objective observer of poetry, and the efforts to come to so-called objective conclusions are embedded in subjective decision making. Ron had a hunch about how and why poetic language created meaning, and he wanted to test whether it would withstand a full-on assault: not just an interpretive dissection, but a literal shredding of the text. His magician's eye saw the need to separate sense from the lines more fully to test how this as yet undisclosed hocus-pocus might allow any sense from the originals to come back reassembled.

Ron proposed printing copies of each poem in roughly equal sizes and laying one over the other. He'd then take a box cutter to both, cutting across the words and lines instead of extracting letters, words, or phrases from within the lines. This crisscross cutting would leave him with two identical poem-puzzles with pieces to mix but also to fit together. What might this sort of controlled destruction offer by way of poetic meaning, he wondered? Wouldn't that be a truer, because tougher, test of the ability of a poetic line to retain its meaning? Or as he put it in the first version of his essay,

> Poetry is a combination of concise word choice and effective diction, but must also leave the reader with some sort of meaning. To produce poetry, a writer must take all of the words available to him and create order. Therefore a poet's purpose is to exert dominance over vocabulary in order to create harmony. The purpose of this activity is to test this assertion by disrupting that harmony and exploring the results.

Ron's choice of poems was also a test of the theory: he saw Frost's lines rigidly framing simple language for narrative and imagistic effect, and Wright's more discursive lines capturing the mood of a dissipated stream of consciousness.

Another student, Ashley Matson, was simultaneously considering a similar disruption of poetic harmony by juxtaposing William Shakespeare's "Sonnet 73" and Langston Hughes's "Harlem," poems and poets separated by four centuries and nearly, she notes, "polar opposites." However, not wanting "to deal with slivers of paper" that might result from the procedures outlined on the assignment sheet or from something like Ron's plan, Ashley formulated an entirely different derangement of poetry that would break down poetic lines into semantic units. She would number the words and phrases, and then reorder them based on a computer-generated random number list: a relatively simple process using an Excel-type spreadsheet to line up phrases in one column and to generate the random numbers through the RAND function for the adjacent column. With this emphasis on operating "scientifically," Ashley deliberately chose works that differed in time, style, and purpose so that they might more forcefully pull against harmony and sense. This beginning dissonance between the texts and poets, she thought, would offer the best challenge to the notion that language sought its own harmonious meaning. The result of "adjoining these two pieces of poetry," she writes of her motivation, "seemed interesting and complex."

Each student had, without knowing anything about Dada, seemed to adopt a Dada state of mind in wanting to get at the very materiality of the words in their two poems. Tristan Tzara, Dada's "founder," notes not only that "Dada is manifested . . . in violent acts" but that "Dada tries to find out what words mean *before* using them, from the point of view not of grammar but of *representation*" (249, emphasis added). The poetic results of Ron's and Ashley's experiments are below, and they offer a striking picture of words operating in multi-representational directions— connotative and denotative, concrete and thematic. To help trace the origin of the lines in these found poems and to highlight some of their multi-representationality, I have additionally marked the words and phrases from the earlier poets (Frost and Shakespeare) in *italics*; those of the later poets (Wright and Hughes) are in **bold**. Words that could have come from either poet given their placement within the original works and the original lines are rendered in ***bold italics*** (see Appendixes 3.1–3.4 for full versions of original poems).

A Golden Mistake: Ron Shook's "Frosting in a Hammock at William Duffy's Snowy Woods"

> **Over my head** *these are* **bronze butterfly**
> **Asleep** *O is in the village,*
> **Blow** *ill not see me stopping* **shadow.**
> *To watch his woods fill up with* **house,**
> *My little horse must think it queer* 5
> *To stop without a farmhouse near*
> *Between the woods and frozen lake*
> *The* **field of sunlight between two pines,**
> *He give* **pings of last year's horses**
> *To ask if* **golden** *mistake.* 10

The only other sound's the sweep
Of easy wind and downy flake.
The woods are lovely, dark and deep.
*But **I have** promises*
And mil   *15*

As we can see in this concretization of Ron's found poem, not only does the new creation still cling tightly to the phrases and lines of both Wright's and Frost's poems, but it demonstrates the cleaving together of the two poems. Frost's opening passage wedges up into Wright's first line, for instance, occluding Wright's "I see" with Frost's seemingly more neutral and demonstrative "these are." Likewise in lines 8–10, a vestigial trio of Wright's own lines 8–10, which in the full original describe the alchemical transformation of horse dung into "golden stones" ("In a field of sunlight between two pines, / The droppings of last year's horses / Blaze up into golden stones"), unseats Frost's rider from horse; though in Frost's original, horse and rider share some understanding of their lives and work together ("He gives his harness bells a shake / To ask if there is some mistake"). Finally, Frost's "darkest evening of the year" (8) is altogether erased by Wright's "field of sunlight between two pines" (8), resulting in Ron's "**golden** *mistake*" (10). Throughout these alterations, the recombinant lines still manage to maintain some focus on their original sounds and sense. The implied sound invoked when Frost's little horse "gives his harness bells a shake," for instance, is replaced by the "**pings** of last year's horses." Although the syntax is awkward ("*He give* **pings**"), in striking transpositions such as this, we witness a strange doubling effect of the original poems' forms and language.

Other startling juxtapositions are also worth noting for the way they move out from both Frost's and Wright's use of nature to reflect something else entirely. The process is accretive, relying first upon the maintenance of the original meanings, and then upon the gradual and sudden shifts in lines. As Ron notes,

The newly created Frankenstein-like poem still retains some of the elements of Frost's poem. In fact, three . . . verses [lines] remain intact: "My little horse must think it queer / To stop without a farmhouse near / Between the woods and frozen lake" (5–7). However, these verses [lines] rely heavily upon the rest of the original poem . . . The line preceding these ["To watch his woods fill up with snow" (4)] is integral in Frost's poem to developing a coherent picture for the reader.

The transformation of the line *"To watch his woods fill up with* **house**" (4) alters the focus, and seems to comment on nature's destruction and derangement through human agency. What was initially pastoral reverie moves toward a nascent twenty-first-century environmentalism. According to Ron, the original Frost line "creates a beautiful scene of a snowy wooded area, while the second [version] conjures up odd images of houses interspersed with trees, a stark suburban setting." Such an interpretation, of course, is necessarily incomplete—but it is nonetheless an interesting analysis that also happens to be germane to what was our shared regional space in the ever-sprawling urban/suburban/exurban landscape of the New South.

But as incisive as that interpretation might be, it is not sustained by the rest of the new poem. Ron himself notes this problem in his final analysis: "Parts of the new work still manage to make sense, but it is the clashing images that are projected which assert an overall sense of disharmony." In the end, Ron concludes that the "Frankenstein-like poem" he has created is ultimately not itself a poem, in large part because it lacks a connection between the words deployed and an agency or intellect seeking to understand the world through those words. But then, in a sort of concession to my question on an earlier draft for him to "consider what your role as poem-cutter is throughout the meaning-making process," Ron makes a curious observation about the poem and the process: "Perhaps if this experiment had been conducted in a different manner, perhaps even using my own works, there would have been new or familiar meaning in the new work for myself."

Monstrous Truths and Random Beauty: Ashley Matson's "Langston Shakespeare's 'Harlem 73'"

In me thou behold a **dream** or none . . .

ASHLEY MATSON, "HARLEM 73"

Ashley comes to a conclusion very similar to Ron's about the nature of poetry and the results of her experiment. Though she claims that "weaving Hughes's 'Harlem' throughout the tight lines of Shakespeare's 'Sonnet 73' generates twenty lines that cannot truly be defined as poetry," she nonetheless recognizes that the process results in some provocative lines that might lend themselves to further poetic constructions. Both poems have "intense meaning," she notes, but when their words are "strewn about the page in a different order . . . the quality of the original meaning" is stripped from each. Still, the confrontation and collision of the two poems in this manner "forces a new idea . . . allowing no backward glance at what formerly existed." Indeed, as Ashley claims, the assembled poem puts the reader in a precarious cognitive and metaphorical position in relation to the beautiful meanings of the past; she stands like Orpheus or perhaps Lot's wife on the verge of looking back, and the new meaning is a warning that any impulse to nostalgia will be a loss of both the originals and any future meaning. Ashley seems to highlight this tone with her description of both the process and product as an "insanity of convergence," but she suggests that even in the face of such grim prospects, the "monstrosity that developed" from this mad coupling "could, at lengths, evolve into poetry."

The "scientific" technique that Ashley adopted to merge the two poems is obviously much different from Ron's. Despite the orderly matrix Ashley established for her Dada-like reconstruction, the permutation that resulted stays anchored to phrases, and sometimes whole lines, from the original poems in ways that Ron attempted literally to cut through (though no less successfully). Yet contrary to Ashley's initial assertion that the new poem allows for "no backward glance at what formerly existed," her derangement continually tries to pull back toward the poems' original sense. This resilience of the language may be in part the result of maintaining conventional units of language before subjecting them to a reordering. She does not, for instance, separate into discrete units the words in a prepositional phrase or noun phrase; indeed, words remain words and not letters or syllables. Nevertheless, the result is different enough to call attention to the new creation as something potentially poetic and certainly, as Ashley notes, something *interesting*. From out of the "very . . .

formulated yet still random . . . merger of these two poems," emerges a peculiar "coincidence in some of the lines actually having deep, often provocative meaning." Though a "product of random selection," the existence of these poetic fragments is, Ashley concludes, "a beautiful thing." She continues her analysis of "Harlem 73" by noting the capacity of the new lines to carry both aesthetic and thematic sense, often very similar to the despair of Hughes's "Harlem" or the melancholy tone of Shakespeare's "Sonnet 73."

> The line "*In me thou behold a **dream** or none*" suggests the possibility that someone sees potential in him [the persona of the new poem] as a romantic interest . . . A second vivid line, "*Night doth take this away all in **sweet** rest*" . . . is a beautiful line that is easily understood. When troubles become overwhelming, nothing but sleeping and fading fast from the world seems like a solution. The rest that night brings with it is the ultimate cure. A final line, containing personification and strong images, says, "*Death's sunset, **does it sugar** over or **does it run** as the year that well must leave ere long.*" The year that must leave ere long seems to be a year full of memories that are so distant now, and the speaker wonders if death precludes such emptiness or is the sweet satisfaction of ending his pain.

Ashley's keen reading of this new poem—and indeed of both Shakespeare and Hughes—comes from her ability to attend to the language itself first. In considering the possible meaning of "Harlem 73," Ashley is aware of the way that Shakespeare's "verbose . . . more complex" lines continue to dominate the new creation: not surprising, considering the simple 1:2.4 ratio of Hughes's 51 words to Shakespeare's 121. So despite the powerful force of the "visual and impacting" imagery of Hughes's own poem, when combined with Shakespeare's line fragments, many lines end up being "just a mess." Ashley offers one reason for this in the elevated diction and locutions of Shakespeare: his "'thou' and 'which' [make] it difficult to reorder the words [of the two poems] and still allow comprehension." Indeed, despite flashes of startling brilliance, the new poem suffers from an overall lack of "a consistent obvious subject."

And yet, the resulting mess is itself of interest. Perhaps the burden of meaning is too much for the found poem to carry, and like Hughes's dream deferred it "just sags / like a heavy load." But as Ashley describes her decision-making process in assembling the lines, she is confronted with the task of eliminating words, phrases, or combinations that simply do not cohere— "there are still over ten lines [over half of the resulting combinations] that don't tie in"—but to alter anything to make meaning would eliminate what does emerge. So Ashley is left with the claim that the result is not "truly poetry" but also that to try to make it so would somehow diminish what is there. "The interesting nature of the poem would cease to exist," she claims, "because [the] addition of words where I see appropriate could shift the meaning and indefinitely alter the *intention of the entire work*" (emphasis added). Such intention, whatever it might be, of course would be the result not of any *authorial* agency but of the randomly generated number list or of language itself.

Collaboration and Re-Construction

> Dada is a state of mind. . . . [It] applies itself to everything, and yet it is nothing, it is the point where the yes and the no and all opposites meet, not solemnly in the castles of human philosophies, but very simply at streetcorners, like dogs and grasshoppers.
>
> TRISTAN TZARA, *"Lecture on Dada"* (1922, 251)

Despite the apparent success of this invitation to students and their enjoyment with the process, I was somewhat troubled by the conclusions at which they arrived. I knew that something very interesting had happened for a number of my students, and that they had experienced poetry in ways they had not expected. What's more, they had exceeded my expectations for the engagement. Whether they chose the Dada option or composed their own poem in response, or simply argued for a more conventional thesis using several poems as evidence, on the whole the class was able to say something interesting and of personal importance about poetry. But they also had not quite seen what I had seen in their own experiments, and I was curious to see why that was and what that might mean. Even with Ashley's and Ron's rigorous tests of poetic harmony, although they both had sidled up to something fascinating and provocative about the nature of language and discourse, in the end they each reinscribed a student commonplace about authorial intention as a necessary component of literary meaning. Where had all this carefully scripted derangement brought us? What if anything, then, had I really done that helped them understand poetry better than they had before? And what might they be able to show me themselves about what they had done?

The story of "Langston Shakespeare's 'Harlem 41'"—that is, the story of a teaching workshop Ron, Ashley, and several of their peers joined me in presenting at a professional development conference for English teachers—really begins with that query. What I've presented so far about the engagements and student response has followed a rather typical teaching narrative script: teacher wants to shake things up, move away from boring old approaches, and so offers students choice, innovation, inspiration (you can supply your own key word here), and students rise to the challenge, dazzling themselves and their teacher; everyone learns valuable insights about truth and beauty and poetry, which as we know from Keats is all we need to know on earth. Indeed, when we met to prepare our presentation, we were essentially trying to find ways to repackage that teaching-success narrative to convince other teachers to try something new in their classrooms. At the very least, we hoped that our participants would see in the engagement a fun and successful approach to teaching poetry. And based on the written feedback we received from our audience, that is precisely what they saw: a valuable tool they could immediately use in their own classrooms. But they didn't seem to see a need to change their basic classroom structure or teaching philosophy. They liked the activity, they reported, because it was "hands-on," it would "help students get away from thematic analysis and deal with language," and it would in the single option we demonstrated, offer something to "my students." The implied relationship between teachers and students in the classroom would remain largely the same. As successful as the engagement was for me in my own class, however, it raised new questions for me about how I was teaching and how I was conceiving of the learner's position in my classroom. And I wanted those unsettlings to be part of the experience as well.

What if we were to allow the entire engagement, from teacher assignment to student response, to come under a similar process of destruction, derangement, and analysis that Ron and Ashley accomplished? What opposites would such a Dada state of mind bring together at the corners of our practice? To take the teaching-learning script and transpose the positions? What would we discover not just about poetic meaning but about the *teaching* of poetry? And how might we invite others to experience a similar discovery? As I was beginning to formulate those questions over the months after the class, I received an invitation to present at the UNC Charlotte Writing Project's Fall Conference. It seemed an ideal forum to share some of our experiences in the class and to test again what might happen when we unsettle conventional ways of teaching and reading poetry. When I asked Ron, Ashley, and several other students to join me in making a workshop presentation to English teachers at the conference, it was a decision to turn over this work that students had done for me to their own critical razors, to take it apart, reassemble it, and themselves argue for it—or against it—before classroom teachers. In my invitation to them the following September, I highlighted the pedagogical nature of the presentation and the crucial aspect of their collaborative presence. As I told them in my email, I wanted them

> to be co-panelists with me at the UNCC Writing Project's Fall Conference. This is a conference by and for K–12 teachers in the area, and I want to present a version of the assignment you did last semester. During the workshop portion of the presentation, teachers would participate in the same sort of cutting up of poems and then reassembling them and considering what they have and why. I wanted to share the versions and the insights you made in your papers, but I also thought if you were willing and had time, you might want to share that information yourselves with the teachers in the workshop and to talk about the process from the student's perspective.
>
> So, I realize that this is sort of short notice, but if you are interested please let me know as soon as possible. We can then set a time to meet and talk about the organization of the panel, and I can let the organizer know to include your names on the program as co-presenters. If you are unable to present, I will still make sure that you and your work are given full recognition.
> Thanks,
> Dr. Staunton

What I didn't quite realize at the time was that in inviting students to be involved directly in the planning and delivery of the presentation, I was allowing them to redirect the nature of the presentation and the experience participants would have. By the time of our organizational meeting, however, I began to realize that they had a whole set of experiences and insights about the assignment that cut through my assumptions about the nature of their discoveries six months before. What's more, I saw an opportunity to extend the initial focus of the workshop from a teaching-tip format to something that would begin to put students in the fore of both pedagogy and content for classroom encounters with poetry. In short, by becoming co-presenters, our perspectives began to pull and push at each other in ways remarkably similar to Ron's and Ashley's poems.

What I want to share is the results of this extension and the implications it has for such engagements with literature, but also for the preparation of future and current English teachers. First, though, I want to disclose some elements about the presentation that may not at first seem important, but which have shaped later ways of my thinking about teaching. The title for the presentation came from my own *mis*remembering of Ashley's title for her essay and the poem that resulted when she adjoined William Shakespeare's "Sonnet 73" and Langston Hughes's "Harlem." Quite sensibly she dubbed the new creation "Harlem 73"; inexplicably I told the conference organizer that our title, in honor of this student's title, would be "Harlem 41." I suppose I could claim that somewhere in the dusty corners of my memory I knew that Hughes had published a volume of poetry called *Shakespeare in Harlem* (1942), and that the title poem itself was written in 1941. It may simply be that—with all due respect to my student's observation—"Harlem 41" just sounded better to me and I was the one with the power to name the presentation. Whatever the origin, having arrived at that title, I've committed myself to following it where it leads me. Ashley's title captures her inquiry, not mine; hers names an instance of found poetry, while mine seems directed to an instance of found *pedagogy*. In the closing sections I want to sketch out the implications of that transition and the prospects for classroom practice.

From Found Poetry to Found Pedagogy

> If we are to advance our instructional effectiveness, we must struggle to our own resolutions. We must examine our pedagogical problems and be truly puzzled by them, with all the risks accompanying such perplexity. (Fishman and McCarthy 2)

In between my students' encounters with poetic meaning in the spring and our presentation about teaching to arrive at poetic meaning in the fall, I had the opportunity to teach for the first time a course through the Writing Project, a curriculum with the motto "teachers teaching teachers." It's a powerful pedagogical model, both for teaching writing and for professional development of teachers. During the second week of our two-week intensive open institute, my co-teacher and I invited our students, all of whom where classroom teachers, to offer their own engagements for teaching writing. Several shared their best lessons for teaching a range of genres as well as for using writing to support the reading and analysis of literature. The demo week was designed to give all the teachers a pool of strategies and resources for their classrooms and the chance to offer their own practice up for analysis and critique. In seeing these teachers share their thinking about putting students more centrally in the learning situation, I began to wonder about my own experience with my students the previous spring. What had we done, really, that moved beyond traditional models of student, teacher, and text?

What I had devised was a series of textual encounters based on my own hunch about language and poetic meaning. I was, in Fishman and McCarthy's sense above, truly puzzled, for I didn't know where it would take students, nor did I know what it was likely to produce in terms of their opportunity to understand literature or even literary devices. Still, I did have a suspicion about the process. I trusted in the ability of language to cohere enough to give them something to work with. I knew enough about discourse and the nature of utterance to submit myself and my students to a process in which we would have to grapple with the sudden emergence of the idea that language itself carried meaning apart from any human agency or intention, and that sometimes that meaning might even bear traces of the aesthetic or poetic. But how could I possibly reduce all that to a classroom demo or conference presentation such as the Writing Project teachers were showing me?

Thinking about the possibilities of sharing this discovery prompted the following reflection in my daybook about what I had begun referring to as *found pedagogy*:

> It's what you discover you're capable of doing in the face of student confusion, textual resistance, or serendipitous collisions— it's not the easy-breezy free-for-all that simply gives over to students the reigns of the classroom, especially without a sense of what they are taking them over for.

I was thinking about the stereotype of the student-centered classroom as the scene of pedagogical chaos, but also of the idea of teacher as naïf, blindly pursuing any and all questions and curiosities. But I realize now that a found pedagogy often can or does emerge out of some initial failure or setback or misunderstanding between student-text-teacher.

The notion of found pedagogy, like found poetry, opens teaching to the same sorts of meaning-making processes that we imagine are involved in *learning*, and allows us to move beyond a sense of teaching as merely the distribution of knowledge, or even as a process of helping others co-construct knowledge. Teaching in this view is itself a process of knowledge construction and meaning-making. Stephen Fishman notes the inherent aspect of struggle in such a view of teaching and learning, whether in the classroom or in the world at large. "Learning, in its broadest, nonschool sense," he says, "is a reconciliation of tensions between the self and its surroundings. It happens when desire is frustrated, attention is aroused, and we investigate our surroundings with purpose." We see each of these moves carried out by Ron and Ashley and me throughout the engagement; we each resolve the tension created by the discontinuity of our interpretive acts by continuing to engage the texts. Fishman makes this connection to the classroom as well when he advises that teachers "must encourage students to find genuine problems which excite their interest, *problems* which can be explored and ameliorated by engagement with the curriculum" (19). Applying

Fishman's observation to the "students" of our presentation, my co-presenters and I helped create problems of poetic meaning and poetic pedagogy for our participants. To resolve both their teaching and thinking about teaching poetry, all of us would have to get physically involved with the texts.

Our session description invited participants to join us "in discovering ways that poetic meaning can be created and learning how to teach and interpret poetry through a series of hands-on engagements." The shifting focus between teaching and learning in the invitation reveals the collaborative nature of the panel as well as the tension between students' desires and expectations for learning and my own. But it also suggests that any teacher-participants of the session will themselves learn to interpret poetry differently as they discover ways to teach the poetry they presumably already know. That dual aspect of the presentation was frequently mentioned by the participants as one of the things they liked or learned or would take from the session. All the participants saw in the activity something they could or would take into their own classrooms, but perhaps more interesting for me and my students was how many of them also indicated their own pleasant surprise at finding something valuable in interacting with their teaching peers—something Joanne, Gloria, and I likewise mentioned in Chapter 2 as a happy surprise of our collaboration. Similarly, these experienced teachers seemed genuinely surprised that a group of students, of all people, had in fact been able to offer them something from the other side of the teacher's desk that could change their way of thinking not only about students, but about their own teaching and content areas.

This surprise about the nature and character of student insight surprised me, though I had myself experienced something similar just six months before. In that shock of recognition that students can follow their own inquiries, lie the seeds of transformed practice and possibly of critical pedagogy. Had these teachers' struggles with poetry been really a struggle with letting go of the reigns of the classroom and the province of knowledge? I realize in posing this question that I am myself implicated, for my initial invitation to derange poetic understanding had been delivered not for my students, but for myself. Nonetheless my students had used the pretext of my question to pursue ones of their own. As a result, my question about poetry turned back to an investigation in teaching.

As our session drew to a close and participants offered feedback and reflected on the process, I began to see that what we had created was a space for an approach to teaching that did not fall into traditional or authorized ways, which as Knoblauch and Brannon note, can endure without "change through the years and without concern for any larger context of public action" (7). "Langston Shakespeare's 'Harlem 41'" was not the result of such authorized teaching, but it did authorize students to direct their own learning. Not only did students get to name poetic meaning, but especially for those who presented with me, they helped name what counts as knowledge about poems, poetry in general, and the teaching-learning/student-curriculum nexus.

The situation recalls for me another poem by Robert Frost, a lengthier and much more narrative poem, "The Axe-Helve." As do many of Frost's narrative poems, this one opens on an encounter between neighbors: Baptiste interrupts his neighbor, who is also the poem's speaker, in midstroke of his wood chopping—"He caught my axe expertly on the rise" (10)—to caution him about the dangers that might result from using an ill-fitted axe-helve. "'Made on machine,'" Baptiste observes in his French-English to his Yankee neighbor; "'You give he' one good crack, she's snap right off'" (22, 26). The speaker lets himself be convinced to visit Baptiste's residence to obtain a better tool, knowing that the neighbor is primarily interested in finally being able to host the speaker in his home. After this cross-cultural encounter, the poem ends with a rather curious turn toward questions of teaching, learning, and schooling:

> Do you know, what we talked about was knowledge?
> Baptiste on his defence about the children
> He kept from school, or did his best to keep —
> Whatever school and children and our doubts
> Of laid-on education had to do
> With the curves of his axe-helves and his having
> Used these unscrupulously to bring me
> To see for once the inside of his house. (83–90)

Having begun this inquiry with my students by hacking away at assorted and selected poems from our anthology, I was stopped by students' inquiry to consider the consequences of laid-on education. My hope is that for our presentation, these participants, just like Frost's speaker and Baptiste, in stopping for a moment their own systematic chopping up of poems for the sake of utility and meaning, of churning out machine-like interpretations, may have had a different sort of connection with students, with poetry, and with each other. For in recognizing each other as co-learners when traditional roles of teacher and student are transposed, we may find a pedagogy of our own.

"Anchoring Points" in the Fabric(ation) of a National Literature: Connecting Students and American Literature through Inquiry

Pedagogical Reckoning

Have you reckoned a thousand acres much? Have you
　　reckoned the earth much?
Have you practiced so long to learn to read?
Have you felt so proud to get at the meaning of poems?

Stop this day and night with me and you shall possess the
　　origin of all poems,
You shall possess the good of the earth and sun . . . there are
　　millions of suns left,
You shall no longer take things at second or third hand . . .
　　nor look through the eyes of the
　　　　dead . . . nor feed on the spectres in books,
You shall not look through my eyes either, nor take things
　　from me,
You shall listen to all sides and filter them from yourself.
　　　　　　　　WALT WHITMAN, *SONG OF MYSELF* (1855)

It's mid-April 2007, and I am reading the first two sections of Whitman's 1855 version of *Song of Myself*—ending with the lines above—to students in my American literature survey class. The text of the poem is both in front of them on a handout and in their class text. We are nearing the end of a long, intense, and distinctly deranged semester filled with literature from more than

400 years of American continental history, written in at least three different original languages and multiple genres, each laying claim to a particular vision of American literature. For some, Whitman's lines will be an "anchoring point" of signification (Lacan's *point de capiton* [154]) that weaves together a coherent story line about the nature and meaning of American literature. For others, it will be yet another in a series of curricular ravelings pulling at the threads of their prior conceptions of *the* American literature story. For me, Whitman's lines do both—and they also pull through a very particular deranged thread marking the fashioning of an inquiry approach to teaching content that was initiated by the experiences of Chapter 3. In the found pedagogy that emerged in the transposition of student and teacher inquiries, the pride at getting to the meaning of poems fled in the face of new reckonings about what teaching literature *for* and *with* students—rather than *to* students—might look like.

Before reading these lines from Whitman, I give students very specific instructions for reading and listening along with my reading:

> As you read/listen to these lines, think about when or if you may have heard them before. Then do A or B.
>
>> A. If you think you *have* heard these lines before, what was that prior experience like for you? Take some time in your writing notebook to tell about it, describing perhaps how it felt, or something that happened when you heard the lines, or someone else who was there with you when you did.
>>
>> B. If you are pretty sure that you *have not* heard the lines before, try to pay attention to how you are experiencing them now. What does it feel like to hear/read the words? What do they remind you of or make you remember? Write your impressions down in your notebook. Try to imagine where these lines are coming from or perhaps who is speaking them originally: describe or draw the place and speaker in your notebook. What do the people look like who may be listening?
>
> After doing one of the response options above, consider these questions: What do you think these lines mean? How are your experiences while listening just now related to that meaning for you? Write these down.

Of course, almost all the students have *read* the lines before, at least before this particular class meeting, and I expect some of them to refer to these prior experiences. But I also suspect that few have had a chance to *hear* Whitman's words outside of their own heads. It can be a daunting task to read aloud a poem that places such a high premium on the sound of the human voice; indeed, throughout *Song of Myself* Whitman figures voice as both point of interpersonal contact and hermeneutic conduit for understanding the world. As he says in a later section, "My voice goes after what my eyes cannot reach, / With the twirl of my tongue I encompass worlds and volumes of worlds" (567–68). Ideally this engagement will anchor a hermeneutic process of understanding for my students and not simply a desperate attempt to call a halt to the endless play of signification in their literary studies. But what I am hoping for in my brief reading is something slightly more modest: I simply want the sound of the words at this moment in mid-April to allow students another opportunity to think about how literary meaning is mediated by its context(s).

The student responses on the whole tend to focus either on the imagery of the first few lines, as they imagine outdoor scenes in the campus gardens, on the quad, or just somewhere generically "in nature." Or else they stay with the ideas at play in the "commands" of the last two lines and consider what it might mean to "listen to all sides and filter them from yourself." But some also consider this particular classroom rendering of the poem. As one student notes anonymously on the exit writings I collect at the end of class, "He read it completely different from in my head. He read it soft, but strong and matter-of-fact. In my head, it was still soft but seductive as well." Another student, Brandon, observes that "such poetry should be read out loud and not read in silence," adding in Whitmanesque fashion, "Each word vocalized evokes a passion alongside its brother."

Other students make connections to their own lives. Kyle connects the poem to a conversation with his fiancée the night before about the things they feared: "She asked if I fear death and I said no. The [earlier] parts of the poem speaking about the perfumes struck me. In this way life is a perfume, smells, tastes, we all want it. But the atmosphere is beyond all that. Life death and soul. To be in love with that is somehow more powerful and more fulfilling." Ashley, whose hybrid "Langston Shakespeare" poem was featured in Chapter 3, seems to struggle syntactically to put in words both her suspicion that I'm up to something with this invitation and her desire to engage Whitman's ideas more directly: "In your asking what it means and nothing more, this resistance to forcing thought process is the epitome of meaning of the experience. It is a . . . realization that ideas must be self created and 'filtered' for [one]self." Her observation is echoed in another anonymous response, which also seems to capture something of Whitman's own opening gesture from the famous first lines of the poem, "I celebrate myself, / And what I assume you shall assume . . .": "Sitting here reflecting on Whitman's *Song of Myself* is reflexive to the point of the poem—to reflect on yourself and your inner dialogue. Especially how inner dialogue becomes the reference point for exterior communication." Each of these responses is both interpretation and description—here's what is happening to me and here's what that means—but in the "filtering" process, students are doing more than "getting at the meaning of poems." They are also involved, as Ashley claims, in an act of self-creation and self-understanding mediated through the poetic experience.

As these and other students begin to share some of their responses, first in pairs and small groups and then with the whole class, I experience an interior dialogue of my own about what Whitman's closing lines might herald for the teaching of American literature and American literature teachers. This particular read-aloud engagement has a complex history that is tied to my efforts to organize a course around inquiry into American literature that could also derange the typical survey course focus on canonical authors and traditional teacher-directed classroom. The Whitman engagement itself, though certainly dealing with a canonical author, had been suggested to me through collaboration with several former students from another section of the course almost two years previous to this one, whose inquiries into American literary history had developed into a workshop presentation for teachers at another Writing Project fall conference. As did their peers in Chapter 3, when these student-learners were able to become what Harste and Leland call "curricular informants"

(7), moving from the sidelines of the curriculum to the frontlines of the knowledge base of what and how American literature means, they set in motion a shift in my own practice and thinking about curriculum.

They also raised the questions that I am seeking to investigate here, with this class, two years later. So as I read now the lines by Whitman in the final weeks of the course, I wonder: What is it that I—we, they—assumed about American literature that I now want these students to assume? How might these students filter the origin of all poems from themselves, as Whitman suggests? Or have we practiced "so long to learn to read" and "to get at the meaning of poems" that when confronted with the sound of language struggling with the mysteries of being in the world we are struck dumb and at a loss for words? What sort of act of observation—whether of a spear of summer grass, or of a poem about observing a spear of summer grass, or perhaps of a classroom engagement about a poem about, and so on—allows for this understanding? In the moment of reading, I realize that I have come back to a challenge to teaching American literature that a simple transposition of student and teacher roles could not quite answer. I need to reckon with a deeper question about the nature of teaching anchored to another moment of pursuing inquiry together in a discipline.

Some Origins of the American Literature Story

> There was once a boy who had no home. His parents were dead and his uncles would not care for him. In order to live this boy, whose name was Gaqka, or Crow, made a bower of branches for an abiding place and hunted birds and squirrels for food. / He had almost no clothing but was very ragged and dirty. When the people from the village saw him they called him Filth-Covered-One, and laughed as they passed by, holding their noses. No one thought he would ever amount to anything, which made him feel heavy-hearted. He resolved to go away from his tormentors and become a great hunter.
>
> "The Origin of Stories" *(Lauter 30)*

In the fall of 2005, some eighteen months before this reading of Whitman, I am sitting with some former students in a conference room at my university. Like the preparation for "Langston Shakespeare's 'Harlem 41'" the year before, this time around the students and I have spent considerable time preparing a teaching engagement, and we are eagerly awaiting our as yet unarrived audience of English teachers. We have hopes that our session will help them find new ways to connect their students to American literature. One of the student co-presenters is in the honors program and preparing for a yearlong internship in the local schools before going on to student teach. The other two student co-presenters are both preparing to graduate that winter, and, although pessimistic about the future of the country, they too are considering a possible future in teaching—among other options. If the three are nervous about presenting in front of experienced classroom teachers, they don't let on; instead they talk easily of plans that are perhaps typical of cautiously idealistic college students, that is, of students who want to make a difference in the lived realities of others. They mention the Peace Corps, teaching night classes at one of the local community colleges, prospects for studying abroad. One is married and thinking of starting a family, another is under indictment by the FBI for video piracy and intellectual property violations, and the third has never left the country. Some of this I know already, and some I won't discover until months after, as they individually get in touch with me about recommendations for applications or job advice. For now, though, we sit in the conference room, watching the clock, waiting for the teachers to come, if not quite in Whitman's words to "stop this day and night" (33) with us, then at least to pause with us for forty-five minutes or so and take another, closer look at some nineteenth-century American authors.

We are armed with many handouts that include excerpts from Whitman's *Song of Myself*, Emerson's *Nature* and "American Scholar," and Chopin's "Story of an Hour." These sit neatly stacked on the tables in our conference room. We have a specific plan, created in the days prior, to get things going. The message below is my reframing and reporting back to my co-presenters after one of our meetings:

> Here's what I have put together as the first version for the presentation based on our conversation last Thursday. Let me

know what you think about the sequence and range of activities. Does this seem to capture what we were saying last week? Are there things to change or modify or cut out altogether? Do you have preferences for the Table Activities? Etc. JS

Overview of our presentation: What we'll say to the participants . . .

Where we are coming from: I'll explain a bit about the course content and share some descriptions of the activities and assignments, specifically pointing to the ones that the three of you took on. (I'll create a packet of materials for the participants with some sampling of the essay questions and the criteria for the group presentations.) This will take about two minutes.

Then I'll invite you three to speak briefly about the artifacts and creative options you ended up choosing, and then we'll get into the session.

Some suggestions for how to do this:
Mention why you chose the activity/artifact you did for your presentation and/or essay response. Why this seemed like the one for you, given what you wanted to say or help the class understand.

So for instance, [A] might say something about the film clip or the Sufi poems: "I used these because I wanted people to be able to understand X about Whitman's poetry, and these examples let us see X by . . ." Or [B] might say about his Emerson Magic Goggles essay: "I really just thought it would be less boring/difficult/time-consuming than the traditional essay. What I discovered was . . ." Or [C] might talk about the bark and twigs and Thoreau: "We grabbed a shovel and headed over to the Glen because . . ." Or whatever happens to be the actual story behind your decision. The important thing, I think, is not so much that the reasons be really high-minded or deep and insightful (though of course I'm sure they were), but that they were yours, and that they ended up yielding interesting and provocative results. In other words, be honest and forthcoming but not overly modest.

What strikes me now, as I look back over this recasting and forecasting of our experience, is the excitement that the students and I seem to have in planning our presentation. The agenda unfolds to reveal the first attempt at the Whitman engagement that began this chapter. I am trying to get my co-presenters to confirm that what I am saying is in fact a faithful rendering of what they've suggested.

> **What we want to provide participants with:** Starting with Whitman's poem (excerpts), which will offer something difficult, but accessible—that is, the language is easy enough to read but the meaning is tricky. We want to help them tap into some of their own experiences with story to discover something new about the poem. And then after the first whole-group experience, each participant will be invited to choose one of the stations (run by you three—each with a different activity/text) to dig a little deeper into Whitman, but also into the way that story works in American literature.

The activities are drawn directly from the students' own prior work in class, but are not simply a repetition of their earlier transmediations for their exam essays and presentations. This is significant, I think, in the way that this presentation has managed to shape my own future teaching and curricular planning. So for instance, the student who had linked Whitman's poem to Rumi and to Dustin Hoffman's Existential Detective, who shows his client how everything is connected through the use of a blanket in the film *I Heart Huckabees* (2004), wants to return to one of the early stories in our course readings, the Seneca tale "Origin of Stories." In that story, whose opening I cite at the beginning of this section, Gaqka, or Crow, goes on a quest of self-discovery only to return with stories that explain the community's history and origins to itself. In addition to being rather comical—Gaqka learns his stories from a mountain with a tobacco craving; "Give me tobacco and I'll tell you a story"

(Lauter 31) the mountain demands—the story has the potential in the student's eyes to disrupt the traditional classroom story of teaching American literature by underscoring the reciprocal and transformative nature of stories and storytelling.

The student whose group literally brought pieces of nature for us to examine during a class presentation on the Transcendentalism of Emerson, Fuller, and Thoreau wants to extend Fuller's feminist perspective and put the "natural" hierarchies of gendered power under our gaze with Chopin's story. Chopin's ironic coda in "The Story of an Hour" has the potential to unravel what we think we know about offering students freedom to explore their ideas in classroom settings that then close the door on any real application or test of that freedom. And finally, the student who has surprised himself with his ethical discovery of other lives by trying to imagine himself as Emerson's transparent eyeball, puts the popular discourse version of Emerson under the microscope to tease out evidence of community amid his rhetoric of individualism.

Disrupting the Transmission of American Literature

> Are you he who would assume a place to teach or be
>   a poet here in the States?
> The place is august, the terms obdurate.
> WALT WHITMAN, "BY BLUE ONTARIO'S SHORE" (1856)

But unlike the earlier "Langston Shakespeare" presentation, this time the teachers never show. And so the story this chapter tells cannot be a simple narrative of success, not entirely, or at least not in the way that the genre of the classroom story has scripted it. Nor is it a narrative of failure, though, for we would not have been in that conference room at all had we not first had a rich, shared history of successful inquiry and discovery about American literature, which I was able to return to in those opening two sections of Whitman's *Song of Myself* eighteen months later. On this border of success and failure lives a deranged possibility to see what has perhaps always been lurking in the shadows of American literature and classroom pedagogy: a hybrid act of being and knowing that is ever in the making.

That is not what I tell those students at the time, however. Instead, I make allowances for the absent audience: after all, our session is up against several that promise a veritable toolkit of strategies for helping students pass the state writing test or finally learn to love grammar. These are not unimportant issues that occupy teachers' lives in our district, I say. The students nod. What we don't have to say is that what we've really come up against is the seductive appeal of what John Mayher describes as "commonsense learning" (49), that view of schooling and teaching which assumes that students only learn what has been taught or transmitted to them by a teacher, and which decontextualizes student encounters with meaningful content. Drawing upon specific intertextual connections/transmediations from students, our session (we hope) will unsettle those commonsense views of teaching literature and move toward Mayher's "uncommon-sense learning," focusing on learning in context and on multimodal and multi-genre ways of knowing (104). We are likewise hoping to demonstrate how teachers might be able to turn Gordon Pradl's claim about good teaching, that "teaching/learning works best when teachers and students manage not to get in each other's way" (125), into effective practice. Derek, one of my student co-presenters, is less politic: he'd like to create an experience that will make it impossible for teachers to return to the mind-numbing pedagogy he remembers from his recent past. "I want them to stop ruining literature for us," he says.

In our blurb in the conference program, we make no promises for student achievement on standardized assessment instruments, although in our invitation to participants "to explore practical and creative ways to write about and understand American literature," we do give a nod to the pragmatic impulse of many conference participants. Our description ends with a specific plug for the student perspective on learning that seemed to have captivated the teachers who participated in the "Langston Shakespeare" poetry session the year before: "The session offers a unique student perspective on connecting with some of the best and often most difficult classic American texts." The title of our presentation attempts to capture both the texts and the approach: "Whitman's Blanket, Thoreau's Twigs, and Emerson's Magic Goggles: Connecting Students and American Literature." What it does not reveal is that we also hope to engage participants in the work of other American authors and traditions: native tales, nineteenth-century women writers, and the participants' own on-the-spot writing about America, Story, and Nature.

Some Consequences of Canonical Inquiry

Any number of things might have accounted for our audience-less session, of course, but in the end I suspect it had less to do with any appeal of an easy fix for statewide testing than the last part of our description of our content—"some of the best and often most difficult classic American texts." For whatever reason, we couldn't generate an interest among teachers to put students and American literature—or at least Whitman, Thoreau, and Emerson—into meaningful contact. Early in his 1836 essay, *Nature*, Emerson makes a claim about the nature of inquiry that I challenge students in my survey course to turn back on their own situations, and which my co-presenters had claimed for themselves: "Every man's condition is a solution in hieroglyphic to those inquiries he would put. He acts it as life, before he apprehends it as truth" (692). As we had prepared to tell our audience, unless American literature is helping you and your students understand yourself and your own conditions, you're not asking the right questions about it or with it. Despite these grand schemes for making the world better for teachers and students with a stroll through American literature, we eventually had to accept that our panel did not convincingly suggest a Rosetta stone to the student-content hieroglyphs of twenty-first-century classroom teaching. The possibility exists, of course, that our condition itself was simply a positive sign of the way that American literature is happening in the schools. It seems more likely, however, especially given the presentation's origins in my students' own inquiries into American literary history and pedagogy, that our lonesome wait in the conference room signals an uneasiness among classroom teachers with American literature in general and with questions of canonicity more particularly.

Some of this unease is rooted in the long history of American literature's attempt to gain a foothold in the academy as a serious object of study and not just as a derivative and lesser instance of a British tradition. If English classroom teachers understand this vexed history of American literature canon-making, the material conditions of schools allow little opportunity to complicate it, and too often teachers, students, and textbooks fall back into familiar though suspect routines that keep American literature undefined, unexamined, and certainly under-appreciated (see Applebee; Yagelski, *Literacy Matters*). As currently figured in secondary schools, American literature lacks a certain sexiness or caché among both teachers and students that other literary periods and traditions have, and it suffers from a general confusion about its own content.

Consider, for instance, that nearly every state in the union and most large metropolitan areas have some sort of annual Shakespeare festival, usually with inducements or discounts for classroom teachers to bring their students. By contrast, and despite the centrality of Emerson to most versions of the American literary canon over the past century (Shumway)—not to mention his place among the powerful discourse of American individualism—a classroom teacher of American literature anywhere in the United States (outside of Concord, Massachusetts, perhaps) would be hard pressed to find a parallel opportunity for teacher and students so consistently to immerse themselves in multiple works by a major U.S. author. They might be able to sift through the leavings of consumer culture to find fragments of Emerson's texts, ephemera on the back of tea boxes, cleaning solutions, even automobile advertisements, or else draw from the rich public store of artifacts on such Web sources as the Library of Congress. But they would never have the pre-established shorthand of Shakespeare-as-Literature that is embedded in the public discourse about "literature" in America. Indeed, college English departments, secondary textbook websites, even default computer image files, assault American literature teachers with the icon of Shakespeare governing their content. One publisher of a very popular and widely adopted eleventh-grade American literature textbook actually has a cartoon medallion of The Bard anchoring its online unit outlines and table of contents. Rather than see this sort of pairing as an infelicitous gaff, I believe it shows a knowing inaccuracy deployed in the service of a larger and, of course, very problematic audience expectation: teachers, students, parents, and administrators want their American literature to be washed clean of any controversy and subsumed into the generic currency of universal literature.

This tendency too often leads teachers and students to imagine that they are encountering texts both chronologically and historically—as one of my former graduate students, who was a classroom teacher seeking an advanced license, claimed—when in fact curriculum packages offer an idiosyncratic mix of texts, which sometimes may share a thematic focus, such as "Colony to Country" or "The Spirit of Individuality," but which more often simply share a convenient length for instruction. My graduate student reported his frustration with "*having* to teach chronologically," based on the curriculum schedule adopted by his department, instead of thematically as he would have liked; but in fact, his schedule of Nathaniel Hawthorne's *The Scarlet Letter* followed by Arthur Miller's *The Crucible* and then John Steinbeck's *Of Mice and Men* was neither. His textbook itself proceeded through broad historical moments with a heavy weighting toward twentieth-century works that reimagined the colonial or nineteenth-century past. So the unit on Puritan literature offered very short excerpts from Jonathan Edwards and some seventeenth-century accounts of the Salem witch trials as prelude to the full text of Miller's McCarthy-era play. Nonetheless, the common pairing of Hawthorne and Miller can allow for an interesting quasi-thematic focus that my student could have made more of in discussing at least the conventional American literature story starting with the impact of Puritan thinking on American literature and culture.

In what follows, I want to pursue a different American literary-historical trajectory—both chronological *and* thematic—that will trace the origin of my students' inquiries, situating them within the context of my own deranged American literature survey course. In doing so, I hope also to allow my students' suggestions for classroom practice to find another hearing, just as they did in my own classroom. In particular, I want to foreground their own struggles with the "American Literature Story" as they had previously received it (in ways similar to that of my graduate student) and then tried to refigure it through a series of transmediations, interdisciplinary juxtapositions, and independent inquiries.

Transmediations of the "America" Story: Jacopo Zucchi and/or Bishop Berkeley

> The Muse, disgusted at an age and clime
> Barren of every glorious theme,
> In distant lands now awaits a better time,
> Producing subjects worthy fame . . .
> GEORGE BERKELEY, "ON THE PROSPECT
> OF PLANTING ARTS AND LEARNING IN
> AMERICA" (1726 [1752]; IV: 365–66)

In early January 2005, some nine months before our ill-fated wait in the university conference center, I meet my future co-presenters and their classmates for the first time as students in my American literature survey course. Some are in fact students from my previous classes in world literature and in writing about literature —and two were among my co-presenters for the "Langston Shakespeare" engagement. So several students have a sense of what is to come, but none is quite prepared for the twelve-page, single-spaced syllabus they receive the first day. The course is itself something of an oddity among the surveys required of majors, since it compresses the entire history of American literature into a single semester offering. This sort of compression often eliminates the possibility of including a broadly inclusive *and* representative selection of authors and texts. I have decided to take the short-ened space as an invitation to do something a bit different from what my American literature colleagues do, without neglecting those canonical, mostly nineteenth-century, authors who have typically dominated American literature curricula at both the secondary and post-secondary level. My sense of this sort of survey course, and of my own teaching, has changed in light of my continued thinking about classroom research, student learning, and pedagogy. I have designed an ambitious syllabus—twelve pages replete with images, readings, semester-long group and individual assignments, rubrics for each, hypertext- and Web-based research links, and a list of some fifteen additional texts (all short novels or story collections) to supplement the hefty anthology they will need for their whole-class readings (see Appendixes 4.1–4.2 for full syllabus and sample engagements). The document is designed to indicate what was in fact the case: this is a course that will demand much of the students outside of our class meetings, and it will deliberately range beyond their expectations of what constitutes American literature.

After a few introductory remarks welcoming them to the class, I turn on the overhead projector and cast them back four centuries to Jacopo Zucchi's 1585 painting, *The Coral Fishers* (Figure 4.1), transposed onto the front wall.

FIGURE **4.1.** *Jacopo Zucchi,* The Coral Fishers *(Allegoria de scoperta dell'America) [1585]. Galleria Borghese.*

I allow the students some time to think about the Italian mannerist painting they are seeing, and to write down anything they think worth noting. After a few more minutes, I ask them to draw a line under what they've just written and to begin a new thought: "What does this painting say to you about the study of—or the meaning of—American literature?" I write the question on the front chalkboard beside the image. When they've had a few more minutes to write, I invite them to talk with the people around them about their responses before these smaller groups report back to the class as a whole.

This process—moving from an initial individual response to a shared engagement, then to smaller groups discussing these first impressions, and finally on to a whole-class sharing and analysis of what the range of reactions might be able to tell us—is one I've used often in other classes. It is, of course, fairly typical of a constructivist approach to teaching and learning, in which student responses help create a knowledge base about a common experience, theme, or idea. What differs from that pedagogical approach is that this activity is also specifically tied to an implicit understanding of what we will be pursuing throughout the class in American literature. That is, the process of negotiating multiple and competing responses to a shared reality is itself at the heart of the American project; and the "Vision(s) of America" we will encounter through the course readings and through works in different media, such as Zucchi's painting, are similarly in dialogue with the visions about American literature we will develop on our own. American literature itself seems ideally suited to a constructivist view of knowledge and pedagogy, and perhaps more than any other content area suggests innovative options to draw meaning from the *demos* of the classroom.

The next fall, when my student co-presenters and I sat in the conference room waiting for the classroom teachers to cross the threshold, we framed this parallel quality another way. It simply made no sense to us to approach the literature of the United States in a way that would be anti-democratic, or that would create learning experiences that worked at cross purposes to the goals of the literature itself. So for instance, to read Whitman's lines and *not* allow students a chance to filter meaning from their own experiences is to miss a crucial opportunity to create experiential learning, and to occlude a key component of the poem's own agenda.

Deranging Prospects for American Literature

The course overview and rationale from the syllabus poses these questions more generally for students in terms of their thematic goals, but it also suggests in its varied components a pedagogical model that might represent the themes, values, and tensions of American literary history. In the language of my syllabus, I invite students to consider what role individual and community values and identities play in understanding "fundamental questions at the heart of American Literature and American literary history: What makes 'American literature' distinctly *American*? Or *literary*?" In light of these questions, the painting by Zucchi offers a useful place to consider the origins of the colonial project(s) and European representations of "Americans." What's more, it raises the problem that so often besets the teaching of American literature in today's schools, when teachers are frustrated by the seemingly competing pulls of history and theme: any chronological or historical approach to American literary or cultural history reveals that even at the beginning of this history, the thematic question and narrative construction of that history is already in play. Zucchi's allegory of *prospect* imaginatively attempts to re-create and explain the meaning of an event almost a century past. Emerson's own opening complaint in *Nature*, that "our age is retrospective" (691), hides the fact that both retrospect and prospect are equally selective fictions, although both have real consequences for the present.

My students make the following observations about the painting, though they don't really know what, if anything, a painting has to do with what they imagine they should be doing in an English or American literature class. They note that the figures with the darker skin are turned away from the viewer's gaze— they have no faces and thus, the students say, they lack subjectivity or individuality; these same figures also seem to be doing most of the work. The female figures in the foreground are idle, European in appearance, and seem to be enjoying the fruits of the darker figures' labor. They adorn themselves with the riches of this new land.

The students also have questions. Who was Zucchi? Had he ever been to the "New World"? Who is the old guy in the lower right foreground? And what's up with the monkey and the baby at the bottom foreground? Are these women supposed to be beautiful or ugly—that is, does Zucchi criticize them or celebrate them? *What does the painting mean*? I offer some contextualizing information in terms of title and date of composition, but the students point to other features of the work, and together we make some attempts about what we can say for sure about this painting and its relationship to America.

Before the first hour is up and we take a break, we have assembled a list of things on the board. The painting was made nearly a century after Columbus's first voyage and slightly predates Raleigh's failed Virginia settlement (a history of the Lost Colony and Virginia Dare that my North Carolina students perhaps still remember dimly from their state history class in elementary school). So even without its second title deliberately invoking America as both idea and story, the painting's glance on the New World comes at the end of a relatively long history of European, but non-English, colonial engagement with the New World. It promotes the notion of the New World as a place of wealth and ease—for Europeans—and of exploitation, both for those brought there to labor and for the indigenous people forced into collaboration. The painter himself could not have seen this scene in any realistic way; we agree at least that he was certainly not present at a First Contact event. Indeed, it seems highly unlikely that he has ever been to the New World at all, and he has just borrowed a real local site to imaginatively stage his allegory of American discovery. His audience is not American but European—the sashes of the women seeming to indicate the European powers engaged in exploration. Noticeably absent from these sashes are the colors of England.

When the students and I regroup after our short break, I finally introduce one of the pages of the syllabus: the sixth page carries a copy of Bishop George Berkeley's eighteenth-century poem "On the Prospect of Planting Arts and Learning in America" paired with a nineteenth-century reproduction of a print of

Minerva in the Library of Congress. I ask students to read the poem with me and consider the image. First I read the entire poem aloud; the Zucchi painting is still projected on the front wall. I then pose a series of questions to start the next part of our session:

> What questions does the poem raise for you, either on its own or with respect to the painting and/or other image?
>
> What connections do you make between the poem and painting?
>
> What connections between poem and yourself? Painting and self?
>
> What surprises do you encounter after viewing and reading?
>
> What happens to your claim about the painting's meaning in light of this new work?

I begin to read the poem again, but this time I ask students to join me as they feel inclined. I read the first couple of lines and then pause, letting those who want to read do so, and for as long as they like. This "drop-in" or "popcorn" reading takes more time to move through the entire poem, of course, but it also creates a nice effect of allowing students to participate in a non-threatening way.

Again the common technique of the read-aloud is deliberate for this content and course theme, for I want us to experience many individual voices building one whole piece. After this second reading and time to reflect, the responses to the works and to the experience vary—several students want to know what *clime* means; others begin to reframe their observations about the painting in terms of the poem's imagery, as if Berkeley's poem were a deliberately ekphrastic work—a poem in response to a painting. And some students still want to know what the monkey is doing there in the lower foreground of the painting. In making connections among the works and between the works and themselves, however, they begin to draw from an interesting store of prior knowledge. They pull from their early British literature survey to reference Shakespeare's *Tempest* (figuring Berkeley as Prospero), or from their knowledge of five-act dramatic structure or Atlantic slave narratives. They also make links to contemporary world and national history, remarking on the twenty-first-century perspective of the United States as colonial and imperialist power; or the ongoing racial and class tensions in America; or the real or chimerical benefits of free trade and global capitalism, which is again an issue especially germane to our region, a major international banking center surrounded by outlying and dying textile towns. What has happened in their reflections is a simultaneous consideration of an idea—"America"—and the historical development of the aesthetic rendering of that idea in art and literature. It is a successful start to the course, not simply because students are engaged or interested, though for the most part they are, but because it models a way of approaching history and literature that allows both to speak to contemporary contexts without being totally unmoored from their own fields of production. And finally, it demonstrates a process of transmediation that will begin to take a central place in students' engagement in the class and with the material.

"My Xocoyote/a," Sor Juana, and a New World Hybridity for Twenty-First-Century Americans

. . . I shall give you a metaphor, an idea clad in rhetoric of many colors and fully visible to view this shall I show you, now I know that you are given to imbue with meaning what is visible . . .	. . . Que en una idea metafórica, vestida de rétoricos colores, representable a tu vista te la mostraré; que ya conozco que tú te inclinas a objetos visibles . . .

SOR JUANA INÉS DE LA CRUZ, *LOA FOR THE AUTO SACRAMENTAL* THE DIVINE NARCISSUS (c.1688; 229–31)

The lines above are from a seventeenth-century Mexican nun who sought out religious life so she might more consistently pursue a life not so much of holiness and seclusion, but of inquiry and intellectual engagement with the mysteries of the world. "Called by her contemporaries 'The Tenth Muse' and 'the Phoenix of Mexico,'" Sor Juana had become "a favorite in the viceregal court [of New Spain] before entering the convent in 1669" at the age of twenty-one, and was "renowned as the finest Latin

American poet of the Baroque period" (de la Cruz i). The passage above comes from a *loa,* a short dramatic précis for a longer dramatic or liturgical work. The "playlet" details the Spanish colonial enterprise in the New World and in these lines announces its own design—to demonstrate, through spectacle and literary language, the allegory of Spanish success in New Spain. The *loa* includes scenes of battle, conflict, conversation, and finally a merging of indigenous culture (in the allegorical characters of America and Occident) with European religion and power systems (figured by Religion and Zeal). It's a useful corollary to the theme of America begun on the first day of class through the juxtaposition of the Zucchi painting and Berkeley poem. What's more, coming from Sor Juana herself, whose writings bear witness to women's power and frequently argue for female education, the lines emphasize a uniquely "American" subject and way of seeing—transmediation across sign systems to further understanding.

The speaker here in Sor Juana's *loa* is Religion, although it is also most certainly the voice of Sor Juana herself justifying the choice of medium. The specific plan, which is outlined, for a New World hybridity through the visual rhetoric of dramatic spectacle has a historical prefiguration in one of the earliest writings from the settlements in the New World, "The History of the Miraculous Apparition of the Virgin of Guadalupe in 1531." That text was among a set of readings on "Discovery, Captivity, Contact" in the second week of my course, which lined up the differing accounts of European-Native American encounters with and through religion in New Spain, New France, and the British colonies of New England and Virginia. In this account of the Virgin of Guadalupe, Juan Diego, a local campesino on his way to mass, encounters a beautiful Náhuatl woman attired in native dress, who addresses him in the familiar terms of his people. "My xocoyote," she calls: my child, my son (de la Cruzr 73). She instructs him to direct the local bishop to build a church on the site of her appearance, which also happens to be a site associated with the Aztec fertility and harvest goddess. Juan Diego appeals to the skeptical bishop several times before finally bringing a physical sign of the truth of the apparition—a bunch of roses, which have bloomed out of season on the hillside where the woman has appeared. Juan Diego allows the woman, whom he also addresses in familiar terms as "my xocoyota" (my daughter, my child) (75), to arrange the flowers in his mantle before he takes them to show the bishop. When Juan Diego opens the mantle before the bishop, the flowers fall away to reveal the likeness of the woman transferred onto the fabric itself. The bishop, Juan Diego, and others take the image and the woman to be the Virgin Mary herself, but manifested as *la Virgen Morena*, the dark lady.

In the centuries since this account, the historical (and religious) truth of the story has often been called into question as an obvious manipulation by European religious and colonial leaders to overlay Christian iconography onto indigenous beliefs and practices to help advance the colonial enterprise. Nonetheless, as Gloria Anzaldúa notes, "*la Virgen de Guadalupe* [remains] the single most potent religious, political and cultural image of the Chicano/*mexicano*," having in its history eclipsed "all the other male and female figures in Mexico, Central America, and parts of the U.S. Southwest" (29–30). That range of influence continues to grow with the patterns of migration and immigration across the southeastern and midwestern United States, which was of particular interest for my students and me in the Carolinas, where the Spanish-speaking population has increased throughout these two states and in the Charlotte-metro region alone has increased over 500% in between the last two census counts.[1] These shifting linguistic, ethnic, and religious demographics of our local community call us to take stock of the ways such icons have entered into twenty-first-century American culture, not to mention American Catholic culture more broadly,[2] as cultural/literary/religious symbols with powerful connotations that ripple beyond their own immediate contexts.

For the purposes of our survey of American literature, however, the religious associations are less important than both the discursive mechanism by which this "history" inscribed a new process of Americanization, and the discourse of gender and power embedded in the account. That is, what students witness in this *mestiza* figure is not the traditional myth of American assimilation but a hybrid refiguration, a merging of cultures and identities. And though it most certainly is a problematic fusion that has been used to maintain restrictions on women's subjectivity, it nonetheless offers a radical leveling of the divine with the human, for when both Juan Diego and the apparent Virgin Mary address each other in Náhuatl as "my xocoyote/a," they claim each other as spiritual, ethnic, and linguistic kin. This relation gives rise, according to Anzaldúa, to "a new *mestiza* consciousness, *una conciencia de mujer.* It is a consciousness of the Borderlands" (77). Anzaldúa's merging of gender and geography also offers a new way of seeing and understanding not just American literature, but *teaching* a literature which itself is caught up in questions of linguistic, cultural, and even geographical origins.

A "Solution in Hieroglyph": Curricular Transmediations as Inquiry

The hefty syllabus I distribute to students underscores this aspect as a positive, or at least a potentially welcome, unsettling from an "English-only" account that simply starts with the Puritan experience in New England and trudges forward to American high modernism, say, with T.S. Eliot, a figure who is claimed by the British canon as well. The overview and rationale for the course points to a different approach:

> American Literature Survey spans over 400 years of American literature, from the Colonial Period (including literature of the First Contact and early works from New France, New Spain, and of course New England) to the Modern Period. Through shared readings from an anthology (poetry, histories, essays, fiction, and drama) and through individual and smaller group readings of novels focused on particular themes and genres (American Utopias, Borderlands, Romances/Adventures), we will investigate the fundamental questions at the heart of American literature and American literary history—What makes "American literature" distinctly *American?* Or *literary?* Who writes it, who reads it, and why?

Again, Anzaldúa's description of a *mestiza* way of thinking is instructive for the cognitive shifts—and metacognitive discoveries—that are possible in this sort of design.

Every increment of consciousness, every step forward is a *travesía*, a crossing. [As knower] I am an alien in new territory. And again, and again. . . . Knowledge makes me more aware, it makes me more conscious. "Knowing" is painful because after "it" happens I can't stay in the same place and be comfortable. I am no longer the same person I was before. (48)

In this view, knowing and coming-to-know are themselves *deranged* activities. The task of the syllabus is to describe as completely as possible what path this derangement would take and what the journey might allow students to discover about themselves as knowers, and about American literature as an object of knowledge.

The printed schedule of readings itself offers a mix of traditional syllabus information—titles of readings, page numbers, authors—with accompanying images from popular culture, history, and other disciplines that similarly blur the line between high and low, literary and nonliterary. Some of these images are perhaps familiar to students, such as an illustration of the landing of Columbus (taken from Washington Irving's 1828 *History of the Life and Voyages of Christopher Columbus*, which remakes Columbus's explorations for Spain into a proto-American/U.S. narrative of self-fashioning). Others are a bit more strange, though somewhat directly representational. For instance, below the second week's readings listed under the heading "Discovery, Captivity, and Contact," is an image of a contemporary Southwestern *ritalbo* of *la Virgen Morena*, a folk-art form that captures something of the hybrid *mestiza* qualities of the 1531 *History* in its use of found materials to create devotional artifacts. Alongside this seemingly benign encounter of European religious figures with indigenous people of the South-Central Americas are equally strange and more violent encounters involving torture, abduction, and "invisible bullets" (Harriot 124): Thomas Harriot's astonishing 1588 "Brief and True Report of the New Found Land of Virginia"; the account in *The Relations of 1647,* by Father Jerome Lalement, of the "American Martyrs" of New France (which actually occurred in the middle of current upstate New York); and Mary Rowlandson's *Captivity.* Behind the list for the following week's readings from *The Bay Psalm Book, The New England Primer,* and the works of two religiously influenced poets, Anne Bradstreet and Sor Juana Inés de la Cruz (both identified in their times as "the tenth muse" in the New World) is a multitextual and bilingual version of the Lord's Prayer designed for the religious and literacy education of the coastal northeastern Miqmaq tribe. The prayer appears in three simultaneous versions: in the ideoglyphs of the Miqmaq; in an apparent transliteration of native dialect; and in eighteenth-century English (Le Clercq 411).

Images such as these hint at the requirements for student transmediations of their understanding throughout the course, in which they demonstrate their understanding of texts in one sign system or genre (usually the written literary and historical texts of their anthology) through another sign system (original or contemporary visual, musical, or inter-mediated texts). But these juxtapositions of historical texts also point to the complicated intersection of European politics, language, and colonial enterprise that inflect the writings at the beginning of the survey, and which becomes available for student inquiry and critique through the encounter of multiple and competing perspectives. As Collins and Blot have noted about colonial literacy practices, the very

> framing of natives in writing as colonial subjects begins with justifying the writing process itself as imbued with the power to record history accurately and with complete disinterest. . . . Without [native] writing, native history is delegitimated. . . . Without [their own] history, the natives can more easily be remade (inscribed in texts) using molds provided by the right of conquest and Christendom. (126)

So in the case of the short multitextual scripture used as background on the syllabus, we can examine how the use of English makes a claim for the Miqmaq as allies against their French-speaking Acadian neighbors on Nova Scotia—a people whose own forced resettlement in the mid-eighteenth century is termed *Le Grand Dérangement*. The pairing of Harriot's "Virginians" and *la Virgen Morena* helps establish a timeline of intercultural interaction in the Americas that allows students to make their own discoveries about just how civilized much of the Americas were even before the English arrived and tried to argue otherwise in accounts such as Harriot's and Rowlandson's.

Establishing parallel or sideshadowing timelines around the weekly readings is a key element of the student presentations, and paired with the transmediations, puts students in the position of bringing these disparate but contemporaneous texts into a coherent picture. The full instructions for these activities, the assessment criteria, and the scoring guides are all included in the syllabus packet. Every student is required to work with a group of two to three others to deliver a short in-class presentation on a reading or set of readings. Their task is not simply to report on the biography of the authors, but to create an engagement for the class about some aspect of the readings for that day that is of particular interest to the group. By the time one of my student co-presenters and her group make their presentation on Thoreau and Transcendentalism in the seventh week of the semester, several groups already have brought transmediations that kept alive the question of the Americanness of our readings. The very first group has taken up the religious and gender discourses of Anne Bradstreet, Sor Juana, and *The New England Primer*, noting that at the same time the Salem witch trials are going on in Massachusetts, halfway across the continent Sor Juana is writing from her convent in defense of her right to learn and to write, asking her bishop and protector, "What then is the evil in my being a woman?" (65). Through a subtle and theatrical cross-dressing, one of the women in the group even appears for the presentation in the guise of a typical college male to underscore the troublesome rhetoric of the back-handed compliment Sor Juana receives from an admirer of her poetry, who says that "she would better be a man" (137). This embodied transmediation gives new force to Sor Juana's own poem "In Reply to a Gentleman from Peru," which the class has read in advance of the presentation.

Another group considers Crèvecoeur's foundational question "What is an American?" and wonders why he allows for an admixture of nationalities and ethnicities but omits the Africans and Spanish, who have already been long resident on the continent. Another group delights us with Benjamin Franklin's seeming embodiment of the quintessential American bon vivant, with one student updating an eighteenth-century Anglo-American ballad on her guitar for the class. The group embraces Franklin's financial advice from *Poor Richard's Almanack* by bringing in

copies of the fine print and high interest rates from the ubiquitous credit card offers targeting college students. Each of these
presentations leaves the rest of the class with multiple resources
to assist their thinking about course goals, and allows me to clarify,
supplement, or cover other texts omitted by the presenters. The
transmediations themselves become useful course reference points
for later readings and assessments, as students bring them back
as examples in their papers, online talking points, and even exam
essays.

Virtual, Real, and Ethereal Americans: Moving Online Discussion into Classroom Practice

> Students, to you 'tis giv'n to scan the heights
> Above, to traverse the ethereal space,
> And mark the systems of revolving worlds.
> PHILLIS WHEATLEY (1773, 7–9)

In each of the cases above, the presentations have been shaped
by the weeklong threaded talking points on the class's online discussion page. These discussions are established early on as a means
for us to stay connected during the week. I try to stay out of the
conversations unless there seems to be obvious misunderstanding, or some event or happening on campus seems especially topical to our conversation. So for instance, after the first week, I
share with students the calendar of campus events organized to
celebrate and honor Dr. Martin Luther King Jr. His "I Have a
Dream" speech is one of the selections for the following week,
paired with excerpts from the *Journals* of Columbus's voyages.
In a February posting under the subject "Cabeza de Vaca's Kangaroo," I offer some links to help students think about what the
animal with a pouch that the Spanish explorers encounter could
possibly be. "That's no kangaroo," I write. "It's *didelphis
virginiana*, or a 'possum to us in North Carolina; and apparently
it's the only naturally occurring marsupial in North America,
reigning supreme for almost two million years, according to the
Florida Fish and Wildlife Conservation Commission website link
'Critters/Opossum.'"

After encountering a number of texts that make extensive religious allusions and references, several students express their frustration both at not recognizing these references because of a lack of any formal religious training (whether for familial, theological, or regional reasons; that is, they never went to church, or they're [insert denomination here], or they're from the North) and at feeling they ought to know these because of the overtly religious culture of their Bible Belt peers. I direct them to a link at the National Humanities Center TeacherServe project called "Divining America: Religion and National Culture," which I suggest may help supplement their reading of colonial and nineteenth-century American texts. At another time, to help clarify the location of the "New France" accounts in *The Relations of 1647,* I post a link to the Shrine to the North American Martyrs at Auriesville, New York. But these remain periodic professorial interruptions, and for the most part, the discussion list evolves week-by-week into a tentative conversation space where the talkers in class still talk but where, too, the more silent students have a chance to think through three or four items that have drawn their attention in the readings, and which they present as talking points for the coming in-class discussion.

Before the presentation on Thoreau midway through the semester, however, these talking points have included only a few extended student-to-student exchanges; most postings do engage the readings, but in a way that seems to indicate that the students do not quite believe that anyone else (including me) is reading all the responses. In fact, one student remarks in the middle of a posting, "Let's be honest, not a lot of people read over all the talking points." The readings from Thoreau (both "Resistance to Civil Government" and a large chunk of *Walden*) mark a significant shift in the way students engage the texts online. Though several students take up certain passages from *Walden* that seem to be inspirational, they are largely preoccupied with the way that "Resistance to Civil Government" seems to speak to their fatigue with political rhetoric and two-party politics, and with the way its argument echoes much of the "discourse on the Iraq war"—which perhaps accounts for the hotly contested postings about Thoreau's apparent contradictions or hypocrisy. A particular passage from "Resistance to Civil Government" that students return to seems to advise a sort of libertarian self-sufficiency with respect to governmental systems:

> This American government . . . is excellent, we must all allow; yet this government never of itself furthered any enterprise, but by the alacrity with which it got out of its way. *It* does not keep the country free. *It* does not settle the West. *It* does not educate. (752)

Some students who had not posted more than a few lines prior to this are now posting several pages—and they seem to be reading every bit of each other's postings. By the time the discussion comes back around to one of the original discussants and a member of the group presenting that evening, they are eagerly awaiting the evening's presentation and discussion.

But something else also emerges. Despite this spike in activity, unlike many of the previous week's postings, not everyone in the class makes a response to the online forum. The drop-off in number of participants may result in part from what several students identify as the "really long," "ridiculously long," "extremely long" readings; perhaps the silent students had yet to finish the readings in time to post talking points. But it also seems likely that the flurry of political-leaning discussion kept more timid students from entering the fray. For instance, one student who does end up posting very late in the week begins by giving voice to a sentiment shared by many students who feel disaffected by what is sometimes construed as a liberal bias or anti-establishment drift of twenty-first-century American universities: "I hate it when people talk about the government." If the class has begun to feel like a close-knit group, the sort of community of practice or "family" atmosphere we teachers often say we want to establish in our classrooms, then this week we are engaged in a protracted sibling rivalry that threatens to make the upcoming class presentation a spirited and tense evening.

When it comes time for the class presentation, however, the group chooses to focus its attention on the very point of contention that many students have been identifying in their postings: Thoreau's apparent contradictions. A member of the group gives the discussion list an advance notice of what the group has been thinking. They plan to start from the notion that Thoreau's "hypocrisy" may actually be

> him thinking of all possible outcomes and situations . . . He's exploring all options and keeping an open mind. He wants to start with a clean slate, so he separates himself and indulges in nature to really gather his thoughts.

It's a shrewd maneuver to deflect the tension but also to incorporate it into the analysis itself: "What should we make of Thoreau's ability to polarize us so markedly?" they ask. "How has he manipulated us into being invested in the outcomes of *ideas*?"

This group rewards our participation with treasures from the dollar store related to nature, for giving "correct" answers to their questions—really open-ended invitations allowing for a range of valid responses. One student receives a CD with sounds of the forest; another a butterfly net; all of us receive a piece of wood gathered from the campus's Van Landingham Glen, which is across the street from our classroom building and home to the university's old-growth nature walk. The group invites us to observe this material closely and through as many senses as possible, including taste, although only a brave few put twig to tongue before writing (after all, some of these twigs have bugs on them!). Perhaps because several members of this group are also teacher candidates, the presentation highlights the pedagogical aspects of transcendentalism: "What does transcendentalism *teach* us or allow us to *learn* about the world?" they ask. It is this direct engagement with teaching and content that plants the idea for the fall conference presentation.

Pedagogical Fragments: The Ends and Origins of Inquiry

> Standing in the empty Gallery, I stared at the walls. How do you ask a picture what it's trying to say?
> CHRISTOPHER (from exam 3 option B, ENGL 3300 final exam)

Despite the failure of our fall conference presentation to attract any participants, that experience of collaborating with students during the previous spring's class to develop inquiry invitations for others continues to influence my practice as a teacher, particularly in the way I ask students to engage American literature. The quote from Christopher above is the closing scene of his final exam response in the most recent version of this course. His response offered a dialogue between himself and three of his classmates as they strolled through an imagined exhibit of American visual artworks and talked about the key issues of the course. In the course of this "Colloquy on the Art and Nature of American Literature" section of the exam, Christopher and his peers reference themes and passages from the course readings, with special focus on Emerson (*Nature*), Phillis Wheatley ("On Being Brought from Africa to America"), Edward Albee (*The Sandbox*), and Crèvecoeur ("What Is an American?"), all in an effort "to determine which (or any) of the pieces on display is artistic, distinctly American, and indispensable to understanding American literature and culture." Several images from a mix of genres, styles, and time periods were available in a folder on the course website, and the four Christopher focused on in his dialogue were typical of the range of works: Frida Kahlo's *Two Fridas*; Christopher Cranch's cartoon caricature of Emerson's "Transparent Eyeball"; a Walker Evans photo of an African American couple on a city street; and an untitled William Eggleston photo of a rusted-out, upside-down car on a dirt road. This last was the image before which Christopher's fictive self stood puzzling at the end. This sort of option for the final exam allows for student creativity, but not simply for its own sake. It also offers an opportunity to think across artistic modes about a central idea—in Christopher's case, what a "true" American identity might be—in a way that students have experienced throughout the course.

Another option for this final exam likewise invited students to imagine texts and authors in dialogue with each other, but this time as physical artifacts. As I've mentioned, part of the local economy used to be heavily tied to the textile industry. Imagining a collaboration between the National Humanities Center and the North Carolina Center for Applied Textile Technology—both very real organizations, both located in North Carolina—I invited students to construct a new textual artifact that could be woven together from existing materials/texts, and which would offer both an *artistic* and *educational* experience to a diverse set of readers/viewers so that the experience of witnessing/viewing/ reading these artifacts will help them to understand something indispensable about American literature and culture, but also about themselves in relation to these artifacts.

The students who choose this option became *bricoleurs*, pulling together disparate texts to create a (usually) coherent text held together by their own themes and argument. Aimee's long apprenticeship growing up in a family of quilters allowed her to turn the invitation into an extended transmediation with pictures of quilts themselves transmediating several of the readings from the course. A large window-pattern quilt, with repeating and alternating panels of ships and waves appliquéd on, became a textile interpretation of discovery and exploration narratives such as Columbus's *Journal of the First Voyage to America* and John Smith's *Generall Historie of Virginia, and New England*. As Aimee notes,

> these texts show the . . . meeting of the European explorers and the Native Americans as the previous quilt [used to interpret "Creation of the Whites"], but from a divergent viewpoint. Here we see from the point of view of the explorers. . . . These texts are important because of this change of view from the natives to the Europeans. At this time in history, the culture began to shift, and the literature with it. It is important, from both historical and literary standpoints that we recognize this shift from an existing culture to a newer one.

Aimee's transmediation helps both to demonstrate her own understanding about these works and to articulate something important for her about the contextuality of literary history.

The final option for the exam was the one most selected by students, perhaps because it allowed them to make explicit their preferences for and against particular texts. The invitation required them to argue for the continued inclusion of at least two of the texts from the semester, the replacement or exclusion of at least one text, and the further addition of one that we had not read as a whole class. By far the most common text listed for exclusion was Mary Rowlandson's *Captivity*, surprising perhaps given the way that particular text's resurgence through the eighteenth and early nineteenth centuries was deployed to rekindle patriotic fervor, but not out of character with earlier class discussions of the narrative itself. Erin's take on this argument took the form of a story. "The world in which my story is placed is very strange," she begins; "it mixes the 1600s and present day with modern court proceedings and polytheism, among other things . . . The American Literature Witch Trials." The trial unfolds with Rowlandson, Thoreau, and Hawthorne accused of being literary "witches," those who "jeopardize the very canon of American literature and must be removed as one removes a gangrenous limb." I am figured as the judge, and Erin is sent "by the gods of American literature. They bestowed great knowledge upon me of the meaning that lies within its depth, and charged me with the quest of saving these innocent writers from harm." After vigorous defenses of Thoreau and Hawthorne, the fictional Erin stumbles in her defense of Rowlandson, all but consigning her to the fate many of her peers had already determined, when Kurt Vonnegut appears from beyond the grave to chasten Erin,

> You were to defend ALL the writers. . . . It is true that the work of this woman is quite boring, and filled with righteousness, bigotry, and whining, but my fellow humans, *that* is part of America as well! Just because we don't like a part of our history doesn't mean we can hide it . . . We are so very diverse that we can't pick and choose our identity; we can't try to breed a pure identity by casting out all the ones we see as unfit; that's literary genocide, and it's WRONG.

If you can guess the ending (Rowlandson saved, Vonnegut added to the canon, Erin the defense attorney garnering an "A" for Erin the student), no doubt it's because of the very familiarity of such genres, which themselves are part of the shared literacies of American culture. In addition to being great fun, Erin's scenario is also quite astute at deconstructing the very canon game that a survey course is supposed to establish.

But not all the responses have such happy endings, especially those that take up the question of the canon. There are some who argue against the texts that deviate from a strict Anglo and Protestant vision of America, excluding on the basis of religion, language, or ethnicity those native texts, such as "The History of the Miraculous Apparition of the Virgin of Guadalupe" or Southwestern folk tales, that seem more "Mex" than "Tex," to name just a few. Others implicitly discount the work of women writers or those on the margin of the dominant discourse of nation. This sort of response seems to follow Whitman's advice to filter meaning from oneself without recognizing his condition to first "listen to all sides" (l. 29).

Although I am certainly troubled by these responses, both for their content and the fact that they clearly are resisting the very class experience I've tried to create, they also suggest the need to continue to work against the facile transmission of a master narrative about American literary history that is both historically and ideologically suspect. But until classroom teachers have an opportunity to acquire a deeper understanding of American literature from exposure to primary texts, historical and contextualizing documents, and cultural artifacts from across media and artistic modes, it will be difficult for them to present students with experiences to engage this literature and history on their own terms. They'll have to rely on the sort of history packaged by their anthologies and curriculum guides, which, as I've noted, frequently send mixed messages about the content of American literature. The good news is that every one of the texts I've mentioned in this chapter—including the visual images—is freely and easily available through a quick Web search, at sites like the Library of Congress's American Memory Project, Wikipedia Commons, and others. But unless the teaching of American literature happens differently and more extensively in English departments connected to university teacher education programs, it's unlikely that classroom teachers or their students will see in this literature anything that speaks to their situation as readers, writers, and thinkers in the twenty-first century. And that is a reckoning we can ill afford.

Notes

1. See the State of North Carolina census and demographic data at http://demog.state.nc.us/.

2. Indeed, the Virgin of Guadalupe has been designated by the Catholic Church as the Patroness of the Americas and more recently as the Patroness of the New Millennium.

Of Blackbirds and Backpacks:
Images and Models of What Counts
as Knowledge in English/Education

What Everyone Already Knows about Teaching
English and Teacher Education in America

> Students, parents and educators intuitively believe that a teacher's
> knowledge of subject matter is critical if students are going to
> achieve to high standards. As Sandra Feldman, president of the
> American Federation of Teachers, says, "You can't teach what
> you don't know well." [7] In addition, research shows that teach-
> ers who know the subject matter they teach are more effective in
> the classroom. [8] Having teachers who know well the content
> they are teaching is good practice because it leads to improved
> student learning.
>
> A TOOLKIT FOR TEACHERS,
U.S. Department of Education (2004, 10)

I concluded Chapter 4 with a call for greater immersion in the
content of American literature, which would seem to be in
alignment with the claim above about the importance of subject
matter expertise. But of the many obstacles facing future English
teachers as they seek to put students and subject matter into productive conversation, the No Child Left Behind Act (NCLB) of
2001 is one of the more daunting and opaque. In support of
reinforcing this legislation among teachers, the U.S. Department
of Education has offered its own *Toolkit for Teachers*, which
seeks to dispel some of the "myths" about the law, and ostensi-
bly tries to help teachers navigate the thicket of arcane language
in the act. Within this document several key terms and phrases
recur: "highly qualified," "scientifically-based research," "program effectiveness," "core knowledge." The overall intent seems

to be to instill confidence in teachers to embrace the goals of the Act. Voices from within the English/Education research community have already taken exception to NCLB's easy elision of scientific "facts" with ideological and commercial agendas, especially with respect to the reading focus of the law. Those critiques deliver a close rhetorical and discursive analysis of the language of the law and its mandates, so my purpose in invoking the law and particular passages of it here is not to engage in a lengthy dismantling of its problems—though I believe that it does have serious problems. Rather, I want to use it to demonstrate an aspect of what James Gee calls a public "discourse model" that shapes the expectations and assumptions of and about teacher candidates. "Discourse models," says Gee, "are 'theories' (storylines, images, explanatory frameworks) that people hold, often unconsciously, and use to make sense of the world and their experiences in it" (61). Such models give utterance to what "everyone already knows" about, say, what counts as American literature or the nature of teaching, learning, and schooling, though they are in fact socially situated meanings and practices that hide powerful assumptions about people, communities, and even literary value. An analysis of discourse models of teaching English is especially important in the formation of teacher candidates, so the latter half of this chapter will take up that question in the context of actual student work from preservice and post-baccalaureate teacher candidates in English.

The quote above comes from a section of the *Toolkit* answering the FAQ "Why No Child Left Behind Focuses on the Importance of Teachers Knowing the Subjects They Teach." We see a curious appeal not to scientifically based research (though it is cited as such) but to the court of public opinion: "Students, parents and educators intuitively believe," we are told, that teachers' content knowledge is critical to student achievement. But as Gee notes of discourse models, they "often involve us in exclusions that are not at first obvious and which we are often unaware of making" (72). These exclusions remain in the shadows of the mainstream practice of these discourse models, however, and can become visible to our inquiries when we look closely at how language is operating. For instance, the language of the claim above invites us to join in believing this assertion as if we were the educational elect—certainly we must somehow be among the students, parents, or educators hailed by the *Toolkit*. But it also dissuades our dissent in the same gesture, for if we choose to believe other than what seems to be known by all, then we must perforce position ourselves outside the realm of knowledge about our own practice, either as educational apostates or simply the woefully uninformed (think: the anti-teacher caricature of the "unqualified" teacher, which, critics claim, the institution of tenure in public schools has allowed to persist in the pedagogical damage of students).

If we examine more closely the two citations (referenced as [7] and [8] in this chapter's opening quotation from the *Toolkit*) supporting this "intuitive belief" about teaching content, however, we see that they hardly meet the very standards of reliability defined later in the *Toolkit* document for "scientifically-based research." The first claim comes from a speech made by Feldman, which the citation simply notes was "at a White House Conference on Preparing Tomorrow's Teachers, 2001" (62, fn 7). As *Toolkit* readers, we don't know the nature of Feldman's utterance, whether it was part of any larger research findings, or whether it was simply a personal conviction; for that, we need to follow *another* series of government links to get to Feldman's entire speech. We would need to be more than intuitive; we'd need to be critically inquisitive. When we are—but only *if* we are—we see that the lines cited in the *Toolkit* come nearly at the end of a talk in which Feldman, drawing from her own experience as an alternative licensure track teacher in English, offers a long narrative account of coming to the profession and reflecting on her own practice. So the use to which the *Toolkit* puts Feldman's account decontextualizes it from its narrative and reflective framing, but also occludes Feldman's own advice drawn from her experiences, in which she (1) explicitly cautions against teacher-training programs based solely on subject matter expertise and divorced from pedagogical instruction; (2) stresses the importance of collaborative work among teachers throughout their induction years—work of the kind that was so important for both my students in Chapter 4 and for my own collaborators in teacher-research; and (3) puts special emphasis on the need for ongoing and purposeful professional development and onsite mentoring of new teachers.

None of these recommendations is highlighted in the *Toolkit*, but each has been advocated by NCTE and CEE for some time, and each has more recently been identified again by the research on teacher induction by McCann, Johannessen, and Ricca. It is also the kind of sustained inquiry and collaboration I've been describing among my students and my own teacher-research. Whether the U.S. Department of Education in fact shares Feldman's perspective on the need for collaboration and sustained professional inquiry among teachers or is simply unaware of other recent studies, we do not know from the *Toolkit* itself. As the *Toolkit* validates intuitive belief about content expertise, it simultaneously discounts teachers' reflective knowledge of their own experiences, and by extension their pedagogical knowledge drawn from their own inquiries about what works in the classroom.

We perhaps should not be surprised by this governmental blind spot to the work of actual teachers and researchers on what works in the classroom. Rarely is such extensive investment in maintaining a climate of professional growth part of the public or political discourse about education. The general disregard of teacher knowledge *about teaching* by policymakers has been well documented, although it is no less dispiriting for being so. Cathy Fleischer's opening anecdote in *Teachers Organizing for Change* gives a particularly stunning and sobering account of how teachers, teacher educators, and educational researchers were serially and summarily dismissed by state officials during public hearings for standards reform, only to have officials accept the same information and findings from parent advocates (1–2). In light of such dismissals, it is remarkable (though encouraging) to me that anyone even continues to consider teaching as a worthwhile profession. The image of the teacher as the privileged knower of student learning needs and as constructor of pedagogical knowledge is simply one that does not fit the already "known" storyline or discourse model about teaching and schools in the United States. This omission is one of the major exclusions of the "content knowledge" discourse model. What's more, the storyline excludes the possibility that teachers already *do* have knowledge of the subject matter when the knowledge they have, as I argued in Chapter 4, deviates from the master narrative of what counts as the subject of English. Instead, the focus of politicians and the local and national news media has typically been on failing test scores, abysmal student grasp of "core knowledge" relative to other countries and disciplines, and sensationalized accounts of school violence.

The second citation in the *Toolkit* ([8] in the opening quote) in support of this intuition about teacher knowledge is from a 1994 article in *Economics of Education Review* by David H. Monk on "Subject Area Preparation of Secondary Mathematics and Science Teachers and Student Achievement." The content-specific focus of this article may indeed indicate reliable information about math and science teaching, but to extend Monk's survey-based findings in a wholesale fashion to all teachers and every content area, as the NCLB *Toolkit*, through its citation of his work, tacitly recommends that teachers themselves do, again strains the demands of the document's own definition for research. This is not to say that either Monk's or Feldman's work is to be discounted, or that teachers should not have knowledge of their content areas, but rather to recognize the highly problematic elision of disparate data and learning claims when they are brought together under policy rhetoric and then turned toward the ideological subject formation of teachers. More troubling for me and for my English/Education students is that this passage from *A Toolkit for Teachers* clearly does not assume a teacher readership that has the capacity or interest to critique research claims, despite the need for these same teachers to be "highly qualified." Instead, the document seems rather deliberately to construct a teacher audience that is unqualified to know their own classrooms and will passively accept the findings of researchers because of their authority claims.

Jennifer Buehler's recent essay, "The Power of Questions and the Possibilities of Inquiry in English Education," makes a similar observation about the current educational and "political climate of high-stakes testing, teacher accountability, and assaults on public education" in which "federal mandates put pressure on teachers not to pose questions but to offer up results and answers." Faced with the needs of real students and a recognition of our own imperfect knowledge of content, Buehler argues, teachers inevitability are confronted by what she calls the "big questions" of English education: the ones that "remind us that there are no easy answers and no one-size-fits all approaches to teaching English." The role of the English educator, especially in our work with classroom teachers and teacher candidates, is to create a space where such questions can be raised. "Professional growth and educational change become most possible," she says,

> when groups of teachers come together to reflect, to question, and to devise a collective course of action . . . If we in the field of English Education . . . could lead teachers to articulate their own big questions, could provide teachers with opportunities to engage in a collaborative process of exploring those questions, and could guide teachers to establish a questioning stance that would evolve throughout their careers, then teachers could become researchers and a questioning stance could become the norm. (286)

Buehler acknowledges the difficulty of establishing such networks, especially since they require the sorts of partnerships among schools, administrators, and university faculty that are often vexed by existing institutional and pedagogical histories based on uneven power sharing. The place of the teacher candidate, the primary denizen of the methods course, within these networks remains especially vulnerable.

Nevertheless, as I've discovered in my own classes and attempted to describe in the previous chapters, fostering an inquiry stance among preservice teachers, or simply undergraduates interested in questions of pedagogy and curriculum, is certainly possible. Indeed, such a stance can foster a deeper investigation of subject matter without losing sight of the students who will encounter it. In *Teacher/Mentor*, Peg Graham, Sally Hudson-Ross, and their partners in the UGA-NETS collaboration of classroom teachers, university teacher educators, and English teacher candidates at the University of Georgia describe a more systematic rethinking of the traditional student teaching experience. McCann, Johannessen, and Ricca's *Supporting Beginning English Teachers* describes the challenges that face new teachers in their induction years, and recommends that methods courses and teacher training programs more generally focus on the teaching of "procedural knowledge" (151), or how students learn content, rather than assume that content knowledge can simply be transmitted from teacher to student. New teachers can be supported in this shift by maintaining "dialogues with peers, mentors, and supervisors so that the various perspectives can guide and enrich the establishment of [teaching and curriculum] priorities" (149). Again, these partnerships amid a richly engaged network of practitioners acknowledge the delicate balance that sustains the group and emphasize the need for ongoing professional development among all the partners and stakeholders.

Studies such as these help maintain an emphasis on *theorized practice* during what most teachers and teacher educators would describe as difficult times. Such times create the climate that confronted my American literature co-presenters and me during our Writing Project Fall Conference, when we met head-on the climate change of the current educational regime. As Cathy Fleischer and Dana Fox noted in their final issue as editors of *English Education*, in these situations "administrators, legislators, even teachers . . . turn to an emphasis on the very practical:

> how to help students (k-12 *and* preservice) pass the test, how to design curriculum to meet the standards, how to make sure lesson plans demonstrate a strong correspondence to standards and test questions. These reductive yet very real demands on teachers, of course, ignore the larger theoretical and contextual issues in which these discussions need to be placed. In times like these, it is easy to respond with more practical knowledge and suggestions, practicalities that help the overstressed and overworked teacher simply cope . . . easy for the overarching theoretical frameworks that inform our work to get lost in the day-to-dayness of the crisis. Theorized practice—practical solutions that are firmly situated in the questions of *why* and *how* and *so what*—is what we believe can lead us forward. (256–57)

For teacher candidates in my English Methods course, the move forward emerged through a looking back on their own experiences as individual and collaborative literacy learners (and users); then by examining the discourses and knowledges that students bring to the school setting, but which remain hidden from or discounted by school literacies; and finally in a sustained reflection on the meaning of English/Education in their lives as teachers.

/-ing Conceptions of Teaching English

> We must erase the lines which have become inherent to the [educational] system through centuries of indoctrination and stop trying to teach students and start trying to teach people how to learn.
>
> JUSTIN, *"Erasing the Lines," Teaching Philosophy, Z version (May 2007)*

At the end of my spring 2007 course Teaching English/Communication Skills to Middle and Secondary School Learners—known to students and faculty alike by the shorthand title English Methods—I invited my students to work in their semester-long reading groups one last time so they could list thirteen things that had been important or memorable for them about the course. The number allowed roughly one thing for each of our weekly meetings, and it deliberately invoked Wallace Stevens's well-known poem, "Thirteen Ways of Looking at a Blackbird" (92–94; see Appendix 5.1), which I myself had used thematically to organize the course schedule. Stevens's stanza 2 ("I was of three minds . . .") and stanza 4 ("A man and a woman are one. A man and a woman and a blackbird are one"), for instance, were the poetic headnotes for the weeks that included a focus on different types of peer review engagements. Stanza 5 ("I do not know which to prefer, the beauty of inflections or the beauty of innuendos . . .") was prelude for a week focused on the use of literary theory and interpretive acts in the secondary school classroom. Alas, I wasn't able to sustain the conceit quite so directly through the entire semester; though the blackbird may have been "involved in what I know," I never quite figured out how to deal with those "thin men of Haddam" in stanza 7. Whatever the poem may mean, it certainly gave rise to thinking about perspective, placement, and the struggle for coherence amid the indeterminacy of even the most well-planned classroom.

It's an apt metaphor for the very process of English teacher candidate education as well, for in these sorts of methods-course and end-of-semester reflections, English/Education students are faced with the daunting task of making all their previous experiences as students, learners, English majors, and teachers in training fit into some grand scheme of meaning about their future practice. Indeed, as teacher educators in NCATE institutions, we want to see just this sort of evidence that candidates *can* make their experiences cohere. With Stevens's poem as a vehicle for reflection, we see that *blackbird* becomes a floating signifier, always moving beyond our "one of many circles" (stanza 9), alternately carrying positive and negative inflections about teacher candidates and classroom teaching: *they* are blackbirds, isolated in a room of inert, unengaged students; their *students* become blackbirds, piercing them with fear, or else joining them in exclusive domains of understanding; or perhaps blackbirds are the *curriculum* they've learned or that they will deliver, through the beauty of inflections or innuendos. For my students and for me, the point of these possible analogues was the realization that the more one looks at blackbirds or uses blackbirds to look at teaching/learning/schooling experiences, the more complicated the act of understanding becomes.

Through my students' reflections, however, I've come to see that this sort of derangement generates a keen focus on the territory *between* English/Education. Like the "sh/ed" at the core of that juncture, it's a site *both* to shelter or store up new understandings *and* to slough away or cast aside old ways of thinking and doing "English." It's a forward-leaning territory where "English" content slashes its way into "Education" practice. And the methods course that is at the deliberate center of this encounter—the anchor point threading together pedagogy and content—should put into question the nature of English subject matter for teachers, not simply encourage a naïve belief in the efficacy of subject matter knowledge to drive good practice. As Dewey notes of subject matter more generally,

> the teacher should be occupied not with subject matter in itself but in its interaction with the pupils' present needs and capacities. Hence simple scholarship is not enough. In fact, there are

certain features of scholarship or mastered subject matter—taken by itself—which get in the way of effective teaching *unless* the instructor's habitual attitude is one of concern with its interplay in the pupil's own experience. (*John Dewey on Education* 183)

In the quote from Justin heading this section, we see an echo of Dewey's concern to put student and curriculum into engaged contact. As Justin suggests, such divisions between content and practice, English and education, student and teacher, leave out the needs of students to use the tools of literacy to direct their own inquiries. Justin is close to Stephen Fishman's own Deweyan perspective on active learning, in which the classroom is the site where teachers "must encourage students to find genuine problems which excite their interest, problems which can be explored and ameliorated by engagement with the curriculum" (19). Justin was a post-baccalaureate teacher candidate, and his teaching philosophy statement—like those of his classmates—was a semester-long project that began with a critical reflection on popular culture representations of English teachers and English teaching in film, and evolved into a position statement about what the teaching of English/language arts can and should be in twenty-first-century American schools. Like many post-bacc students, and perhaps not unlike Sarah Feldman herself, Justin had come to teaching through a circuitous route borne of necessity and desire, but without much of the naïve optimism of more traditional licensure-track undergraduates. As second-career professionals, these students do not have the natural cohort of undergraduates living on campus. Perhaps because of the isolation of many post-bacc students within the teacher education program, Justin frequently noted the importance of collaborative learning and a vision of teaching as co-inquiry.

The student responses to the blackbird prompt certainly varied, but tended, like Justin's above, to highlight some signal discovery or transformative moment, perhaps a glint of a piece of found pedagogy to take into their teaching. Embedded in that shift in perspective is some recognition both of the collaborative role that others have played in their sense of themselves as teachers of English, and of the interplay of learner and content in shaping the future of English/Education. I was pleasantly surprised, after invoking Stevens's poem one last time, by the way the responses seemed to cluster around several of the engagements I'd introduced to help them explore that terrain. The full resulting list offers a series of group and individual student snapshots of the class, which figure their relationships with each other and their impressions of my assignments largely in terms of their collaborations and confrontations with the multiple locations of literacy in students' lives. But they also carry with them much of the tension and frustration that come from actually working with adolescents in a rapidly changing local environment.

In addition to the standard methods course fare of lesson and unit planning, curricular design, and reading and writing pedagogy, these confrontations for teacher candidates came primarily though several engagements and reflective activities: the dialogue journal; a personal literacy dig; and a student profile called a Virtual Schoolbag (see Appendixes 5.2–5.4 for a full description of these assignments). I'd like to explore these responses at more length in the remainder of this chapter, to begin to shift the focus of teacher preparation toward inquiry into the territory on the border between English/Education. I do not, however, offer them here as a list of fixed methods or experiences, for as every classroom teacher knows, the local context of teaching is rarely the same as the imagined one of the teacher preparation class. Any methods class that tried to account for every eventuality of the local classroom would simply create a sort of rigid notion of instruction that can end up working at cross-purposes to student interactions with literature, writing, and the world.

Dialogue Journals: Reading Tools for Social Learning and Metacognition

> Two minds came together under a water tower.
> JAMEY AND LISA, *in-class "Blackbird Reflection" (May 2007)*

> When reflecting back on the experience reading *Godless* with Jamey, I find laughter, confusion, random connections, and two ELA teachers with too much in common to produce any real good.
> LISA, *"Dialogue Journal Reflection" (May 2007)*

Many teacher candidates are, in fact, still heavily invested in schooling as a site of stasis, not change. Though I certainly would like to see change in our schools, what I attempt in my class is perhaps not overly revolutionary. I'm not prepared to tell teachers to do things that will lose them their jobs if their districts have adopted particularly reductive approaches to teaching standards of reading and writing and making "adequate yearly progress" on mandated tests. Nor am I going to write anyone off simply because they are frustrated with a roomful of active preteens at the end of a first year in a new profession. But I do want them to know what they are getting into—including understanding whose interests are served by English as it is variously taught in our schools; who their students are when they are not being students; and when to know that it's time to stop perpetuating a system that treats teachers and students unjustly. Those will always be personal reckonings, but to help teacher candidates consider the possibilities of something other than the rigid hierarchies of the status quo, I try to create opportunities for them to develop their teaching identities *together* in dialogue—and sometimes in collaboration—with other teacher candidates. This *is* something a methods class can and should do, to establish networks of inquiry and an incipient community of practice within the often overly bureaucratic teacher-training systems in place at most universities.

That is why I am drawn to the possibilities carried in Jamey and Lisa's in-class response to my blackbird prompt. Two minds coming together here and now also means two minds thinking together, supporting each other, and offering a way out of isolation. Their line refers to a central image of Pete Hautman's award-winning and controversial young adult novel, *Godless*, in which a group of teens jokingly begin their own religion organized around the town's water tower. The tower becomes their deity, and things get wildly out of hand for the newly elect believers. Lisa's individual reflection on the dialogue journal experience captures that spirit of camaraderie, and jokingly suggests that what she and Jamey pursued was a sort of guilty pleasure amid the more serious work of teaching adolescents to read and interpret literature. Each student in the class had a similar dialogue journal project for a book from a class-generated list. We listed books that we had wanted to read for some time, or that we had found ourselves recommending to others, or that others seemed to be recommending to us. Genres and styles ranged from young adult realistic fiction (*Godless, Speak*), contemporary literary fiction (*I Am One of You Forever, Big Fish*), science fiction (*Do Androids Dream of Electric Sheep?/Blade Runner*), and philosophy (*Zen and the Art of Motorcycle Maintenance*).

Then each student tried to enlist a reading partner, so that in the end the groups were self-selected and organized around a work of shared interest. As the partners read, they were to engage in a written exchange about the book and their reading, a dialogue journal that ended up becoming, for many of the groups, a shared pedagogy journal considering how they might teach this book to adolescents, use it to anchor a unit of instruction around a particular theme, or offer it as one of several selections for literature circle groups.

The commentary that Jamey and Lisa offered about their experience with the dialogue journal, however, suggests more than just a moment of intellectual convergence through a shared reading (though it certainly does that as well). Like Justin, they were post-bacc students, but unlike him and unlike the traditional undergraduate teacher candidates, they were already employed as teachers on probationary licenses, so they had the opportunity to use the methods class to reflect on their current practice in the classroom. Both had doubts about their own teaching, occasionally struggled with some of the course positions about multiliteracies and the home knowledges students bring with them to the classroom setting, and questioned the ability of all students to learn at high levels. Still, as Lisa noted in her reflection on the dialogue journal, "We must make changes [in our habits and dispositions] when reading with others . . . to reach a common goal." Jamey had already read the novel in a similar dialogue journal engagement the summer before in my Writing Project Open Institute, so his knowledge of the book and the process made him more expert than Lisa throughout the process. Her response seems to acknowledge how that aspect of their pairing forced her to read closer to Jamey's understanding of the text, though leaving her in a liminal space between her regular reading habits and her desire to function within a group.

These student-directed and -sustained dialogue journals were among several course activities that began to shift teacher candidates from individual and sometimes idiosyncratic perspectives on English learners and teaching reading/literature toward a shared vision of something more enduring about English/Education: if not yet a theorized practice, then at least a belief about the necessity to learn from each other and through multiple perspectives. In Jamey and Lisa's case, this shift encompassed a view of what it means to be novice middle school teachers in a rural school district. Joy Ritchie and David Wilson have identified such shifts in perspective as a crucial element in preparing teachers to engage critically the discourse of their "accidental apprenticeship as teachers"—which they estimate involves some thirteen thousand hours of observing teachers in the contexts of compulsory schooling, not to mention the additional influence of popular discourse and media images of teachers and teaching—and to recognize its ideological function in their current practices. Often this shift challenges received notions of what it means to be a teacher and "unsettle[s] their conceptions of who they are and how the world operates." The methods course is one of the components in the "deliberate apprenticeship" of teacher education, which should "suggest that there are other ways of thinking about teaching, learning, and literacy—and that these conceptions might require a different role for the teacher." To do so, Ritchie and Wilson acknowledge, is to do more than place familiar pedagogy at risk; "students' very conceptions of the kind of life they want to live and their most basic reasons for entering teaching are unsettled" (39). With all this deliberate derangement amid the methods course, students naturally seek some point of stability or ground for crafting new narratives of teacher identity. For Jamey and Lisa, that ground was a collaboratively discovered and shared space of the water tower.

Even in their deliberate lightness, the reflections from Jamey and Lisa, like the responses of other students who simply listed key phrases, ideas, or fragments from the class, capture something of their lingering concerns about the teaching of English that remain at the end of a course designed to help them meet those challenges. Since Jamey and Lisa were already responsible for their own classrooms, they had some perspectives on the classroom that the preservice teachers had yet to acquire before their student teaching. All of this made for an interesting and often delicate balance for me as the English educator, since the class was almost evenly split between graduate/post-bacc students and undergraduate teacher candidates. This demographic aspect of the class helped facilitate the confrontation between old and new assumptions about teaching that Ritchie and Wilson note is necessary for any sort of transformative moment in teacher formation, for the lived history of our classroom—I was not the oldest in the room—tapped into the history of English instruction in the late twentieth and early twenty-first century in a way that might otherwise be unavailable to traditional college-age preservice teachers. And what Jamey and Lisa both seem tacitly to recognize in their reflection on the dialogue journal, and to capture in their blackbird lines, is Ritchie and Wilson's point that "without ongoing critical dialogues between their old and new assumptions about teaching, learning, and literacy, their assumptions could not become fully transformative" (53). Yet, in some of their other reflections and comments in class, I heard Jamey and Lisa (and others) continue to characterize students and student-learning in very traditional ways, in tacit resistance to the descriptions offered in our readings. I was at a loss for what to make of this apparent collaborative discovery and nontraditional experience in learning that somehow still managed to conclude, as Jamey did in his final teaching philosophy, that perhaps the task of the English teacher might be easier if we simply tracked students by their intellectual abilities. Or else, as Lisa suggested in her own teaching philosophy, that *real* student engagement with writing and literature can't really happen before high school.

Other dialogue journal pairs drew different conclusions about teaching and learning, however. Lynn and Theresa's reading of Daniel Wallace's *Big Fish* shared some similarities with Jamey and Lisa's adventures with Hautman's water tower: both partners were alternative-track licensure candidates, although Theresa had pursued teaching years before and even had a valid teaching license from a neighboring state; one of the partners (Lynn) had read the novel before, allowing her to serve as the slightly more expert reader of the text; and the two clearly enjoyed each other's written company. Lynn sets the model for engaging the text with her first entry, starting with a passage from the text and then offering a response related to her own life, and to herself as a previous reader of this and other texts:

> "The day Edward Bloom was born, it rained."
> I love this imagery. For those of us who have had the pleasure of bringing another human being into the world, we know the rain. The rains pour down from within us as we bring great joy, enormous hope, and change into our lives.
>
> Although I have taken this journey with Edward and his family before, I find the anticipation and knowing create a sense of excitement. The memories, the relationship between my own dear father who left my world nearly ten years ago. I understand the love, the not knowing just who this person was who occupied so many of my days. I recently made a DVD compilation of my dad's photos. What an amazing man. Like Edward, he was a great man. A myth. Although Daniel Wallace has said that *Big Fish* is purely fictional, it's difficult to believe that one could create such a tale without there being something personal. Perhaps this is why I become so emotional while reading this story. It strips us to the bones and reveals so much about who we are, where we've been, and where we're headed. I refuse to believe that Wallace has simply created this story. I suspect it has been created for him by those in his life. (February 13, 2007)

The entry also serves as a personal introduction of Lynn to Theresa. Lynn is a mother and a daughter, and she has thought about the images that are linked to both those identities for her. She also reminds Theresa that she has read the novel before, but offers reassurance that she is perhaps even more excited than Theresa by the anticipation and knowledge of what is to come. Theresa's response a week later takes up some of those invitations to link the text to self, but also moves the exchange forward in new directions through a slight alteration of the form, turning reflection into dialogue.

February 19, 2007
Dear Lynn,
I too was taken with the imagery. At first I laughed at the mythic proportions (page 2) the narrator's father had taken on. The stories on the surface are just so fantastical, but it does remind me of the way members of my family talk about those family members who are deceased. They remember the good over the bad and it becomes more than it really was—hence the "walked twenty miles in five feet of snow to school every day during the winter months" stories.

Though, in each of these stories the father is telling the son, there is a more basic point to them. The narrator mentions that his adult life is just beginning when his father sits with his feet in the stream and tells him these stories of his boyhood, and I was able to discern life lessons in many of the stories, such as "How He Tamed the Giant" (acceptance and open-mindedness will allow people to live in harmony) and "The Day He Left Ashland" (it's scary to leave what you know—especially if you grow up in a small town, but you can do it if you set your mind to). I grew up in a small town, so these are stories and ideas that I can relate to.

I do think we all have the desire to be a big fish in a big pond. For some, they see how they can become a big fish in a small pond, and are content with that—fearing that in the bigger pond, they would actually be a small fish. You'd never know it by the way these people tend to act, but all that boasting and ego tends to hide self-doubt. Then there are those who try to become a big fish and fail, ending up eaten by the piranhas in the water. That's always sad to witness because often these people have a great deal of potential. Most of us are just swimming along growing a little more day by day, avoiding the dangers and enjoying the passing beauty.

What makes a big fish? This is something that is different for everyone, and I'll be curious to see how that question is answered in the remainder of the book.

Theresa

The next several entries through the end of the dialogue journal maintain Theresa's salutations and anticipatory ending questions, and the two even begin to add brief personalizing signoffs, such as (☺-emoticons); "I'll see you on Monday." Throughout the dialogue both readers are engaging key passages from the text that have captured their attention or somehow arrested their reading, and forged a connection to other texts, other lives, themselves, and the world at large.

Virtual Schoolbags: Discovering Traces of Multi-Literacies

> The school knowledges that are at the top of the cultural capital league table are not only those required for university entrance but are also the cultural knowledges of those who are socially, economically, and politically privileged and who determine what counts. In other words, the rules of the schooling game are geared to perpetuate particular kinds of knowledges. (Thomson 4)

This connection beyond the text itself is something that Lynn takes up again in her final reflective essay on the class. In the context of thinking about student reading and the knowledges they bring to school with them in their Virtual Schoolbag (VSB), Lynn remembers her own reading of Judy Blume as an adolescent:

> [She] wrote characters who knew what it was like being me. Her creations experienced much of what I lived or thought I wanted to live. So when I see my kids walking around the room, sharing novels like *Revenge of the Wannabes*, *Sisterhood of the Traveling Pants*, and *TTYL*, I don't push them toward Austen or Hawthorne. I ask them about the book and what it's about. I realize the importance of what kids read for pleasure. These are vital pieces of the child's VSB and I need to embrace the value of these books.

In honoring her students' reading practices, Lynn is allowing for some literacy work to happen beyond the purview of the English teacher; in engaging them about their interests, she is allowing their literacy practices to alter the definition of what counts in school. This is the pedagogical shift that is enabled through an inquiry like the Virtual Schoolbag profile. Pat Thomson has used the term to help teachers understand the role of "cultural capital" (following Bourdieu) in schooling, identifying the traces of literacy practices that count in schools, and which remain hidden by the discourse models schools enable and privilege. In inviting my own students to conduct a profile on a particular adolescent by examining the contents of his or her Virtual Schoolbag—that is, the knowledges the he or she has in the myriad social, familial, and cultural domains—I've shifted Thomson's focus somewhat. I've tried to help my students discover what *their* students already have so they can focus on those things as potential assets for instruction, rather than consider the discontinuity between a student's home literacies and school literacy as a problem to be solved (usually by replacing home literacies and values with school values).

Lynn's final reflection shows her making this realization but also thinking about how to use an assignment like this in her own class, allowing her students to become informants about their own strengths as learners. Initially, she conceived of the activity as an inventory of a student's traditional literacy skills: "I chose a student I have worked with since last year and dutifully wrote about his lack of phonics knowledge, his troubled educational past, and considered his future." After I shared samples from previous classes and from a former colleague, Lynn began to think differently.

> The displayed VSB delved deep into the featured student. The author had a great deal of "inside" information about the child and that's when it made sense to me. Schoolbag—baggage. This activity was about what a student brings into the classroom—not the skills or lack of them—but the baggage . . . the world and literacies they know. . . . I have always considered myself a holistic educator. However, I confess, I tend to look at what a student *needs*—rather than what a student *has*. The VSB has made me more aware of this flaw. I now look beyond simply needs. Rather, I think of how I can use what the student already has and enrich these skills. This is something I hadn't really considered prior to the VSB activity.

In her Virtual Schoolbag assignment, Kristen, an undergraduate teacher candidate, ends up advocating for the student she profiles to embrace his hidden knowledges as assets in the school setting.

Every day, Juan makes use of his bilingualism, and taps into that resource, both covertly and sometimes openly. I think that sometimes the pressure that Juan seems to feel to assimilate into the white, middle-class dominate culture at his High School causes him to feel like he needs to hide his Mexican heritage. . . . Based on what I have learned from my case study on Juan, I believe that he needs additional support from teachers and classmates. Juan seems to value what his classmates and teachers think about him. If his classmates could encourage Juan's bilingualism in some way, and let him know that he can and should embrace it as an additional resource, I believe he would benefit in many ways, both educationally and socially.

Through these profiles, Lynn and Kristen and their classmates begin to reorient themselves to the "big questions" about teaching, literacies, and schooling that Buehler recommends. Their new knowledge of their students' lives and literacies helps them pose the questions at the heart of English/Education: Who is "English" for? What is it for? And what do we do when we are doing "English"?

As I mentioned to my students on the first day of the course, the posing of such questions is one of the chief tasks of a methods course, for it helps candidates to envision both likely and possible futures for themselves as teachers. The questions lead to the inquiries and investigations that both prepare future teachers to be critically reflective practitioners and help them endure in a profession that seems bent on driving them out. The task is, in Robert Yagelski's characterization, a potentially utopian enterprise, one in which the work of English is "the analysis, critique, and production of discourse . . . pursued in the service of some larger social vision" ("English Education" 277). He continues, "The purpose of [this] work should be the larger Utopian project of defining, examining, and fostering that 'future social subject' who can contribute to the building of just and sustainable communities" (278). Before the candidates in my class peered into the Virtual Schoolbags of their students, this utopian vision appeared, if at all, only dimly on the horizon of their imagined practice.

Beyond Methods and Training

> Though it is surely easy to love those who love what you love (or even love you), it is the students who do not demonstrate such a love who need, perhaps, the most attention. And they need a teacher who will sit with them and patiently talk about their writing, not a desk jumper. But that just doesn't look as good on the big screen.
>
> MARK, *"Final Reflection" (May 2007)*

As Mark notes in his reflection above, our practice changes when we put our students, and not our pet techniques or curricula, first. It's an important reminder for those of us in English/Education responsible for the preparation of English teachers, and it offers a useful closing sideshadow on my end-of-semester blackbird reflection about the experiences students had in my methods course. A dozen years ago Smagorinsky and Whiting attempted to represent the state of English teacher education classes as revealed in an extensive survey of programs, syllabi, and teacher educators. They offer recommendations for effective methods courses: they should be theoretically informed and not just an exercise in assembling a "trick bag"; and teacher-candidate learning should be "good work," transactional, holistic, process-oriented, situated in meaningful activity, always leading to critical reflection. My hope is that the work my students and I did was the sort of good work that Smagorinsky and Whiting recommend, "activities that are compelling yet challenging, requiring them to draw on a great many resources to learn about the profession of teaching" (28).

Mark was an undergraduate candidate, who in the quote above is trying to separate himself from the discourse model of the hero teacher, embodied in his case by Mr. Keating of the film *Dead Poets Society*. The quote comes from his final version of his teaching philosophy, which he ends by merging Mr. Keating, Whitman, and Ginsberg to point to a turn in his thinking away from mere critique and toward reflective practice:

> However, in light of the content of my Unit Plan, I find it humorous that I am so critical of Keating. Though the plan does not

encourage the instructor to celebrate himself as much as Keating does and also incorporates a more diverse group of writers, the celebration of Whitman and a number of other dead white men is clearly present. Students are asked to imitate and perform, to extend themselves to new activities and thinking about poetry through doing poetry. They are not required to jump on desks, play in the woods, or address the instructor as "Captain," but still engage with poetry on a more than passive or analytical level. I guess I cannot escape the specter of Keating, therefore: I make a pact with you, Robin Williams / I have detested you long enough / Let there be commerce between us.

Mark acknowledges in this ending that any model of teaching must engage the power of the images that have come before if we are to create spaces for students to explore questions of their own. Justin makes a similar point in his reflection that "assignments should be vital to the student, not to the curriculum; there isn't a student anywhere that says, 'today I want to write an alternate ending to *The Catcher in the Rye*.'" These observations come of both candidates' evolving sense of who they are and what English should be, a process they and their peers pursued through a semester-long inquiry into their own philosophy and convictions about teaching English language arts.

Reflection and inquiry are explicitly or implicitly mentioned in each of the CEE belief statements about coursework in the preparation of English teachers, especially amid the social and ideological contexts that shape content/curriculum history, pedagogical practices, and the teacher candidate's own subject position (see CEE, "What Do We Know and Believe about the Role of Methods Courses and Field Experiences in English Education?"). On that final in-class reflection on the final day of our methods course in spring 2007, the thirteen-plus ways that my students choose to think about English/Education point to these aspects of their own activities and resources in the course:

1. $X + Y + Z = A$ [referring to designations for multiple versions of written assignments]

2. two great minds came together under a water tower

3. working in groups

4. guest speakers provide real-world knowledge/strategies

5. dialogue journals are awesome!

6. there is an academic interpretation [of literature] but room for an argument

7. author talk (with Urbanski)

8. communication through writing

9. student individuality

10. importance of writing process

11. grammar is not the end-all, be-all of writing assignments

12. a text doesn't have to be canonical to be useful

13. knowledge is constructed, not passed on

14. different methods of making poetry accessible

15. grammar: to teach or not to teach? that is the question

16. Wallace Stevens as framework

17. The minds whirled in spring winds / It was a small price to pay / regardless of the tuition

18. O youth of campus / What do you imagine / teaching will be like? / Do you not know parents / will pick apart everything you do?

ENGL 4254/5254, "Constructed Reflection" (May 2007)

After we had generated this list, putting the responses on the board for the rest of the class to see, I asked the class to think about what they thought the list meant. What surprises or connections or extensions to their own thinking about teaching did it raise? What seemed to be left out by these attempts?

Adrian, another student who was also a post-bacc teacher, noted that although every one of the responses comes as a result of student reflection, none makes explicit reference to the *process* of reflection itself. As I've noted above, reflection was so embedded within the structure of the class that it seemed to disappear from view, and yet it was a crucial element in the students' growth in the class. Mark and Justin both observed that in many of the items listed, we saw evidence of growth within community and not just individual change or development, although items like #9—student individuality—stress seeing learners on their own terms, a focus derived from observation and especially the Virtual Schoolbag profile. Several of the undergraduate teacher candidates, Anna, Melissa, and Kristin, placed particular value on a visit by Cindy Urbanski, a local teacher consultant with the UNC Charlotte Writing Project, whose book *Using the Workshop Approach in the High School English Classroom: Modeling Effective Writing, Reading, and Thinking Strategies for Student Success* we had used in the class. Urbanski put a local face on the sort of practices that the teacher candidates had already read about from Atwell, Daniels, and others, and that they had experienced in miniature in their own writing for me; but it wasn't until this face-to-face question and answer session with someone who had tried these theories and succeeded under the same pressures the candidates felt, or were anticipating, that it suddenly seemed like a viable pedagogical choice for them. What Cindy confirmed was that for many secondary school students in workshop or process-oriented classrooms, this sort of learning "doesn't look like school." It was supposed to be different and strange, and she, we, they hoped it would be transformative.

After these analyses of the list, I then invited the students to return to Stevens's poem. On the first day of the class, I had asked them to identify which of the thirteen stanzas seemed best to capture what they thought was at the heart of teaching English or who they wanted to be as teachers. Back then, in the dim cold of a January evening class, few had even seen the poem before, so we spent quite a bit of time engaged in both literary interpretation and pedagogical reflection. With a full semester with Stevens's blackbirds staring back at them from the pages of the syllabus, as well as additional teaching demonstrations by me modeling poetry instruction or perspective-taking in writing, which referenced the poem, they were perhaps done with blackbirds. But I asked them anyway to choose a stanza that best captured their experience in the course. We didn't need to use the poem to create this opportunity for reflection, of course; any document from the first days of the semester in their daybooks, or that I could have collected and saved for the purpose of returning on this final day, would have sufficed. But there was something added by the lingering strangeness of the poem then and now, and so the poem became a way for them to figure their teaching perspectives metaphorically. For me, stanza 9, "When the blackbird flew out of sight / It marked the edge of one of many circles," seemed to point to my experience with constantly trying to balance the many personal and pedagogical spheres in my life. This class was one of many circles. I then asked them to choose a stanza (though it might be the same one) that captured best what they *now* saw as possible for themselves as teachers. Stanza 8, "I know noble accents / And lucid, inescapable rhythms; / But I know, too, / That the blackbird is involved / In what I know," seemed to offer a counter to the escapist impulse of the first selection, reminding me that I'm connected to this community, this circle of teachers and teacher candidates, whether I know it, whether I like it, or not. It also offered a pointed claim against mere intuitive belief about effective practice, underscoring the situatedness of knowledge about teaching, learning, and schooling.

In sharing our responses, we were of course tending toward the rhetoric of conversation narratives and resolutions for new practice that are not uncommon at the end of any course. It's the sort of language that promises to be a different, better, more student-centered teacher, one who will value the backgrounds and experiences of each student. But just because those stances may be expected—or because teachers may succumb to pedagogical backsliding once they begin a new year—doesn't mean that they aren't real for teacher candidates. In the space between those two stanzas, for me, lies not just a history of teaching, but a history of *thinking* about teachers and teaching. No doubt the same is true for my students as they simultaneously look back on the class and toward their own future classrooms. And of course, the images they construct over time to capture their sense of who they are and what they do as English teachers will continue to evolve. That's as it should be, I think, and it suggests again that the task of the methods course is not to help fix a static identity as teacher with a plentiful though finite bag of tricks or strategies to use on students for the next twenty years. Rather, pedagogy courses in the teaching of English ought to unsettle fixed positions and allow for explorations into the very hermeneutic and interpersonal nature of the classroom and teaching. Pedagogy is about the making of understandings, after all, which means that our task isn't simply to articulate meanings about literature or texts more broadly, but to put those meanings into conversation with others. Teacher candidates ought to be able to examine pedagogical thinking in light of the unique capacities of English, and literacy more broadly, to highlight the processes of understanding.

Stanza 8 of Stevens's poem, then, illuminates this context-ualized nature of knowledge and understanding: "the blackbird is involved / In what I know." Understanding both requires and generates a community of inquirers. As Richard Bernstein observes about the role of hermeneutics and praxis in understand-ing, "We belong to a tradition before it belongs to us," and "tradition, through its sedimentations, has a power which is constantly determining what we are in the process of becoming" (142). Bernstein's concern as a philosopher is to find a path that, in the title of his study, can help us move "beyond objectivism and relativism." In the end, he locates the possibility for such movement in the establishment of communities of practice that come from shared conversations. His conclusion is instructive for the work of English/Education, which similarly is beset by competing discourses and agendas about what constitutes knowl-edge and practice in the discipline of English. It is not sufficient, as Bernstein cautions, simply to show, "once and for all, what is wrong with objectivism and relativism; such a movement gains 'reality and power' only if we dedicate ourselves to the practical task of furthering the type of solidarity, participation, and mu-tual recognition that is founded in dialogical communities" (231).

For the English teacher educator and English teacher candi-date, the challenge in a methods course is, in part, knowing how to clear away the sedimentations of English as discipline, prac-tice, and content, to find one's own path. The task is more than pointing to the failings of "scientifically-based research" and "in-tuitive belief" about teaching, but recognizing that either posi-tion throws us into existing and powerfully defining discourses about who we think we are when we are teaching English. This *thrown-ness* into a discursive wilderness pedagogy marks the boundaries of one horizon of understanding. What we do and are able to do is marked by what has come before us. The way out is one that can be discovered through shared inquiry and a recognition of those students who join us on the way.

At the Thresholds of English/Education

Change is the order of nature.
ALICE CARY, "My Grandfather" (*Clovernook*, 1852)

Learning Content(ion): After Derangement, What Next?

In the opening lines of Alice Cary's "Learning Content," from the second series of *Clovernook* (1853), Mrs. Polly Williams gives voice to a curious wish for self-doubling. In the process she captures a desire for replication and reproduction that occupies a peculiar place both within the ethos of nineteenth-century regionalist literature and among mainstream literary and cultural arbiters attempting to fashion a national American subject. Brought to the edge of patience and self-control by the desperate calls of her rambunctious boys to pay attention to their imaginative play, Mrs. Polly Williams responds by wishing herself made multiple: "What on earth am I to do now? I'd just like to know—here you are crying out 'Mother, mother, mother!' a half a dozen at a time—may be if I could make myself into two or three women I might get along" (93). For Mrs. Williams, such a mirroring forth of her self might, she imagines, allow her to find some measure of contentment in an otherwise harried life as a farm wife in rural Ohio. Her comment emerges from her desire to get outside or "out of place" (in Fetterley and Pryse's phrase) from her role, routine, and identity—if even for a moment. And her final statement, "May be if I could make myself into two or three women I might get along," carries the story's eventual thesis (93). Once Mrs. Williams and her nearest neighbor, Mrs. Emeline Giles, have a chance to visit each other, the two discover that things are really not so bad, that the things they have (one, a nice dress; the other, a set of knives) are sufficient for their rural lives.

But Mrs. Williams's imaginative gathering of two or more women also calls forth a strangely vexing presence that lurks throughout Cary's story and carries the haunting sense that all is perhaps not well in this idyll of the American frontier. In marking the similarities of the two women as a possible solution, Cary also reveals an unsettling effect of their multiplication. Rather than become more singularly themselves by becoming a plurality, they each experience a reduction of self through their doubling. The *Ladies' Repository*, that magazine whose name had become synonymous with Alice Cary by the 1850s, frequently carried engravings in its front and back matter to encourage just such a corporate merging of female subjectivity. But seen through the prism of Cary's own "honest relations," images such as "Education of Nature" (Figure 6.1) and "The Verb 'To Love'—'They Love'" (Figure 6.2) from the 1851 volume of *Ladies' Repository* make a doubling desire such as Mrs. Williams's into something obsessively and eerily self-regarding. The images underscore the dilemma of the women in Cary's fictions: they conform to the ideal vision of "woman" at the risk of losing the particularities of their local lives.

A similar, but far more grim, duplication of women confronts the unnamed female narrator in Cary's "Uncle Christopher's," from the second series of *Clovernook* and the Cary story most frequently included in twenty-first-century anthologies of American literature. In this strange tale of domestic tyranny, a young woman is inexplicably brought out by her father in the middle of a midwestern blizzard to meet his uncle Christopher, and is then left there with the uncle, presumably to learn how best "to mind." At this remote outpost, she quietly faces an eerie panel of identical women—a mother and several daughters, each of like manner and appearance—who sit silently knitting identical blue stockings and waiting for Uncle Christopher to speak or give instruction.

Cary's stories richly engage the discourse models of nineteenth-century domestic life, and they offer an incisive depiction of the pedagogical aesthetics of regionalism of the type that I

Figure 6.1. *"Education of Nature."* Ladies' Repository *(January 1851)*

Figure 6.2. *"The Verb 'To Love'—'They Love.'"* Ladies' Repository *(April 1851)*

invoked in Chapter 1. I return to Cary here at the end of this deranged journey, however, because I am tempted to find my own situation at the threshold of English/Education to be very much like that of Mrs. Williams and Mrs. Giles. I am hoping to conclude that things are not as bad as they seem in English/Education if I can only find my double or counterpart on the other side of that division to reassure me—we in English (or education) have the nice dress; our colleagues in education (or English) have the shiny new set of knives. All we have to do is keep our old uncle "Christopher" from trying to make us all alike through standardization, testing, accountability, and a retreat into a common, restricted canon. And in that identification, I recall the lines of Rich's poem with which I began the first chapter: This is *still* the place, and I am *still* here, the mermaid/merman circling about the wreck, diving into the hold. I am he; I am she.

But I have not yet learned to be content with the state of English/Education, and this transaction with Cary's stories risks being little more than an experiment in intellectual cross-dressing unless we seriously consider what it might mean to examine critically images of our teaching selves, and to cross the threshold of each other's practice. Throughout the previous chapters, we have seen moments at precisely those liminal spaces that are simultaneously openings and closings, entrances and exits, beginnings and endings. Joanne, Gloria, and I quite literally walked across the thresholds of each other's classrooms, and in the process we saw ourselves, our profession, and perhaps most important, our students in new lights. This result, too, was a threshold moment, the point at which a new physical, cognitive, or pedagogical effect begins to be produced. Ashley, Ron, and their peers brought classroom teachers through another such moment in their "Langston Shakespeare" engagement, which in turn marked the beginning of a different way of thinking about student inquiry in my own practice. Though my American literature students and I were unable to induce teachers the following year to step through the door we thought we'd opened into new ways of thinking about American literature, the experience again shifted my own practice and helped me develop a curriculum for American literature that might open borders to thinking and reading differently about America.

There are other moments, however, in which I find myself or my students lingering at those openings and instead of entering into new conversations, closing off opportunities for change or effecting the utopian vision of social change that Yagelski calls for from English/Education (see "English Education"). For many of my students in English methods, the work they do in English remains separate from and alien to the things they do in their pedagogy courses. And perhaps most troubling of all is the continued difficulty that students themselves encounter when they make their own threshold movements into their own classrooms. These are the moments that keep me from being content, and they also remind me that the elision of English/Education through a sustained derangement of the territories along the border dividing our practice is not yet a reality for many teacher candidates or for their students.

Framing Social Justice in English/Education

Throughout the stories and discoveries of these chapters, the intersection of teaching, literature, diversity, and student learning has brought the teaching of English into contact with questions of social justice—what, ultimately, is English/Education in a democratic society *for*? This concern for social justice has been an undercurrent throughout this book, but I want to draw it out briefly and more explicitly here.

My own path to teaching and to thinking about issues of social justice came through a slightly more sustained inquiry into what stories alternately enable us to do and prevent us from doing for each other and for ourselves, and an investigation into why only some stories about our culture seem to count. But I am reluctant to attempt a story of myself as a teacher of English concerned with questions of social justice, in part because of the tendency for these, too, to become discourse models that advance a myth of the heroic and self-sacrificing teacher at the exclusion of the teacher community. The teacher-hero script that teacher candidates, politicians, and virtually every movie made about a teacher popularizes, risks keeping teachers from joining each other to support the learning of all students; from challenging each other to be critically reflective about their practice; and from being willing to let students shape the course of their inquiry and learning. To turn the popular truism of this discourse model back on itself: if only one teacher can make a difference, what do we need the rest of them for?

In keeping with that traditional awareness narrative, I could tell a story of my family's history with linguistic and English oppression by tracing my mother's Acadian or my father's Irish heritage. Certainly, both have contributed to my sense of injustice in the world, and indeed *Le Grand Dérangement*—the forced deportation of the francophone peasants in Nova Scotia by British colonial leaders in 1755—gives this book its title and central metaphor. I could tell a story about how those English majors in my classrooms, who wanted to be English teachers in high school and yet boasted of their own dislike of reading and writing, led me to think about how and why the teaching of literature matters. Or how those same students' resistance to thinking about the complex history of canonicity as a part of their pedagogy brought me to become a professor of American literature *and* English education. But those stories—with me figured as the protagonist in a family story triumphing over hardship, or in an individual story blazing new paths of enlightenment for the sake of less adept others—risk occluding my concurrent history as a beneficiary of the systems of privilege, for my own race, class, and gender have given me access to institutions and systems of power that are simply not readily accessible to others. And as Jill Swiencicki and others have cautioned about the rhetoric of awareness narratives, like the scripts of teacher development Ritchie and Wilson identify, such personal narratives too often follow a pattern of "turning a gap in consciousness" that doesn't ever quite move out of a reification of guilt and into a larger discursive field and field of social action (337). They *poach* upon, in Michel de Certeau's phrase (xii, 165–76), the experiences and pain of others, talking about cultural or pedagogical change without necessarily enacting it in everyday practice.

So without seeking an origin story for why I am doing so, I want to tell about when I received my PhD in American literature from a Jesuit university in New York. Like most important teaching moments, it was fully embedded in the course of my everyday routine—on my way back from a first-year writing class I was teaching and on the way to a graduate seminar on non-canonical American writers I was taking. It captured for me how teaching and the study of literature both were and still are implicated in questions of diversity, representation, and social justice. As part of its stated institutional mission, the university promoted "excellence" in teaching and learning; at the same time, it called faculty and students alike to pay heed to "the option for the poor." The mission was especially salient given the low socioeconomic status of the local community living just beyond the walls and gates of the university. This perhaps odd statement of mission has stayed with me long after I received my degree and has been gnawing away at my teaching and research ever since. Though admittedly this statement of mission was not always foregrounded in my early courses (indeed, I didn't even know the school *had* a mission statement until almost my fourth year of teaching there), these two ideals of teaching with and for excellence and teaching to foster social action, especially on behalf of the poor, however contradictory, still seem to me worthy of consideration and pursuit.

The building where I taught first-year writing sat adjacent to campus just outside the stone and iron wall that separated the campus from the community. Every fifty-five minutes the building emptied into the street, and students and teachers alike made their way through a narrow gate onto campus. At the gate was a security guard, who was putatively required to ask each person to show a valid university ID before letting him or her go any further. Rarely did the guard ask me for my ID, whether I was dressed to teach (coat and tie) or just coming for a class (jeans and T-shirt). I was not much older than many of the students walking from the building, and several were much better dressed than I on my meager grad student budget. Really, it was just a short walk of about twenty yards, and we moved en masse to the gate, filing through two or three abreast and heading up to the interior campus. I noticed that the security guards—and this was the case irrespective of any guard's own race—only requested IDs from certain students; and they clearly *were* students, carrying books in their hands or book bags over their shoulders, but they were all either black or Latino young men. On this particular day, I made a point—what point I'm not sure—of removing my ID card from my wallet and flashing it to the guard. He gave it a cursory nod as if I were wasting his time, and I walked on. It finally occurred to me that my access was assumed even before I showed my card. As a white male, I was presumed to belong to the university and not the community around it.

In the graduate seminar moments later, we were talking about the way in which the development of the American literary canon had systematically disappeared the work of women and writers of color, largely by positing a certain storyline to literary history and valuing certain genres, which happened to resonate with the handful of white male academics of the last century seeking to find the greatness and excellence in American literature. Here again, I was presumed by the existing literary history to belong, to count. And my own reading up to graduate school had continued this exclusion of others. I had not been required to read a single novel written by a woman, for instance, until after I graduated from college (with honors, no less) as an English major. My knowledge of English and American literature was apparently sufficient without such encounters. It was part of an acceptable script.

The dual dilemma of teaching and learning for "excellence" and "for the poor" besets the question of social justice and English/Education in an especially acute way, I believe, since both literary value and social justice notions of fairness, equity, and access must be offered *through language*, through alternative scripts (but scripts nonetheless) still awaiting enactment or refiguration in the lives of those who speak it. This is nothing new, of course, as Gee reminds us about the nature of discourse and language-in-use (27). In the story of American literature and learning (though not always within its canonical account), we have several examples of those on the margins speaking back to those in power, and in the process challenging the conception both of literacy and literature. For instance, Phillis Wheatley's 1773 poem "To the University of Cambridge in New England" reminds Harvard students to "Improve your privileges while they stay / Ye pupils, and each hour redeem, that bears / Or good or bad report of you to heav'n" (21–23). Alice Cary's mid-nineteenth-century poems and sketches similarly call white middle-class readers to allow aesthetic experience to help them imagine new moral and ethical possibilities for those on the class margins of mainstream society. A stanza from her poem "The Washerwoman" offers a typical reminder: "Nobody ever thought the spark / That in her sad eyes shone, / Burned outward from a living soul / Immortal as their own" (45–48). The experience of that graduate seminar in non-canonical American writers—especially as it happened on the threshold of lived reminders of gender, class, and racial privilege—introduced me to a different narrative and rhetorical tradition from American regionalist literature, a tradition with its own pedagogical as well as ethical concerns, and which as I have argued in the introduction, has much to teach English/Education.

Cary's work is especially useful in limning this intersection, and the words from her story "The Sisters" are worth recalling here. Deploying the techniques of sentiment to focus the attention of readers out of their own condition and into sympathetic confrontation with the condition of another, the narrator observes that "Orphaned as we are, we have need to be kind to each other—ready with loving and helping hands and encouraging words, for the darkness and the silence are hard by where no sweet care can do us any good" (*Clovernook Sketches* 64). The shared orphaned status Cary posits creates a double need and exists in tension between individual isolation and community. Her language here underscores the physicality of her ethical pedagogy, for it is the "loving and helping hands," which will keep those on the margins of power from the "darkness and silence," that are "hard by." The process of learning to draw community out of isolation, however, also undermines the self that is taught. And it is this threat of losing the self—alternately in isolation or absorbed, assimilated into a larger social or discursive collective—that always lurks on the borders of this regionalist pedagogy and which should caution us about how to think about justice in the English classroom.

Ending Reflections

I began this inquiry with the notion that a deranged perspective on English/Education could foster new ways of thinking about teaching and learning. The chapters have offered a series of glimpses at such a perspective in practice across grade levels and stages in the life of the teaching profession, and within different institutional and regional settings. What I hope has become clear is that those practices are not anchored exclusively in *my* teaching of *these* texts or with the success of *my* students. I am not content to be the single or singular teacher who thinks it is enough just to want to make a difference in the life of a single student. It has been through working as part of a collaborative, as student, as teacher, and as researcher, that I have been able to move past my own assumptions and to interrogate the stories they are a part of, and the power they have over others. Readers should do the same with their encounters in these chapters before considering the shape they will take in their own lives, but they should also consider the lives these practices may enable in their own classrooms. Part of that process lies—for me, for you, and for our profession—in recognizing that voices other than our own, particularly those who share the space of our classrooms, need to be allowed a hearing about what "English" is for.

I want to close with a final deranged image of English/Education from an experience that on the surface is perhaps rather unremarkable, a mere optical effect that has probably happened to countless people walking into a school or office building. Nevertheless, as a situated event in the life of someone constantly on the border of English/Education, it demonstrates the question I posed at the end of the introduction: given the present educational situation and the state of English/Education, what sort of creatures are we going to be?

In the early spring of 2001, I was walking into the School of Education building at Indiana University, preparing to meet my graduate students in my academic writing class. I was planning to share with them one of my recently published articles, a piece from my dissertation on American regionalism which had been through a number of revisions and reviews before finally being accepted for publication, some fifteen months after I had submitted the first version of the article. But I was also thinking about the next couple of weeks; my DeScriptophiles colleagues were scheduled to arrive for the next week's class, and so teacher-research was very much on my mind as well. I was feeling overwhelmed by the schedule and also torn between the success of my English past and the uncertainty but excitement of my Education present and future. Still it was a rather pleasant day; the long gray days of the midwestern winter were just starting to end, and though it was still cold, it was very sunny. There were a few people walking out of the building, but mostly folks were going in for work or class, a steady stream of us walking in pairs or singly on the long walkway from the parking lot to the entrance. It wasn't until someone had entered the building ahead of me that I noticed that I could see myself quite clearly in the glass windows of the double doors several hundred feet away.

At first it was a little uncanny: one moment I'm staring blankly ahead at the back of someone's head, trying to hold two ideas in my own head at the same time, and the next moment I can see myself fully framed simultaneously in each of the doors. Here in the dual reflection of the glass was Mrs. Polly Williams's desire made manifest—if only "I could make myself into two or three . . . I might get along" (Cary, *Clovernook* [1853] 93). I was doubled, and it was weird. I had often jokingly compared my entering a second doctorate program after finishing my PhD in English to trying to grow a second head or catching one's shadow, and now here I was walking into the School of Education with two fully formed reflections walking back at me. Which was the "real" me, and which the ghostly double?

I paused. If I moved to the left, the reflection on the right disappeared. If I moved to the right, the left image vanished. It was getting late. Class began in a few minutes, and ironically I still had copies to make. I saw one of my students pull into the parking lot, and I quickly walked toward the building. I didn't want anyone to see me hopping back and forth on the sidewalk, making faces at the School of Education building.

But as I continued walking, I noticed that something was starting to happen. The twin figures in front of me were starting to pull toward the frame between the two doors. At first this just made for a ghastly merger of my twin reflections—two arms, one leg, three eyes, no nose—until just as I reached for the door, I was greeted by a single merged reflection reaching out from the door to me. When I opened the door, of course, the reflections disappeared, and the long hallway of the main floor stretched out before me. The sounds of the footsteps echoed somewhere beyond the first-floor atrium, and I paused at the threshold briefly to hold the door for the walkers behind me, including my breathless student who had caught up quickly, apparently not wanting to get to class after the professor. My student gave me a sheepish smile, and the others nodded their thanks to me for holding the door and then walked past. I followed them in and made my way slowly to class, letting my student get well ahead of me to arrive on time.

This strange encounter with multiple reflections of myself raises, of course, the question of which self—English? Education? Both? Neither?—greeted me at the door. The truth is that I'm still not sure what to make of what happened, though I remember feeling on that long, slow walk as if something had finally fallen into place. This book has been an attempt to think through what the proper alignment between English/Education might be, and to reflect on the possibilities contained in each of the images offered. In the end, though, mirrors can only offer back to us what we have already placed before them. They can't tell us what we are—only what we just were. What we are or might become can only be revealed in what happens during that long walk toward our classrooms and in what inquiries we pursue for ourselves, with students, and with each other, once we cross that threshold.

APPENDIXES: MATERIALS FOR DERANGING ENGLISH/EDUCATION

Appendix 1:
First Steps to Deranging English

The materials in the appendixes that follow are either texts that have been directly referenced in one of the chapters or are extensions from engagements mentioned there.

I include the page from *Harper's New Monthly Magazine* where I first encountered the merman juxtaposed with Cary's poem. Following that image are suggestions to pursue the recommendations in the section titled "The Future Praxis of English/Education: Opportunities and Obstacles" in Chapter 1.

Appendix 1.1: "A Passing Wish"

A PASSING WISH. 31

Man alone, the head and the chief of animals, is lost without immediate exercise of a quality which education alone can make to take the place of instinct—presence of mind. Wild struggles are certain death; rest, and yielding to gravity until only the two avenues of life are free, are the next step; and to advance at all, he must either paddle like a dog, or perform a series of movements with legs and arms and respiratory organs which, it is true, no beast could execute, but which man himself must learn.

FIG.14.—Merman. (*From a specimen in Agassiz's Museum.*)

A PASSING WISH.

O FOR the life of a Gipsy!
    A strong-armed, barefoot girl;
And to have the wind for a waiting-maid
    To keep my hair in curl;
To bring me scent of the violet,
    And the red rose, and the pine;
And at night to spread my grassy bed—
    Ah! wouldn't it be divine?

O for the life of a Gipsy!
    So gloriously free;
Through the world to roam, and to find a home
    'Neath every green-wood tree;
To milk my cow in the meadow,
    Wherever she chanced to stand;
And to have my corn-fields planted
    By every lad in the land!

O for the life of a Gipsy!
    With the dew to fringe my gown;
And to have the sun for a sweet-heart
    To come and kiss me brown;
To take each little chubby-cheek
    That I chose, and call her mine,
And teach her to tramp from camp to camp—
    Ah! wouldn't it be divine?

O for the life of a Gipsy!
    To lie in the lazy shades;
And to predict sweet fairings
    To all the village maids;

To give them caps of pretty flowers,
    And shawls of wool so white,
And troops of lovers to sing them songs
    At their window-panes at night!

O for the life of a Gipsy!
    To hunt the hare for play;
And to take my trap on my shoulder
    And hie away and away—
Away to the tents by the water,
    When the stars began to shine—
To my glad wild crew, with hearts so true—
    Ah! wouldn't it be divine?

O for the life of a Gipsy!
    To be up at the dawning gray;
And to have my dog, like my shadow,
    Beside me all the day;
To have a hat of plaited straw,
    And a cloak of scarlet dye,
And shoot like a light through the glens at night,
And make the owlets cry!

O for the life of a Gipsy!
    To roam the wide world through;
To have the wind for a waiting-maid,
    And the sun for a sweet-heart true;
To say to my restless conscience,
    Be still; you are no more mine!
And to hold my heart beneath my art—
    Ah! wouldn't it be divine?

Appendix 1.2: Wondering, Asking Questions, and Pursuing Inquiry

Most English teachers are thoughtful about their practice, wondering why something (a favorite text, strategy, or engagement) works with one set of students and something else works for another set; why some students immediately latch onto a piece of literature as if it were speaking to their current moment, while others cast their interests widely and deeply among contemporary media. Rare is the English teacher who simply does not think about what she did yesterday or what he will do tomorrow. These wonderings guide our day-to-day practice—how can I get students to be more involved during peer review tomorrow, say, or what would happen if I let the students pose their own questions about that poem before we begin to analyze it?—and they sometimes lead us to question our successes and failures in teaching—why didn't that engagement work today when it *killed* last semester?

The difference between posing these questions to ourselves, or even to our colleagues between classes in the hallways or over coffee in the faculty lounge, and what people do who write articles and books about the practice of teaching is a matter of degree. In those wonderings are the first stages of thinking like a teacher-researcher. But the day-to-day demands of teaching often prevent us from taking the next step of pursuing these stirrings of inquiry further and recording what it is we think is happening when we teach "English." In *The Art of Classroom Inquiry: A Handbook for Teacher-Researchers*, Ruth Shagoury Hubbard and Brenda Miller Power offer several useful tips for getting started in classroom research, turning these teacher wonderings into potential research questions that might generate data and rich descriptions of teaching and learning in practice. Hubbard and Power urge us to "try to love the questions themselves" (1), for if we do, we are more likely to sustain our inquiries into what life is *really* like in our classrooms for us and for our students.

This was the text my colleagues in the Indiana English Teachers Collaborative recommended for novice classroom inquirers, and it remains one I recommend especially for its insistence on the capacity of classroom teachers to become researchers. But loving the questions only takes you so far if you don't have a way to record how they change what happens in our classrooms. One solution that draws from Hubbard and Miller's recommendation is for teachers to keep a "teaching journal" to reflect "on what you have noticed in the classroom" (7). Sally Griffin, my teaching partner in the Open Institute of the UNC Charlotte Writing Project and co-author of *Thinking Out Loud on Paper: The Student Daybook as a Tool to Foster Learning*, has turned her practice of writing daily with her students in her own daybook into a hybrid tool for writing, research, and teaching. As she describes, "My daybook, the same one I had used for so long to write with my students and occasionally to record ideas to use or more things to think about, was about to become an ethnography—a chronicle of my journey through theories and ideologies to an understanding of myself and my students" (114). She then goes on to recount her work with two students in particular whose challenges navigating home and school literacies brought her to think differently about what should happen in her classroom.

This sort of reflective inquiry through writing can become not just a catalogue of tips and strategies for the coming week, but what Cathy Fleischer describes as "a way of thinking about issues of power and representation and storytelling and much more" about our classrooms (*Composing* 4). I want to offer a few questions that teachers of English/ Education at all levels might pose for themselves as they begin to think about what that contact between disciplines might mean for us and for our students. The questions certainly are not exhaustive, but they can begin to unsettle us from our received sense of who we are and what we do as English teachers.

Step 1: Try to picture your classroom. If you need to, draw a map or quick sketch of what it might look like from above or from a point in the room familiar to you. Where does learning happen in your classroom?

Step 2: What does learning look like when it happens in your classroom? Draw a picture of it—use stick figures or symbols but try to limit your use of words. Show who is there. Is everyone involved in the same type of activity? If so, why? How does that involvement happen? If not, why not? What are they doing? What is distinctive about how they are doing what they are doing?

Step 3: What's something you want to know about #1 and/or #2?

Step 4: What's something you want others to know?

The next step is to think of how one might go about finding some answers to the questions in steps 3 and 4, but even without that "how" question, these steps do two crucial things for teachers: (1) they invite us to construct an image of instruction in our classrooms as it is and as we might want it to be; and (2) they position us as capable knowers of our own practice about the field. They work against what for many of us is the opacity of our pedagogy, certainly to our students, but often to ourselves, allowing us to point to and name what it is we do and why. Those are important steps for English teachers to be able to take if they are to shape the nature of English/Education in the twenty-first century.

Appendix 1.3: Looking at Your Classroom and Making It Strange

The following engagement is one I have used with my Advanced English Methods and Advanced Research in Teaching English classes to help teachers to think about their classrooms as sites of possible inquiry. I have modified the materials and instructions at the research stations when using these strategies with students in other courses, but the basic setup is the same. Allowing for forty-five to fifty minutes for the full engagement, I introduce each of the stations and invite students to work in groups of two or three as they move through the stations. In larger classes, I have multiple tables for each station so that more than one group might be working with the same material at a different part of the room. After ten to fifteen minutes at a station, students get ready to shift to a new table and a new focus. At the end they will have experienced multiple ways of examining data—whether literary text, modes of reading, student writing, classroom talk, or other artifacts—and they will have worked collaboratively through different modes of presenting findings about data.

Station 1: The Jar

Materials: glass jar (1); tape; scissors; copies of Wallace Stevens's "Anecdote of the Jar" (15); copies of John Barth's "Frame-Tale" (15); blank paper; file folder (1)

Step 1: Choose someone to read aloud the poem "Anecdote of the Jar" by Wallace Stevens. As the person reads, the other people at the station should choose and engage in one or more of the following activities:

    Activity 1: Read (silently or aloud) the poem as the designated reader reads. Write something down about the experience that interests you. Put it in the jar.

    Or, **Activity 2:** As you listen to the poem, imagine that you are holding two mirrors in parallel on either side of the jar. Look into the mirrors. What do you see there? Write that down and put it somewhere.

    Or, **Activity 3:** Read the handout "Frame-Tale." Using the scissors and tape provided, make something to wear or put in the jar. On a piece of paper, explain your decision.

Step 2: Empty the jar. With the other people at your station, organize the items to explain what you have found. On the paper provided, record your findings and make a guess about what they might reveal or mean. Place the paper in the folder for the next group. Return the items to the jar.

Station 2: Wheelbarrows and Classroom Maps

Materials: file folder (2); colored pencils/crayons; William Carlos Williams's "The Red Wheelbarrow" (15); classroom map(s)

Step 1: Read "The Red Wheelbarrow." Draw your understanding of the poem in the space below the poem. Share your interpretation and drawing with the other members of the station. On a sheet of paper, record any findings you discover about the drawings. Put those in file folder #1 for the next group. Put the classroom map(s) in file folder #2.

Step 2: Remove the classroom map(s) from file folder #2. What do you notice about the classroom(s) as you look at the maps? Record your understanding of them using the following format: "In order to understand [X—whatever you think is worth understanding about these maps] as it affects the teaching of English, so much depends upon . . ." Put your responses back into file folder #2 for the next group.

Station 3: Digging the Desk

Materials: artifacts from your own classroom/desk/office; a desk drawer; file box (1); several hanging file folders

Scenario: You are scientists from another world or time. You're trying to figure out what people were like in 2008 [or your current year] on Earth. Your colleagues have brought back to your lab several boxes of artifacts from an English classroom. Now your team is trying to figure out what these artifacts might mean, or at least what they can tell you about the person (or persons) they belonged to in 2008.

For first group:
Step 1: With the members of your team, sift through the items in the desk drawer. On a sheet of paper, list and briefly identify each. Make notes or comments that will help organize and explain the meaning, significance, or relation of these items to each other and/ or to the owner of the drawer. Save these notes to attach to the rationale for step two below.

Step 2: Remove each of the items and find new places for them in the file box. With the members of your group, explain the placement decision(s) you have made. Why did you choose *these* items to put in *those* folders? Close the box and place this rationale (with the notes from Step 1) in the now empty drawer.

For subsequent groups:
Step 1: With the members of your station, read the rationale(s) and notes in the office drawer. Open the file box and examine the items.

Provide comments, suggestions, and additions to the notes and rationale(s) from the previous group(s).

Step 2: Put the items in the folders and with other items according to the criteria *your* group considers most accurate and appropriate for offering an explanation of the items from the drawer. Provide a brief rationale for this new organization and place it in the drawer with the previous rationale(s) and notes.

Field Log for Desk Artifacts

ITEM	Description (What does it look like? What is it for?) Explanation (What do you think it tells us about the owner of the drawer)?	Folder (What folder should it go in?) Rationale (Why?)

Reflection: What was easy about this activity? Why?
What was difficult about this activity? Why?
Which do you think is more important: the work that the first group of scientists did or the work that the second group of scientists did? Why?

Station 4: Examining Student Writing

Materials: student papers that have undergone peer (or instructor) response, but have not yet been graded; sticky notes; note cards

For first group:

Step 1: Read through the student papers, noting in particular the comments and feedback peer reviewers have provided, and the questions authors have asked of their readers in the margins and at the beginnings/ends of the papers. With the other members of your station, mark with sticky notes any recurring themes, phrases, comments, or other items of interest that you observe about these comments.

Step 2: On the sticky notes, make observations or comments that will help to organize or explain the type of response marked and the reason(s) it might be worth noting.

Step 3: Write a brief explanation of what you think might be happening in these comments and on these papers. What do you think you would still need to know before coming to any final conclusions or judgments about the peer response? Write these suggestions and/or questions at the bottom of your rationale and put it in the file folder for the next group(s).

For subsequent groups:
Steps 1–2 as above.

Step 3: Read the rationale and questions from previous group(s). Make comments/suggestions/critiques for this rationale. Then, with the members of your station, write an explanation of your own that will make a claim about what might be happening with these comments and these papers. What do you still need to discover before coming to a more final judgment? Write these questions/suggestions at the bottom of your explanation. Put them in the folder.

Appendix 1.4: Image-Music-Text Artifacts/ Transmediations

The following engagements are an extension inspired by the work of Jerome Harste on transmediation, which nicely captures Dewey's claim about the image as primary unit of instruction. The title for the activity comes, of course, from Roland Barthes's collection of essays of the same name. Although I use transmediation as a component in all my literature courses, whether as student invitations or as part of initiating engagements with a text or topic, I have found it to be particularly useful when dealing with literature from time periods or cultures distant from twenty-first-century American life.

What they are

Transmediations offer students an opportunity to demonstrate and share their understanding of the readings experienced in one sign-system (usually print text) through an artifact in another sign system. Image-Music-Text transmediations focus on three different sign systems. Note: a transmediation is not simply a *representation*, but offers an *interpretation* or *critical perspective* on the text. Nor does it stand alone. Each transmediation should be accompanied by a short written rationale/ explanation linking the image, music, or text to the work students are reading.

How students use them in the class

Images: students select period or contemporary artwork (original or reproductions), film clips, photography, or other visual texts (maps, sketches, charts, graphs). I try to dissuade students from simply seeking pictures of the author as their image artifacts since those typically are informational and not interpretive. Music: students provide a short (one to three minutes) sample of music that may be contemporary to the text they are reading; or that is more recent but attempts to portray that era of the text; or that captures for them something of the themes or features of the text they are reading. Text: students provide a short work (no more than two pages) in either prose or poetry (can be original) that takes up similar themes or issues of the text they are reading. Except for Music, students provide copies of their transmediations, and for all transmediations they offer copies of their rationales for everyone in class.

Extensions suggested by student work

A group of my modern world literature students, participating in a literature circle reading of Isabel Allende's *The Stories of Eva Luna*, burned
a CD with a song they associated with each of the stories in the cycle,
and then created the equivalent of liner notes to offer mini-rationales
for each selection. Inspired by that project, or perhaps just trying to
relive the past glory of my days as a college radio station disc jockey
(AM 640—WVFI!), I've made a similar option available to students in
the course as an individual final exam project.

> **Option C: "I am a DJ, I am what I play" (Or I am a *bricoleur*, I
> am what I . . . *bricolage*?): Designing Images/Music/Texts for
> World Literature**
> The folks at CMJ (College Music Journal, www.cmj.com), David
> Dye of "The World Café" (http://www.worldcafelive.com), and
> Muzak (Yes, Muzak! http://www.muzak.com) have joined forces
> to institute the first-ever soundtrack to capture the quintessential
> experience of reading, studying, and understanding modern world
> literature—and they of course want you to design the playlist
> and liner notes for the soundtrack. The release party (including a
> live concert and interactive exhibit) for this experience in *Audio
> Architecture* (the term actually comes from Muzak's own brand
> of programming) will combine visual, musical, and textual arti-
> facts that will offer enduring perspectives on the meaning of world
> literature. It will begin right here at UNC Charlotte before trav-
> eling on as part of a larger fifty-three-city tour of the country
> focusing on classic world art, literature, and culture. The goal is
> to offer both an artistic and educational experience to a diverse
> set of readers/viewers/listeners, so that the experience of these
> artifacts will help them to understand something indispensable
> about world literature and culture, but also about themselves in
> relation to these artifacts.
>
> For this option, your task is two-fold: (1) construct the
> playlist, cover art, and liner notes for the CD—songs and cover
> art may of course be original; (2) provide a written rationale (of
> at least 1,000 words) for the inclusion of your new, twenty-first-
> century text into the traveling exhibit—that is, how is the compi-
> lation *itself* a work of art in the tradition of existing and established
> pieces of world literature and culture? This rationale should lo-
> cate the key elements of world literature and culture that are
> central to the project and explain how this artifact will help con-
> tinue to generate an understanding of the meaning of world lit-
> erature (past, present, and future).

Appendix 2: Red Wheelbarrows and Beyond

The engagement below was first used with Williams's poem and incorporates aspects of each of our classroom approaches to using the poem, but it can easily be adapted to other works.

> **Materials:** deck of standard playing cards (preferably unopened); copies of Williams's "The Red Wheelbarrow" (or other poem); drawing paper; colored pencils
>
> **Step 1:** Designate which of the four stanzas of Williams's poem will correspond to one of the four suits of a standard deck of playing cards—clubs, diamonds, spades, hearts. Mark these designations on your copy of the poem.
>
> **Step 2:** Ask for a student volunteer to open the deck and shuffle the cards. Have another student volunteer cut the deck, shuffle again, and then return the deck to you.
>
> **Step 3:** Fan the deck facedown and, walking through the room, have students draw one card from the deck and then put it face down on their desks until everyone has drawn a card. Then allow them to turn the card over and look at it.
>
> **Step 4:** "As you look at the card, I am going to read a poem to you. I want you to think about what you are seeing and what you are hearing; and when I have finished reading, take some time to write in your notebooks anything interesting or unusual or curious that happened or occurred to you." Allow two to three minutes for brief writing.
>
> **Step 5:** Distribute copies of the poem. Assign each student a particular stanza to focus on, based on the suit of the card on each desk.
>
> **Step 6:** Read the poem aloud again. "As I read, think about your particular stanza, and then draw your understanding or interpretation of that stanza." Allow two to three minutes for brief sketching.
>
> **Step 7:** Match the suits in groups of four (four hearts, four clubs, and so on), allowing for more than one group of each suit. "In your new groups, share and compare your responses. What are things you all noticed or emphasized? What are points of difference? When everyone has had a turn, try to agree on a visional representation that captures what your group now understands about the poem and/or this particular stanza."

Step 8: Shuffle the deck. Have each group send a representative to the front of the class to share their visual representation until all groups have had a turn. This step should allow for whole-class participation and teacher direction about areas of focus or interest in the poem.

Step 9: Have students return to their original seats with their playing cards. "Now consider everything you've heard and seen about the poem. Looking back at your initial writing and your playing card, what do you now know about the poem? How is the card in front of you involved in what you know?"

Extensions

In the Writing Project Open Institute, since my students were teachers themselves, Sally Griffin and I modified my thesis-generator approach to Williams's poem to link the answers to Step 9 to their own work as writing teachers. So for instance, my card, the one-eyed Jack of Hearts, prompted this response: "In order to understand the importance of the Jack of Hearts to my life as a writing teacher, so much depends upon seeing sideways . . ."

Appendix 3: Poetry and Found Pedagogy

Each of the poems discussed in Chapter 3 is printed in its entirety below. Following the poems are several items related to the work students and I did in thinking about poetic meaning: the modified Dada procedure we presented to our conference participants, and then additional resources for introducing contemporary and non-canonical poetry into the classroom.

Appendix 3.1: Robert Frost, "Stopping by Woods on a Snowy Evening"

Whose Woods these are I think I know.
His house is in the village though;
He will not see me stopping here
To watch his woods fill up with snow.

My little horse must think it queer
To stop without a farmhouse near
Between the woods and frozen lake
The darkest evening of the year.

He gives his harness bells a shake
To ask if there is some mistake.
The only other sound's the sweep
Of easy wind and downy flake.

The woods are lovely, dark and deep.
But I have promises to keep,
And miles to go before I sleep,
And miles to go before I sleep.

Appendix 3.2: James Wright, "Lying in a Hammock at William Duffy's Farm in Pine Island, Minnesota"

Over my head, I see the bronze butterfly,
Asleep on the black trunk,
Blowing like a leaf in green shadow.
Down the ravine behind the empty house,
The cowbells follow one another
Into the distance of the afternoon.
To my right,
In a field of sunlight between two pines,
The droppings of last year's horses
Blaze up into golden stones.
I lean back, as the evening darkens and comes on.
A chicken hawk floats over, looking for home.
I have wasted my life.

Appendix 3.3: Langston Hughes, "Harlem"

What happens to a dream deferred?
Does it dry up
like a raisin in the sun?
or fester like a sore—
and then run?
Does it stink like rotten meat?
or crust and sugar over—
like a syrupy sweet?

Maybe it just sags
like a heavy load.

Or does it explode?

Appendix 3.4: William Shakespeare, "Sonnet 73"

That time of year thou mayst in me behold
When yellow leaves, or none, or few, do hang
Upon those boughs which shake against the cold,
Bare ruined choirs, where late the sweet birds sang.
In me thou see'st the twilight of such day
As after sunset fadeth in the west;
Which by and by black night doth take away,
Death's second self, that seals up all in rest.
In me thou see'st the glowing of such fire,
That on the ashes of his youth doth lie,
As the death-bed, whereon it must expire,
Consum'd with that which it was nourish'd by.
    This thou perceiv'st, which makes thy love more strong,
    To love that well, which thou must leave ere long.

Appendix 3.5: Dada/Found Poetry

Below are the instructions for the invitation to Dada/Found Poetry as we introduced them to our conference participants in 2004. The steps can be modified to allow for an appropriate selection of poems from class reading or independent selections. The poems listed here were paired at different stations, which were then led by my student co-presenters, who had used the particular poems in their responses. Any poems or combination of poems that have already generated student interest will do.

Materials: scissors, tape, glue-stick, paper, bowl

Poem Stations
Station 1: Emily Bronte, "Spellbound" and Emily Dickinson, "I'm Nobody! Who are You?" [Poem 260]

Station 2: Robert Frost, "Stopping by Woods on a Snowy Evening" and James Wright, "Lying in a Hammock at William Duffy's Farm in Pine Island, Minnesota"

Station 3: Langston Hughes, "Harlem" and William Shakespeare, "Sonnet 73"

Station 4: Pat Mora, "Immigrants" and W.B. Yeats, "The Wild Swan at Coole"

Procedures
Students may do these steps individually or in small groups, depending on time available. Because the first step takes time, I often encourage students to work together so that all can help with the destruction of the original poems; each takes on a particular role for the reassembling: one draws out the pieces, another glues them into place, a third records on a separate page the new creation. Then the group as a whole deliberates about where to break lines and stanzas, and so on.

Step 1: Take two (or more) poems from the available selections and cut them into pieces (you may do this separately for each poem or combine pieces of some or all of the poems, but you must use all the pieces for this first step). Put these pieces into a bowl and draw them out one by one, placing them in order on a separate sheet of paper as you do. Reproduce this new assemblage in its entirety.

Step 2: What have you created? Is it a poem? Why or why not? If so, how does it become a poem? If not, what would have to happen for it to become a "real" poem?

Step 3: What is the meaning of the product you have created in Step 1? Write your reflections as a group on your reproduction of your found poem.

Extensions

One of the obvious extensions for this sort of activity is to allow individual students to begin to analyze in writing what they have created, arguing for it or against it as a poetic work. This sort of formal interpretive essay would need to allow for a recursive process, with feedback from peers and multiple drafts. But prior to that step, the productions of each of the groups can have a more public showing. Following this activity, teachers can copy and distribute the results of each group for Steps 1–3 to allow other groups to weigh in on the productions and conclusions. This continuing conversation will assist students in refining their thinking about what constitutes poetic meaning and provides artifacts of understanding available to all groups.

Appendix 3.6: Poetry Resources

Many teachers are faced with the same poetic offerings year after year, making it difficult to find something new to say about Williams's red wheelbarrow or Frost's snowy woods. And even cutting them up doesn't necessarily move students to become lifelong readers of poetry. Websites such as the Library of Congress's Poetry 180 site, initiated by Billy Collins when he was United States poet laureate, offer short, topical, and contemporary poems that are easily accessible to secondary and post-secondary students. In my introductory literature courses, I invite students to visit the site and to select a poem to discuss in class. To introduce them to some of the forgotten or disappeared literary history in America, I have them visit digital archives such as New York Public Library's Schomberg Collection of African American Women Writers of the Nineteenth Century. Below is a sample procedure for drawing poems from these sites into the whole-class conversation. These sites, of course, require computer and Internet access; even if students do not have access, teachers can use these sites to offer students poetry that breaks away from the museum quality of so many anthologized poems. Even someone like Phillis Wheatley, whose short poem "On Being Brought from Africa to America" has become a staple of anthologies, takes on a new complexity when seen beside the work of women who came after her.

For tomorrow's class

1. Go to the African American Women Writers of the Nineteenth Century website of the Schomburg Collections of the New York Public Library (http://digital.nypl.org/schomburg/writers_aa 19/). Click on the image to enter the site.

2. Once you enter the site, choose "Poetry" from the drop-down menu under the "Choose a Category" Link.

3. Choose an author link from the new menu (you'll see a list of authors ranging from Eloise Bibb to Phillis Wheatley). Not every work that shows up for a particular author is a poem, so you'll need to browse through the links a bit.

4. Read three to four poems by a single author. Copy/print these poems so you have them for future use—what you begin to assemble here may end up as part of your first exam.

5. Choose at least one poem to talk about for your talking points this week. Post those talking points with a brief summary of the poem and any information about the author or the poem's publication that may be of interest (for this information you may

have to spend some time browsing the "Biographies" link on the main page of the website).

6. Bring all your poems to class on Monday.

or

1. Go to the Poetry180 website (http://www.loc.gov/poetry/180).

2. Browse the poem titles and click on a few links that catch your eye. Read these poems.

3. Which poem is your favorite? What is the best word/phrase/line in that poem? Circle it. Write down your reasons.

4. Reflect on your experience with the poem as a whole. What do you find interesting, amusing, strange, and/or moving about the poem? What are three things that you notice about this poem that you think would interest someone else?

5. Choose a poem to bring to class that you think everyone should read. Why should people care about this poem? Write your reasons on your copy of the poem.

Appendix 4: American Literature Resources

Below are the full syllabus, exams, and engagements from the sections of the American literature surveys discussed in Chapter 4. The syllabus is a composite of the two sections, with variations noted.

Appendix 4.1

The syllabus below is from the most recent offering of the course. Where there were differences in text options I've added that information with the heading [Spring 2005]. Note: for the sake of reproduction here, I have not included the interlinear images that were part of the schedule of readings.

University of North Carolina at Charlotte
College of Arts and Sciences
Department of English

Spring 2007
ENGL 3300 Section 001: American Literature Survey (3)
MW 12:30-1:45 PM, Fretwell 205

Dr. John A. Staunton
Department of English
Office hours: MW by appointment
Phone:
Email:
Course website: WebCT & http://college.hmco.com/english/lauter/heath/
4e/students/index.html

Catalog Description
ENGL 3300. American Literature Survey. (3) Prerequisites: ENGL 2100 and ENGL 3100. *(This course is a survey requirement for English majors who have entered the program since fall 2002).*

Course Overview and Rationale:
American Literature Survey spans over 400 years of American Literature, from the Colonial Period (including literature of the First Contact and early works from New France, New Spain, and of course New England) to the Modern Period. Through shared readings from an anthology (poetry, histories, essays, fiction, and drama) and through individual and smaller group readings of novels focused on particular themes and genres *(American Utopias, Borderlands, Romances/Adventures)* we will investigate the fundamental questions at the heart of American Literature and American Literary History—What makes 'American Literature' distinctly *American?* Or *literary?* Who writes it, who reads it, and why?

Required Texts and Materials (Everyone will need the following):

Paul Lauter, Ed. *Heath Anthology of American Literature. Concise Edition.* Boston: Houghton Mifflin, 2004.

-composition style notebook
-reliable and regular computer access
-an active email account

Literature Circle and Independent Reading Books (You will read at least one book from each group in literature circles and an additional book on your own):

[Spring 2007]
Group A: American Utopias

Bacon, Josephine. *Her Fiancé: Four Stories of College Life.* [1904]. New York: Ayer, 2004. [ISBN: 0836934768].
Bellamy, Edward. *Looking Backward.* [1889]. New York: Dover Publishing, 1996. [ISBN: 0486290387].
Burroughs, Edgar Rice. *Pellucidar.* [1923]. New York: Dover Publishing, 2003. [ISBN: 0486428699].
Gilman, Charlotte Perkins. *Herland.* [1915]. New York: Dover, 1998. [ISBN: 0486404293].
Hawthorne, Nathaniel. *The Blithedale Romance.* [1852] New York: Oxford UP 1991. [ISBN: 0192825984].
Lane, Mary Bradley. *Mizora: A Prophecy.* [1890]. Syracuse: Syracuse UP, 2000. [ISBN: 0815628390].

Group B: American Romances/Adventures

Chopin, Kate. *The Awakening.* [1899]. New York: Oxford UP, 2000. [ISBN: 0192823000].
Ferber, Edna. *Emma McChesney & Co.* [1915]. Urbana: U of Illinois P, 2002. [ISBN: 0252070887].
James, Henry. *Washington Square.* [1880]. New York: Signet, 2004. [ISBN: 0451528719].
Larsen, Nella. *Quicksand & Passing.* [1928/1929]. New Brunswick: Rutgers UP, 1986. [ISBN: 0813511704].
Rowson, Susanna. *Charlotte Temple.* [1791/1794]. New York: Oxford UP, 1987. [ISBN: 0195042387].
Wharton, Edith. *The House of Mirth.* [1905]. New York: Dover, 2002. [ISBN: 0486420493].

Group C: American Borderlands

Cather, Willa. *O Pioneers!* [1913]. New York: Dover, 1993. [ISBN: 0486277852].

Chesnutt, Charles W. *Tales of Conjure and the Colorline*. [1899].
New York: Dover, 1997. [ISBN: 0486404269].

Grey, Zane. *Riders of the Purple Sage*. [1912]. New York: Dover,
2002. [ISBN: 0486424561].

Jewett, Sarah Orne. *The Country of the Pointed Firs*. [1896].
New York: Dover, 1994. [ISBN: 0486281965].

Reid, Christian [Frances Fisher]. *The Land of the Sky: Adventures in Mountain By-Ways*. [1875]. Asheville, NC: Land of
Sky Books, 2001. [ISBN: 1566641772].

Wilson, Harriet. *Our Nig; or Sketches from the Life of a Free
Black*. [1859]. New York: Vintage, 2002. [ISBN:
1400031206].

[Spring 2005]
Group A: Speculative Fictions of America

Baum, L. Frank. *The Wizard of Oz*. [1900]. New York: Tor
Books, 1993. [ISBN: 0812523350].

Bellamy, Edward. *Looking Backward*. [1889]. New York: Dover
Publishing, 1996. [ISBN: 0486290387].

Burroughs, Edgar Rice. *Pellucidar*. [1923]. New York: Dover
Publishing, 2003. [ISBN: 0486428699].

Gilman, Charlotte Perkins. *Herland*. [1915]. New York: Dover,
1998. [ISBN: 0486404293].

Lane, Mary Bradley. Mizora: *A Prophecy*. [1890]. Syracuse:
Syracuse UP, 2000. [ISBN: 0815628390].

Group B: Horrors, Humors, Adventures, and Romances of America

Bacon, Josephine. *Her Fiancé: Four Stories of College Life*.
[1904]. New York: Ayer, 2004. [ISBN: 0836934768].

Brown, Charles Brockden. *Wieland*. [1798]. New York:
Prometheus Books, 1997. [ISBN: 1573921750].

Ferber, Edna. *Emma McChesney & Co*. [1915]. Urbana: U of
Illinois P, 2002. [ISBN: 0252070887].

James, Henry. *Washington Square*. [1880]. New York: Signet
Classics, 2004. [ISBN: 0451528719].

Rowson, Susanna. *Charlotte Temple*. [1791/1794]. New York:
Oxford UP, 1987. [ISBN: 0195042387].

Group C: Frontiers and Borderlands of America

Cather, Willa. *O Pioneers!* [1913]. New York: Dover, 1993.
[ISBN: 0486277852].

Chesnutt, Charles W. *Tales of Conjure and the Colorline*. [1899].
New York: Dover, 1997. [ISBN: 0486404269].

Grey, Zane. *Riders of the Purple Sage*. [1912]. New York: Dover, 2002. [ISBN: 0486424561].

Jewett, Sarah Orne. *The Country of the Pointed Firs*. [1896]. New York: Dover, 1994. [ISBN: 0486281965].

Larsen, Nella. *Passing*. [1923]. New York: Penguin, 2003. [ISBN: 0142437271].

Contexts for the Course:

1) **Attendance:** As the schedule of readings and engagements below suggests, the course will demand much of you as a reader, writer, and thinker. For this reason it is essential that you be in class every day we are scheduled to meet and that you are prepared to participate in conversation about the readings. *Any* absence—for whatever reason—will adversely affect your overall performance in class, lowering your final course grade by 7.5 pts for each absence. More than 5 absences will result in a failing grade for the course. Religious holidays, severe illnesses, and situations beyond the control of the student **may** present special situations. In such cases, consult with me to determine what if any accommodations may be made to mitigate the effect of the absence.

2) **Literature Circles/Group Engagements.** The group and independent reading of the novels in Groups A, B, and C will require of you a willingness to work with others both inside and outside of class. The responsibility for the success of the groups rests with the individual members of each group. For the most part, groups will be self-selected, though I reserve the right to assign or reassign members should the need arise. I will not regularly monitor the meetings of particular groups, but I will always be available should questions or difficulties arise.

3) **WebCT:** In addition to our weekly in-class meetings, we will also have the opportunity to stay connected through the class online discussion site. This resource will allow us to focus our conversation on Mondays and Wednesdays by allowing you to preview questions, concerns, or difficulties with the readings. It will also be a place to share information and issues related to our readings that may emerge from your experiences with literature outside the class.

4) **Technology:** In order to participate fully in all aspects of the course, you will need to have an active email account, and you must be able to access WebCT regularly. To receive full credit, all papers and exams (except for those we conduct in-class) must be submitted electronically as attachments via WebCT either as an MS Word Document (*.doc) or as a document saved in Rich-Text-Format (*.rtf).

Activities and Engagements:

I. **Exams (30%: 3 @ 10% each).** These three exams (**2/5-2/7, 3/19, and 5/9**) will consist of a choice of essay topics and a section requiring you to identify and contextualize passages from the readings. Part of the exams will be in-class and part will be take-home.

II. **Literature Circle Reports (30%: 3 @ 10% each).** Three times during the semester you and up to 4 other members of the class will read (together) one of the texts from Group A, B, or C. You will not necessarily read with the same group of people each time, but each of you must read at least one text from each of the sets. The reading will be conducted outside of our regular meeting times and will be coordinated by the members of each group according to particular reading roles. On the days designated on the schedule (**2/19, 3/14, and 4/25**), your group will come to class prepared with a 300-500 word brief, reporting on your selected text, and an artifact(s) (can be edible) that will engage the rest of the class in some pertinent issue(s) or feature(s) of your novel. You must bring copies of this brief for the rest of the class and be prepared to field questions about your report. (*See Appendix below for full engagement instructions and criteria.*)

III. **Critical Inquiry of Independent Reading Selection (x, y, z versions) (15%).** In addition to the 3 literature circle selections, you will also choose a text from among Group A, B, or C to read individually. Over the course of the entire semester you will conduct an independent inquiry into some aspect of the novel of interest to you, researching the various historical, literary, and cultural contexts that are crucial to understanding the place of this work among the canon of American literature. This inquiry may take a variety of final forms, but it will undergo at least 3 versions (**X version-2/28, Y version-3/26, Z version-4/30**). The final, or **z version**, should be at least 2000 words and is due on the last day of class. (*See Appendix below for full engagement instructions and criteria.*)

IV. **Group Presentation (15%).** Starting the third week of class, student groups (at least 3 and no more than 4 per group) will make a presentation to the rest of the class about some aspect of the reading for that week. There will be a total of 10 student presentations between 1/29 and 4/23. Presentations should be between 30-45 minutes, and they must include: 1) a visual artifact from the period, 2) a timeline of major events surrounding the presentation theme/issue, 3) an **original** artifact/transmediation—in a sign system other than written text, and 4) a typed, written brief to be used as a resource/study guide for other students. (*See Appendix below for full engagement instructions and criteria.*)

V. **Talking Points/discussion list (10%).** Each week **prior** to our class discussions, you will post to the online discussion list Talking Points from the readings for that week. You must have a minimum of 20 postings (including 14 weekly postings). These should include what you consider to be the 4 most interesting, important, surprising, or controversial points from the readings. You should indicate page numbers and provide a rationale for your selection of each point. These should be substantive but brief (about 150-200 words). NOTE: Submissions posted AFTER a particular class discussion will not count toward your weekly total (16) Talking Points, but they will count toward the cumulative total (20). Postings in addition to the minimum may be taken into consideration for extra credit.

Preliminary Schedule (subject to change):

M   1/8   Introduction—Visions of America—Part 1
Jacopo Zucchi, *The Coral Fishers (Allegoria de scoperta dell'America)* [1585];
George Berkeley, "On the Prospect of Planting Arts and Learning in America" [1726];
"Creation of the Whites" (Yuchi) (40);
Handsom Lake (Seneca), "How America Was Discovered" (363-5)

W   1/10   Visions of America—Part 2
Christopher Columbus, "Journal of the First Voyage to America, 1492-1493" (48-57);
Martin Luther King, Jr., "I Have a Dream" (2265-2270);
Phillis Wheatley, "On Being Brought from Africa to America" (575);

M   1/15   MLK Jr. Holiday—No Classes

W   1/17   Fictions, and Frames of America
"The Origin of Stories" (Seneca) (30-33);
John Barth, "Frame-Tale" (photocopy)

M   1/22   Discovery, Captivity, and Contact—Part 1
"History of the Miraculous Apparition of the Virgin of Guadalupe in 1531" (72-80);
Thomas Harriot, *A Briefe and True Report of the New Found Land of Virginia* (118-125);

W   1/24   Discovery, Captivity, and Contact—Part 2
Father Jerome Lalemant, from *The Jesuit Relations*, "The Relation of 1647" (107-117);
Mary Rowlandson, from *A Narrative of the Captivity and Restauration* (206-232)

M   1/29   Presentation 1—The Tenth Muse(s)

Anne Bradstreet, "The Prologue"; "The Author to Her Book"; "The Flesh and the Spirit"; and other poems (187-197);

Sor Juana Inés de la Cruz, "In Reply to a Gentleman from Peru"
(80-86);
W   1/31   Discovery, Captivity, and Contact—Part 3
Alvar Nuñez Cabeza de Vaca (57-68);
John Smith, from *The Generall Historie of Virginia, New
England, and the Summer Isles* (125-135);
William Bradford, *Of Plymouth Plantation* (164-178)
M   2/5   Exam 1—Part 1
W   2/7   Exam 1—Part 2
M   2/12   Presentation 2—Nation and Revolution—Part 1

Benjamin Franklin, "The Way to Wealth" (365-373); *The
Autobiography* (381-423);
Philip Freneau (562-568)
W   2/14   Nation and Revolution—Part 2
J. Hector St. John de Crèvecoeur, *Letters from an American
Farmer* (435-452);
Phillis Wheatley (569-578)
M   2/19   LC 1
W   2/21   Presentation 3—Transcendental US

Ralph Waldo Emerson, "Nature"; "The American Scholar" (689-
707);
Margaret Fuller, "Woman in the 19th Century" (728-748);
M   2/26   Nation(s) and Revolution(s)—Part 1
Elias Boudinot (Cherokee), "An Address to Whites" (650-658);
La Llorana, the Unfaithful Maria, and La Malinche & "The
Devil Woman" (671-675)
W   2/28   Presentation 4—Nation(s) and Revolution(s)—Part 2

X Version Inquiry
Henry David Thoreau, "Resistance to Civil Government" &
Walden (749-801)
M   3/5   Spring Break—No Classes
W   3/7   Spring Break—No Classes
M   3/12   Fictions, and Frames of America—Redux
Washington Irving, "Rip Van Winkle" (940-953);
Nathaniel Hawthorne, "My Kinsman, Major Molineux";
"Young Goodman Brown"; "The Birth-mark" (953-988)
W   3/14   LC 2
M   3/19   EXAM 2
W   3/21   Presentation 5—American Gothic

Edgar Allan Poe, "The Fall of the House of Usher" (988-990;
1001-1014)
Alice Cary, "Clovernook" & "Uncle Christopher's" (1141-1158)

M   3/26   Presentation 6—Captivity and Resistance

Y Version Inquiry
Herman Melville, "Bartleby, the Scrivener"; "Benito Cereno"
(1055-1141);
Frederick Douglass, *Narrative of the Life* (866-931)
W   3/28   Presentation 7—New Americans—Part 1

Walt Whitman, "Preface to the 1855 Edition of *Leaves of Grass*"
(1209-1224); *Song of Myself* (1225-1275); "Out of the Cradle
Endlessly Rocking" (1279-1284)
M   4/2   New Americans—Part 2
T.S. Eliot, "The Love Song of J. Alfred Prufrock" (1900-1905);
Langston Hughes, "The Negro Speaks of Rivers" (2006-2008)
W   4/4   Presentation 8—New Americans—Part 3

Emily Dickinson, Poems (1295-1321);
M   4/9   American Moderns—Part 1
Ezra Pound, Poems (1831-1836);
William Carlos Williams, Poems (1850-1856);
W   4/11   American Moderns—Part 2
Marianne Moore, Poems (1944-1949)
Wallace Stevens, Poems (1954-1960)
M   4/16   Presentation 9—Life on the Edge—Part 1

Susan Glaspell, *Trifles* (1788-1799);
Stephen Crane, "The Bride Comes to Yellow Sky" (1555; 1573-
1581)
W   4/18   Life on the Edge—Part 2
Charlotte Perkins Gilman, "The Yellow Wall-Paper" (1596-1609);
Sarah Orne Jewett, "A White Heron" (1634-1641);
Mary Wilkins Freeman, "The Revolt of 'Mother'" (1642-1655)
M   4/23   Presentation 10—Life on the Edge—Part 3

Eugene O'Neill, *The Hairy Ape* (1856-1889)
Edward Albee, *The Sandbox* (2290-2295)
W   4/25
LC 3
M   4/30   The End (Almost)
T.S. Eliot, "The Waste Land" (1906-1920)
Z Version Inquiry
W   5/9   Exam 3 (11:00 am-1:45 pm)

Bishop George Berkeley (1685-1753)
"On the Prospect of Planting Arts and Learning in America"
(1726 [1752])

The Muse, disgusted at an age and clime
 Barren of every glorious theme,
In distant lands now waits a better time,
 Producing subjects worthy fame;

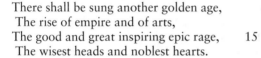

In happy climes, where from the genial sun 5
 And virgin earth such scenes ensue,
The force of art by nature seems outdone,
 And fancied beauties by the true;

In happy climes, the seat of innocence,
 Where nature guides and virtue rules,   10
Where men shall not impose, for truth and sense,
 The pedantry of courts and schools;

There shall be sung another golden age,
 The rise of empire and of arts,
The good and great inspiring epic rage,   15
 The wisest heads and noblest hearts.

Not such as Europe breeds in her decay;
 Such as she bred when fresh and young,
When heavenly flame did animate her clay,
 By future poets shall be sung.   20

Westward the course of empire takes its way;
 The first four acts already past,
A fifth shall close the drama with the day:
 Time's noblest offspring is the last.

ENGL 3300

Instructions for GROUP PRESENTATION Engagement

Time: 30-45 Minutes
 # in Group: 3-4

The week prior to the day of the presentation, the group will meet with me to discuss the group's goals and objectives for the presentation. At that time, the group should have a sense of how it will use its time during the presentation and how the group will attempt to create an experience for the rest of the class that will result in new understanding about the group's topic.

On the day of the presentation, in addition to the engagement that will involve the rest of the class in learning about the group's topic, the group MUST include the following:

1. Copies for the whole class of a *visual* artifact from the period of American literary history that is the focus of the presentation. Examples may include but are certainly not restricted to maps, illustrations, artwork, facsimiles of historical documents, frontispieces from first editions of literary or cultural works, etc. The list of electronic resources at the Atkins Library is a good place to start.

2. A *brief* timeline (no more than 1 page) of major events and figures to provide a context of the 20 years prior to and the 20 years after the focus of the presentation. Copies for the whole class. The textbook's website has a Timeline that may be of use, but also consider some of the Atkins Library sites.

3. An *original transmediation*—an original artifact in a sign system OTHER THAN WRITTEN TEXT—constructed by the group to demonstrate their understanding of the topic and to aid the other students in arriving at a similar understanding. Examples of transmediations from past classes (not an exhaustive list): video/visual text, aural/musical text, culinary text, drama, dance, pantomime, etc.

4. A typed, written brief (~500 words; approximately 2 pages) that will be a resource/study guide for other students. Copies for the whole class.

ENGL 3300

Instructions for LITERATURE CIRCLES Engagement

 # in LC Group: 4-5

I. **The Process.** You and the other members of your group are responsible for establishing meeting times and organizing discussions about the text in preparation for the written 'brief' due on—2/19(for LC 1), 3/14 (for LC2), and 4/25 (for LC 3). To assist you in that process I have created the following roles for your group to assign to individual members. An individual member may take on more than one role, but **each** member must take on **at least** one role.

  a. Roles:

    i. <u>Historical Critic</u>. This person is responsible for finding any book reviews/critiques *contemporary to the book's initial publication* (within a year or two) and then sharing the content and focus of those reviews/critiques to the rest of the group. Some questions to think about as you do this: what were people saying about this book when it came out? What were they comparing it to? What recommendations, observations, or critiques did they make of the book? Why?

    ii. <u>Biographer</u>. This person digs into the author's life, finding and sharing whatever information she can with the rest of the group. Some questions to consider: What sort of life did the author have prior to the publication of this book? What experiences might be significant in thinking about the plot, theme, or meaning of the book?

    iii. <u>Real-world Connector</u>. This person keeps an eye on current events that may relate to issues or features of the book. Some things that the R-W Connector may want to think about: Are the events of today pre-figured or anticipated in some way by the book? What are events of today that might be the result of things mentioned in the book (changes for the better/worse; effects of past causes, etc)?

    iv. <u>Cultural Historian.</u> This person's task is to locate information about the time period and issues of the novel. Some questions to look at: what sort of social issues are important at this time, especially those that might have an impact on the book or the way that the contemporary audience would respond to it? What issues is the book trying to respond to or what social or cultural or literary trends may influence the way the book is written?

    v. <u>Moderator/Editor</u>. This person is responsible for making sure that the other members of the group assume the responsibilities of their roles and stay on task. She is also responsible for compiling the final product for presentation.

II. **The Product (Part 1).** For class on 2/19, your group should prepare a typed brief (1-2 pages) of your novel that you will distribute to the other members of class (make at least 30 copies [some groups may make fewer]—one for me and one for everyone not in your group). This brief should discuss what your group considers to be the most important or challenging part(s) of the novel in respect to a particular issue in American literature or other issue which emerges through the various roles. After thinking about these questions and ones your group itself raises, you are ready to write the brief. But there is a catch. You need to be able to do this in a way that is critical and comprehensive without totally giving away any of what might be key surprises in the novel. The hope is that these briefs will help individual readers determine which books they would like to read next as well as provide a resource guide for those who might be working on this book for their inquiry project.

III. **The Product (Part 2).** In addition to the typed brief, your book group should bring some three-dimensional artifact that will help demonstrate your understanding of the novel and that will support the claims of the brief.

ENGL 3300

Assessment Procedures and Criteria for GROUP PRESENTATIONS and LITERATURE CIRCLES:

You will receive a single grade for your literature circle/group presentation comprised of the following scores:

1. **Your self-assessment. (30 pts)**
2. **Group-assessment of you. (30 pts—average of the scores from each of your group members)**

These scores will be based on the feedback you and your peers provide for the following questions:

_____ (name) was involved in all aspects of the planning of the presentation / literature circle discussions

   not at all   fully involved
     1   2   3   4   5 $x2$ _____

_____ (name) contributed to the success of the presentation / literature circle discussions

   not at all   definitely; couldn't have succeeded without___
     1   2   3   4   5 $x2$ _____

_____ (name) helped other members of the group understand key issues of the presentation / novel

   not at all   definitely; we would have been lost without ___
     1   2   3   4   5 $x2$ _____

3. **Class-assessment of your group (20 pts—averaged from the scores of the class).**
4. **Instructor-assessment of your group (20 pts)**

These scores will be based upon the following questions:

-The presentation created an opportunity for others to learn and understand key issues about American literary history

   Not at all   definitely; the class knows things it didn't
                              know before
     1   2   3   4   5 $x2$____

-The presentation demonstrated creative, unique, or provocative thinking about key issues of American literary history

   Not at all   definitely; this group rocks!
     1   2   3   4   5 $x2$ _____

TOTAL POINTS: ____/100

ENGL 3300

Instructions for Critical Book Inquiry

In addition to the selections you make from Groups A, B, and C for the Literature Circle Groups, you will also select an additional text from among Group A, B, or C for your Critical Inquiry. The inquiry is an independent semester-long project and is designed to allow you to pursue your own question about American literature and/or a particular text. This inquiry will be in dialogue with the course themes and topics explored through our shared readings, but it will also be an opportunity for you to apply and extend your understanding of American literature to areas of interest to you that emerge from your independent reading and through research.

The topic of the inquiry will depend upon the questions you raise as you read your novel and how you pursue them, and so it will likely be different for each of you. The goal for each of you, however, will be similar:

- to produce a final written essay of at least 2000 words (approximately 8 pages, MLA format)
- that will draw from critical and historical sources (at least 5, cited in MLA format and also listed on a Works Cited page, which is not part of the 2000 word total for the inquiry),
- that will demonstrate an understanding of the text and its place within American Literary History, and
- that will focus on one or more of the following:
  - Historical/Cultural Influences and/or Impact
  - Literary Form/Development of Literary Genre/Form
  - Canonical Placement of Text / Challenge to Canonical Assumptions about Text.

To help you get to that end, I am providing the following basic guidelines and criteria. These should not be considered an exhaustive list, though they are meant to focus your approach to help you produce a successful paper.

As you read, consider how the text you choose responds to, challenges, exemplifies, complicates, or otherwise engages American Literary History. Investigate what others have said about this text, author, literary style/ genre, tradition, or period of American literature. In selecting sources, restrict yourself to the following two groups: 1) primary historical documents—ones contemporary to the period of the text's production, and 2) articles and books of literary criticism that are **peer-reviewed**. Indicate through your final project how your insights into the text, author, etc. derive from these sources **but also** how you are synthesizing these sources to offer new and interesting insights about your text, author, etc. When you are making points about what the text is doing or how it is working, make sure that you **quote directly from the text**. Avoid paraphrasing whenever possible, and always leave the last word in any paragraph for yourself and for your interpretations/analysis.

Assessment Criteria for CRITICAL INQUIRY PROJECT

To receive full credit for the final inquiry project, you will submit three versions of the inquiry over the course of the semester. (X Version 2/28; Y Version 3/26; Z Version 4/30).

___/5 pts for X Version Submission

___/5 pts for Y Version Submission

The remaining points will come from the Z Version Submission and will be based on the following instructor and student criteria:

Inquiry Project is free of errors in spelling, grammar, syntax, and mechanics:
No   Yes; ready for the public
 1 2 3   4   5 x2= ____/10 pts

Inquiry Project makes clear and appropriate use of multiple critical sources:
No   at least 5 5; MLA Yes; 5+; MLA
 1 2 3   4   5 x2= ____/10 pts

Inquiry Project demonstrates an understanding of course themes/topics
No   More or Less Yes; clearly knows Am. Lit.
 1 2 3   4   5 x3= ____/15 pts

Inquiry Project shows a command of the text's themes/topics
No   More or Less Yes; clearly read this multiple times
 1 2 3   4   5 x3=____/15 pts

Inquiry Project demonstrates thoughtful/original/provocative ways of thinking about and interpreting American Literature
No   Yes; a delight to read
 1   2 3   4   5 x3=____/15 pts

STUDENT ASSESSMENT (to be completed and submitted with the Z version)

While researching and writing this inquiry project I did work appropriate for an English major and worthy of an 'A' paper
No   Yes
 1 2 3   4   5 = ____/5 pts

While researching and writing this inquiry project I learned something interesting and/or important about American Literary History
No   Yes, couldn't have done it without this
 1 2 3   4   5 x2=____/10 pts

People reading my inquiry project will learn something interesting and/or important about American Literary History
No   Yes, they will be better for reading it
 1 2 3   4   5 x2=____/10 pts

TOTAL____/100pts

Appendix 4.2: Exams and Engagements for American Literature

The questions below are representative of some of the ways that I invite students to make sense of their experiences with American literature. These essays are take-home and complement an in-class identification of short selections from the readings. What's important about this particular format for me is the creation of multiple options for each area of response, and the provision of resources from different media that will allow students to play to their strengths as readers, writers, and thinkers. I also try to include what students call the "creative options," which I model on the case or scenario approach of other disciplines, allowing them to imagine alternative scenarios in which questions of American literature might have some bearing on real world outcomes. Admittedly, some of these options are deliberately fanciful, and the students who choose them have found they offer a respite from the more serious-seeming work of academic study. The centers and websites mentioned in these options, however, are quite real—though the initiatives and technologies described do not, as of this writing, correspond to any real events or items. I invite you to borrow and modify them as they may suit your own classrooms.

Spring 2005

All exams must be submitted electronically via WebCT. Send as an attached document. Attachments not in *.doc or *.rtf format will not be read. All essays must be typed, double-spaced, and follow MLA conventions for format and citations.

> Read the following statement, and attach it to the final exam:
> On my honor, I have neither given nor received assistance on any portion of this exam. All answers are my own.
> Signed,
> _____ [Type in your full name]

Choose <u>one</u> option from <u>each</u> section below. Each response should result in an essay of 500-750 words. You should have THREE essays total, one from each section. You MUST make explicit reference to the text through *direct quotes* for evidence to support your responses. For each of the questions you may also use the links on WebCT for "Visions of America" (Images/Songs/Texts for use with Exam 2).

Question 1: Imagining Americans

Option A: In Letter III of his *Letters from an American Farmer*, Crèvecoeur poses the following question: "What, then, is the American, this new man?" (444). How does his attempt to formulate an answer map out the characteristics of the "American" for him and for later writers? In what way(s) does Crèvecoeur's definition limit or expand the possibilities for later attempts to describe the "American"? (Use at least one additional text.)

Option B: William Bradford's *Of Plymouth Plantation* offers an extended narrative account of an emergent "American" community that makes particular use of the Puritan interpretive strategy of *typology* (165) to explain the founding and settling of the Massachusetts Bay Colony. What typological figures are most central to Bradford's narrative? In what way(s) do these figures become particular "types" of "Americans"? (Use at least one additional text.)

Option C: In his *Autobiography*, Benjamin Franklin provides a recollection of a life that subsequent generations and readers from other nations have come to see as defining "the American self and culture" (367). What are the particular events, characteristics, and/or *errata* (as Franklin calls his missteps) that seem to capture this sense of *the* "American" self and culture? How does this Franklinesque sense of the American emerge in other texts? (Use at least one additional text.)

Option D: Emerson's "The American Scholar" argues for a new way of conceiving of the roles and aims of humans, which he suggests through the phrase *Man Thinking*. Who is this creature? What characterizes its thinking? What impact does such an image have for other attempts to understand the nature and identity of the "American"?

Question 2: Narratives of American Salvation/Transformation

Option A: The *Relation of Alvar Nuñez Cabeza de Vaca* is among the first captivity narratives set in North America. How does Cabeza de Vaca describe the process of being saved or delivered from his captivity? What events seem most central to his transformation? How do later/ other narratives of cultural encounter and/or captivity characterize the process of transformation? What is gained/lost in such transformations? (Use at least one other text.)

Option B: The story of La Llorona emerges from the colonial enterprises in New Spain, and continues to recur in new forms in a variety of media even today. How do the changes that emerge in each new version/telling of the La Llorona tale alter what it means to be American, gendered, and/or faithful to one's cultural identity? What do such transformations suggest about how this and/or other stories create meaning?

Option C: Using at least two of Phillis Wheatley's poems, consider the way(s) in which her poetry articulates an economy of salvation. What are the agents of redemption? And from what does she imagine "America" needs to be redeemed? How do Wheatley's poems seek to challenge or confirm her contemporaries' sense of what it means to be an American?

Option D: In *Walden* Thoreau claims that "I went to the woods because I wished to live deliberately . . . and not, when I came to die, discover that I had not lived" (771). What does he mean? Why is such a move necessary or desirable? What does such a perspective allow one to see about America that was not visible before? How is such a transformation possible for others? (Use at least one other text.)

Question 3: Fashioning American Literary Landscapes

Option A: Using new technologies derived from the application of Precision Metrology (developed by the brilliant minds at the UNC Charlotte Center for Optoelectronics and Optical Communications [http:// opticscenter.uncc.edu/]) to the Transcendental realm, you are able to create a lightweight pair of goggles that allows its wearers to experience the vision of Emerson's *transparent eyeball*. The apparatus can be worn for no more than twenty-four hours, however, without significant (though not certain) risk of permanently degraded vision resulting, in some cases, in total blindness within minutes after the twenty-fourth hour. If you dare, become the transparent eyeball for a day in your life at UNC Charlotte. What do you see or know or understand about the world that you did not before? How are things altered or revealed through this visionary experience?

Option B: Drawing from the readings (and other texts of your choosing), map out (literally or figuratively) the terrain of American literature. What does this landscape look like? How is it populated? Who lives next to whom and why? What might they have in common or talk about to each other? How might one best orient oneself to this range of literature? (Note: visual components of this option need not be submitted electronically but may be turned in as hard copies.)

Option C: Create your own original visual representation of an American Landscape. The representation may take whatever form you think appropriate, but it should demonstrate in some way a theme central to American literature in general.

Spring 2007

Final should be typed, double-spaced, and should adhere to MLA format for citations and document format. Final page lengths will vary depending on the option you choose, but a good target length to aim for will be between eight and ten pages (which has been the average total length for the last two exams).

Append the following statement to the final:

On my honor, I have neither given nor received assistance on this exam. All answers are my own.
Signed _____
[type your name]
Date_____

For each of the options below, you may use any of the images on the course site under the "Visions of America" link for Exam 3. **Through direct citation**, answers **must** refer to authors and texts we have read since Exam 2 and *may also* include references to texts from earlier authors from any point in the semester. In all cases your responses should in some way address the following general questions: What is "American literature" for? Who is it for? What makes it distinctly "American"?

Option A: Canons and Consequences for the Study of American Literature

Throughout the semester we have circled around a particular conundrum that besets any survey class, but perhaps especially plagues a one-semester survey course in *American* literature: what constitutes the *canon* of American literature and what should that canon continue to be? From one perspective, canons are made up of indispensable texts that articulate the core values of a tradition; from another perspective, canons are provisional groupings of texts that may change as traditions and values change. One might further argue that the notion of a canon (from either perspective) exists only insofar as the texts that are part of an apparent tradition continue to be taught and read in *authorized* and *institutional* settings (college/university survey courses, high school curricula, and so on). So from this perspective, what one reads outside of these settings cannot make legitimate claim to the tradition.

For this option, I invite you to argue: (1) for the continued inclusion of *two* texts/authors (at least one from this last section of the course) that you consider to be indispensable to an understanding of American literature; (2) for the exclusion or replacement of at least *one* text (from any portion of the course), providing a rationale from the same criteria; and (3) for the addition of *at least one* text (either from the independent reading or the anthology, or another text you are familiar with but which is not part of the anthology) to the list of texts to be used in a semester-long survey of American literature. Remember to make use of direct citation from any texts used.

Option B: Colloquy on the Art and Nature of American Literature

Many of you have noted throughout your postings and in class conversations that being able to talk with others about texts encountered in common has been especially important in helping you form your own understanding of American literature and culture. Imagine this same sort of conversation occurring in other contexts, with different interlocutors, and while trying to discover the meaning of artwork from other media. How might that conversation go?

For this option, imagine that you and a group of your American literature classmates and/or author friends find yourselves in an art gallery (use the "Visions of America"—Images for Exam 3 link) trying to determine which (if any) of the pieces on display is artistic, distinctly American, and indispensable to understanding American literature and culture. I invite you to enlist the words (through direct quotes) of at least four authors from our readings (at least two from this section of the course).

Option C: Designing Texts for American Literature

Through a National Endowment for the Humanities/American Memory Challenge grant (www.loc.gov) the North Carolina Center for Applied Textile Technology (www.nccatt.org) in Gaston County—it really does exist!—has received funds to construct a series of educational outreach exhibitions. These will weave together the words of a representative group of American authors to create a series of artifacts, which will offer enduring perspectives on the meaning of American literature. The grant stipulates that the artifacts should be able to travel around the state of North Carolina (but also around the world) and be viewed by a broad audience. The goal is to offer both an *artistic* and *educational* experience to a diverse set of readers/viewers so that the experience of witnessing/viewing/reading these artifacts will help them to understand something indispensable about American literature and culture, but also about themselves in relation to these artifacts.

For this option, your task is two-fold: (1) construct a new text—made up of the threads and strands of existing texts (at least two of which should be from this last section of the course)—that will become this artifact. This may be short or long, depending on your artistic vision and educational goals for the piece; and (2) provide a written rationale (of at least 1000 words) for the inclusion of your new text into the Center for Applied Textile Technology's traveling exhibit. This rationale should locate the key elements of American literature and culture that are central to the project and explain how this artifact will help generate an understanding of the meaning of American literature.

Appendix 5: Blackbirds and Backpacks

Below you'll find the full text of Stevens's "Thirteen Ways of Looking at a Blackbird" and full descriptions of the reflective and literacy engagements I used in my English Methods courses for initial and advanced licensure candidates. They are adapted from activities available through the NCTE Reading Initiative and CoLEARN Writing Initiative. I am grateful to Barbara Comber for introducing me to the work of Pat Thomson and to the concept of the "virtual schoolbag."

Appendix 5.1: Wallace Stevens, "Thirteen Ways of Looking at a Blackbird"

I
Among twenty snowy mountains,
The only moving thing
Was the eye of the blackbird.

II
I was of three minds,
Like a tree
In which there are three blackbirds.

III
The blackbird whirled in the autumn winds.
It was a small part of the pantomime.

IV
A man and a woman
Are one.
A man and a woman and a blackbird
Are one.

V
I do not know which to prefer,
The beauty of inflections
Or the beauty of innuendoes,
The blackbird whistling
Or just after.

VI
Icicles filled the long window
With barbaric glass.
The shadow of the blackbird
Crossed it, to and fro.
The mood
Traced in the shadow
An indecipherable cause.

VII
O thin men of Haddam,
Why do you imagine golden birds?
Do you not see how the blackbird
Walks around the feet
Of the women about you?

VIII
I know noble accents
And lucid, inescapable rhythms;
But I know, too,
That the blackbird is involved
In what I know.

IX
When the blackbird flew out of sight,
It marked the edge
Of one of many circles.

X
At the sight of blackbirds
Flying in a green light,
Even the bawds of euphony
Would cry out sharply.

XI
He rode over Connecticut
In a glass coach.
Once, a fear pierced him,
In that he mistook
The shadow of his equipage
For blackbirds.

XII
The river is moving.
The blackbird must be flying.

XIII
It was evening all afternoon.
It was snowing
And it was going to snow.
The blackbird sat
In the cedar-limbs.

Appendix 5.2: Dialogue Journal Instructions from ENGL 4254/5254 Syllabus Spring 2007

Dialogue Journals/Shared Independent Reading Reflection (10%): At the beginning of the semester you will each make a recommendation for a young adult novel, literary text, or other work of fiction that you have recommended to others (or have had recommended to you). This may be a book that you would like to teach in your own classroom some day, but it need not be. Based on these recommendations, you will find a partner who has been convinced of your recommendation or who shares your interest in the text(s). Together you will read this text on your own, keeping an ongoing reading response log of your experience. This log should take the form of a *dialogue journal* in which you write "response letters" to each other about your reading. These letters do not need to take a particular form, but they should be substantive and engage the text(s) and the other reader in conversation about the work(s) as well as make connections to relevant readings and discussions from the course (between 150 and 200 words per "letter" is a good range). You will be expected to exchange these journals every time we meet in class. I will collect these journals at least twice during the semester (un-announced). A final critical reflection on the experience considered in light of the course readings will be due Monday, April 16.

Appendix 5.3: Literacy Dig Assignment

Literacy Dig Procedures — (X Version due 1/29/2007)

I. Background Information (from NCTE Reading Initiative, 2001)

In an article on the ways in which literacy activities are embedded in the ordinary activities of our everyday lives, David Barton (1989) writes:

> In going about their ordinary daily lives, people today are constantly encountering literacy. For someone waking up in Lancashire, England, tomorrow, the first voice he or she will hear in the morning might well be someone reading a written text, a news reader on the radio. Going downstairs, he or she finds a newspaper on the doormat along with some mail, at least glancing at these. Even before this English person's first cup of tea, there have been two literacy events quite different from each other. We could continue through the day with shopping, consulting a calendar, following the instructions for using a new watch, writing a check, on through to leaving a note for the milkman as a final task at night.

Denny Taylor further reminds us that the act of reading or writing is not usually the focus of print activity rather the focus is the accomplishment of some task: "I'm continually pushing my thinking to develop more in-depth understandings of the plurality of literacies that are a part of our everyday lives. Many of us have been acculturated into definitions of literacy that are based upon school interpretations of what it means to be literate" (1994).

II. The Experience (what to do and how to do it)

Schedule some time where you live to dig for evidence of literacy—yours, your family's, roommate's, partner's, and/or that of other members of your house, building, or workplace.

Start in the kitchen, dining area, or other common area, and work your way through the house or building, collecting artifacts as you go. *Dig* is the operative word here. Don't just go for the big, visible items like newspapers and books; scraps of paper and sticky notes may tell you a lot about how literacy weaves its way through your life, your routines, your relationships.

After scouring the house, go through your purse or wallet to find additional treasures. After collecting a range of artifacts, divide a piece of paper into three equal columns to record your findings.

In the first column, simply list the artifacts; in the second column, write the function(s) that the reading/writing experience (represented by the artifact) served in your life or in the life of a member of your household;

in the third column, if the artifact represents a reading experience, write the strategies you used to help make meaning.

Share your artifacts, functions, and strategies with your colleagues (this you will do in your X version).

For future versions and further examination: Reflect on and record the insights you have gained regarding reading process and literacy. What might this mean for your classroom(s)? How might this experience begin to change your definitions of reading and literacy?

Appendix 5.4: Virtual Schoolbag Profile

Virtual Schoolbag Assignment
X Version submitted to PRG
Y Version due

All papers should be 1200–1300 words, typed and double-spaced, and in MLA format.

I will have placed four example papers from previous classes on e-reserve at the library. These are offered to suggest the range of responses taken by students in the past. I have also placed essays by Luis Moll, Pat Thomson, and Deborah Hicks on reserve that I think should be useful in helping you to think more broadly and critically about what happens when student knowledge (developed and acquired through home, cultural, and friendship structures) comes into contact with the expectations for school knowledge and performance within the classroom.

Each of your papers will be different in that the students you are profiling come from a variety of cultural and knowledge backgrounds. Your papers will share, however, a common purpose (and perhaps a common format) in your analysis of how the confrontation between home and school knowledges matters in the educational situation. In fact, your general theses will likely be very similar, not unlike the paragraph below (adapted from what Pat Thomson says in the opening of her article, and later about one of the students she is profiling, and from the objectives for you in this course):

> Imagine two children about to start school. They are both five years old and are eagerly anticipating their first day. Imagine that each of them brings with them to school a virtual schoolbag full of things that they already learned at home, with their friends and from the world in which they live . . . Both children's schoolbags contain roughly equal but different knowledges, narratives, and interests . . . Their teachers must . . . have a repertoire of pedagogical practices that will connect children to knowledges that count through work with the resources that the children bring with them . . . But . . . the congruence between [a student's] schoolbag and the school curriculum, and [the student's] ease in the school setting" put one student at a decided advantage over the other. This disparity raises particular issues for the critically reflective and culturally responsive educator committed to the learning of all students. (Thompson 4)

This opening suggests something of the particular kinds of knowledge that will be discussed; it indicates that those knowledges may be beneficial or deleterious to the student once the student enters the social and institutional environment of the school; and it points to questions that will be raised later as potential topics for future inquiry.

WORKS CITED

Anzaldúa, Gloria. *Borderlands/La Frontera: The New Mestiza*. San Francisco: Spinsters/Aunt Lute, 1987.

Applebee, Arthur N. *Literature in the Secondary School: Studies of Curriculum and Instruction in the United States*. Urbana, IL: NCTE, 1993.

Bauman, Amy, and Art Peterson, eds. *Breakthroughs: Classroom Discoveries about Teaching Writing*. Berkeley: National Writing Project, 2002.

The Bay Psalm Book. Lauter 198–205.

Berkeley, George. *The Works of George Berkeley: Including his Posthumous Works*. 4 vols. Oxford: Clarendon P, 1901.

Bernstein, Richard J. *Beyond Objectivism and Relativism: Science, Hermeneutics, and Praxis*. Philadelphia: U of Pennsylvania P, 1983.

Blau, Sheridan. *The Literature Workshop: Teaching Texts and Their Readers*. Portsmouth, NH: Heinemann, 2003.

Bourdieu, Pierre. *The Field of Cultural Production*. New York: Columbia UP, 1993.

Brannon, Lil, et al. *Thinking Out Loud on Paper: The Student Daybook as Tool to Foster Learning*. Portsmouth, NH: Heinemann, 2008.

Buehler, Jennifer. "The Power of Questions and the Possibilities of Inquiry in English Education." *English Education* 37.4 (2005): 280-87.

Carey, Alice [Alice Cary]. "Peter Harris." *The Ladies' Repository, and Gatherings of the West* 11.3 (1851): 102–104. 28 Mar. 2008. <http://name.umdl.umich.edu/acg2248.1-11.003>.

Cary, Alice. *Clovernook, or, Recollections of Our Neighborhood in the West*. New York: Redfield, 1852.

———. *Clovernook, or, Recollections of Our Neighborhood in the West.* 2nd series. New York: Redfield, 1853.

———. *Clovernook Sketches and Other Stories.* Ed. Judith Fetterley. New Brunswick: Rutgers UP, 1987.

———. "A Passing Wish." *Harper's New Monthly Magazine* 40.235 (1869): 31. 26 Mar. 2008. <http://cdl.library.cornell.edu/cgi-bin/moa/moa-cgi?notisid=ABK4014-0040-5>.

———. "The Washerwoman." Walker 169.

Collins, James, and Richard K. Blot. *Literacy and Literacies: Texts, Power, and Identity.* Cambridge: Cambridge UP, 2003.

Columbus, Christopher. *Journal of the First Voyage to America, 1492–1493* [Selections]. Lauter 49–56.

Conference on English Education. "What Do We Know and Believe about the Role of Methods Courses and Field Experiences in English Education?" *ncte.org.* 1998–2008. National Council of Teachers of English. 28 Mar. 2008. <http://www.ncte.org/groups/cee/positions/122928.htm>.

———. "What Is English Education?" *ncte.org.* 1998–2008. National Council of Teachers of English. 28 Mar. 2008. <http://www.ncte.org/groups/cee/positions/122898.htm>.

Cope, Bill, and Mary Kalantzis, eds. *Multiliteracies: Literacy Learning and the Design of Social Futures.* London: Routledge, 2000.

Critters Home: "Opossum." *myfwc.com.* 2008. Florida Fish and Wildlife Conservation Commission. 27 Mar. 2008. <http://myfwc.com/critters/opossum.htm>.

de Certeau, Michel. *The Practice of Everyday Life.* Trans. Steven Randall. Berkeley: U of California P, 1984.

de la Cruz, Sor Juana Inés. *Poems, Protest, and a Dream.* Trans. Margaret Sayers Peden. New York: Penguin, 1997.

Dewey, John. *Democracy and Education: An Introduction to the Philosophy of Education.* 1916. New York: Free Press, 1997.

———. *John Dewey on Education: Selected Writings.* Ed. Reginald Archambault. Chicago: U of Chicago P, 1964.

———. "My Pedagogic Creed." 1897. *John Dewey on Education.* 427–39.

"Divining America: Religion and National Culture." *national humanitiescenter.org*. March 2008. National Humanities Center: TeacherServe. 27 Mar. 2008. <http://nationalhumanitiescenter.org/tserve/divam.htm>.

Emerson, Ralph Waldo. "Circles." *Pragmatism: A Contemporary Reader*. Ed. Russell B. Goodman. New York: Routledge, 1995. 25–34.

———. *Nature* [Selections]. Lauter 691–94.

Fecho, Bob, Peg Graham, and Sally Hudson-Ross. "Appreciating the Wobble: Teacher Research, Professional Development, and Figured Worlds." *English Education* 37.3 (2005): 174–99.

Feldman, Sandra. "Shaping Our Future." White House Conference on Preparing Tomorrow's Teachers. *ed.gov*. 23 August 2003. U.S. Department of Education. 28 Mar. 2008. <www.ed.gov/admins/tchrqual/learn/preparingteachersconference/feldman.html>.

Fetterley, Judith. "Teaching and 'My Work.'" *American Literary History* 17.4 (2005): 741–52.

Fetterley, Judith, and Marjorie Pryse. *Writing out of Place: Regionalism, Women, and American Literary Culture*. Urbana: U of Illinois P, 2003.

Fishman, Stephen, and Lucille McCarthy. *John Dewey and the Challenge of Classroom Practice*. New York: Teachers College P, 1998.

Flannery, Kathryn, et al. "Watch This Space; or, Why We Have Not Revised the Teacher Education Program—Yet." Franklin, Laurence, and Welles 49–64.

Fleischer, Cathy. *Composing Teacher-Research: A Prosaic History*. Albany: SUNY P, 1995.

———. *Teachers Organizing for Change: Making Literacy Learning Everybody's Business*. Urbana, IL: NCTE, 2000.

Fleischer, Cathy, and Dana L. Fox. "Beginning Words: Envisioning the Future of English Education." *English Education* 37.4 (2005): 255–61.

Foster, Harold. "English in Education: An English Educationist at Work." McCracken and Larson 260–68.

Franklin, Benjamin. "The Way to Wealth." *Poor Richard's Almanack*. Lauter 367–72.

Works Cited

Franklin, Phyllis, David Laurence, and Elizabeth B. Welles, eds. *Preparing a Nation's Teachers: Models for English and Foreign Language Programs*. New York: MLA, 1999.

Frost, Robert. *The Poetry of Robert Frost*. Ed. Edward Connery Lathem. New York: Holt, Rinehart, and Winston, 1969.

Gee, James P. *An Introduction to Discourse Analysis: Theory and Method*. 2nd ed. New York: Routledge, 2005.

Graham, Peg, ct al., eds. *Teacher/Mentor: A Dialogue for Collaborative Learning*. New York: Teachers College P, 1999.

Graham, Peg, Sally Hudson-Ross, et al. "Collaborative Teacher Education for the 21st Century." *English Education* 33.2 (2001): 126–35.

Graves, Donald. "Trust the Shadows." *Reading Teacher* 45.1 (1991): 18–24.

Gray, Donald. "Introduction: What Happens Next? And How? And Why?" Franklin, Laurence, and Welles 1–11.

Grossman, Pamela. *The Making of a Teacher: Teacher Knowledge and Teacher Education*. New York: Teachers College P, 1990.

Harriot, Thomas. *A Briefe and True Report of the New Found Land of Virginia* [Selections]. Lauter 120–25.

Harste, Jerome, and Christine Leland. "On Getting Lost, Finding One's Direction, and Teacher Research." *Voices from the Middle* 14.3 (2007): 7–11.

Hautman, Pete. *Godless*. New York: Simon and Schuster, 2004.

"History of the Miraculous Apparition of the Virgin of Guadalupe in 1531." Lauter 72–80.

Hubbard, Ruth Shagoury, and Brenda Miller Power. *The Art of Classroom Inquiry: A Handbook for Teacher-Researchers*. Portsmouth, NH: Heinemann, 1993.

Hughes, Langston. "Harlem." Lauter 2011.

Knoblauch, C. H., and Lil Brannon. *Critical Teaching and the Idea of Literacy*. Portsmouth, NH: Boyton/Cook, 1993.

Kucer, Stephen B. *Dimensions of Literacy: A Conceptual Base for Teaching Reading and Writing in School Settings*. 2nd ed. Mahwah, NJ: Lawrence Erlbaum, 2005.

Lacan, Jacques. *Écrits: A Selection.* Trans. Alan Sheridan. New York: W. W. Norton, 1977.

Lalement, Father Jerome. *The Relations of 1647.* Lauter 109–16.

Lauter, Paul, ed. *Heath Anthology of American Literature: Concise Edition.* Boston: Houghton Mifflin, 2004.

Le Clercq, Chrestien. *First Establishment of the Faith in New France, Vol. 1.* Ed. and trans. John Gilmary Shea, 2 vols. New York: John G. Shea, 1881. <http://www.alexanderstreet4.com/cgi-bin/asp/eena/imageidx.pl?image_id=S9186-I01&showfullrecord=yes>.

Livingston, Carol, and Hilda Borko. "Expert-Novice Differences in Teaching: A Cognitive Analysis and Implications for Teacher Education." *Journal of Teacher Education* 40.4 (1989): 36–42.

Luke, Alan. "The Trouble with English." *Research in the Teaching of English* (2004): 85–95.

Marshall, James. "Closely Reading Ourselves: Teaching English and the Education of Teachers." Franklin, Laurence, and Welles 380–89.

Mayher, John. *Uncommon Sense: Theoretical Practice in Language Education.* Portsmouth, NH: Boynton/Cook, 1990.

McCann, Thomas M., Larry R. Johannessen, and Bernard P. Ricca. *Supporting Beginning English Teachers: Research and Implications for Teacher Induction.* Urbana, IL: NCTE, 2005.

McComisky, Bruce, ed. *English Studies: An Introduction to the Discipline(s).* Urbana, IL: NCTE, 2006.

McCracken, H. Thomas, and Richard L. Larson (with Judith Entes), eds. *Teaching College English and English Education: Reflective Stories.* Urbana, IL: CEE/NCTE, 1998.

Menand, Louis. *The Metaphysical Club: A Story of Ideas in America.* New York: Farrar, Straus, & Giroux, 2001.

Miller, Nancy K. *Subject to Change: Reading Feminist Writing.* New York: Columbia UP, 1988.

Monk, David H. "Subject Area Preparation of Secondary Mathematics and Science Teachers and Student Achievement." *Economics of Education Review* 13.2 (1994): 125–45.

Morson, Gary Saul. *Narrative and Freedom: The Shadows of Time.* New Haven: Yale UP, 1994.

NCTE's Standing Committee on Teacher Preparation and Certification, Robert C. Small Jr., Chair. *Guidelines for the Preparation of Teachers of English Language Arts.* Urbana, IL: NCTE, 1996.

The New England Primer. Lauter 198–205.

No Child Left Behind: A Toolkit for Teachers. U.S. Department of Education ([2003] 2004). *ed.gov.* 2004. U.S. Department of Education. 28 Mar. 2008. <www.ed.gov/teachers/nclbguide/nclb-teachers-toolkit.pdf>.

"The Origin of Stories." Lauter 30–32.

Pradl, Gordon. "Disrupting the Transmission Cycle in College Teaching." McCracken and Larson 115–26.

Rich, Adrienne. "Diving into the Wreck." Lauter 2347–48.

Ricouer, Paul. *Time and Narrative.* 3 vols. Trans. Kathleen McLaughlin and David Pellauer. Chicago: U of Chicago P, 1990.

Ritchie, Joy S., and David E. Wilson. *Teacher Narrative as Critical Inquiry: Rewriting the Script.* New York: Teachers College P, 2000.

Rosenblatt, Louise. *Making Meaning with Texts: Selected Essays.* Portsmouth, NH: Heinemann, 2005.

Roskelly, Hephzibah. "Still Bridges to Build: English Education's Pragmatic Agenda." *English Education* 37.4 (2005): 288–95.

Rowlandson, Mary White [Talcott]. *A Narrative of the Captivity and Restauration of Mrs. Mary Rowlandson* [Selections]. Lauter 208–31.

Short, Kathy G., Jerome C. Harste, with Carolyn L. Burke. *Creating Classrooms for Authors and Inquirers.* 2nd ed. Portsmouth, NH: Heinemann, 1996.

Shumway, David R. "Emerson and the Shape of American Literature." Shumway and Dione 99–114.

Shumway, David R., and Craig Dionne, eds. *Disciplining English: Alternative Histories, Critical Perspectives.* Albany: SUNY Press, 2002.

Smagorinsky, Peter, and Melissa E. Whiting. *How English Teachers Get Taught: Methods of Teaching the Methods Class.* Urbana, IL: NCTE, 1995.

Stenberg, Shari. *Professing and Pedagogy: Learning the Teaching of English*. Urbana, IL: NCTE, 2005.

Stevens, Wallace. *Collected Poems of Wallace Stevens*. New York: Knopf, 1954. 92–94.

Swiencicki, Jill. "The Rhetoric of Awareness Narratives." *College English* 68.4 (2006): 337–55.

Thomson, Pat. *Schooling the Rust Belt Kids: Making the Difference in Changing Times*. Sydney: Allen and Unwin, 2003.

Thoreau, Henry David. "Resistance to Civil Government." Lauter 751–65.

Tierney, Bob. "Let's Take Another Look at the Fish: The Writing Process as Discovery." Bauman and Peterson 9–17.

Tzara, Tristan. "Lecture on Dada." 1922. *The Dada Painters and Poets: An Anthology*. Ed. Robert Motherwell. 2nd ed. Cambridge, MA: Belknap Press, 1989. 246–51.

Urbanski, Cynthia. *Using the Workshop Approach in the High School English Classroom: Modeling Effective Writing, Reading, and Thinking Strategies for Student Success*. Thousand Oaks, CA: Corwin, 2005.

Walker, Cheryl, ed. *American Women Poets of the Nineteenth Century*. New Brunswick: Rutgers UP, 1992.

Welch, Nancy. "Sideshadowing Teacher Response." *College English* 60.4 (1998): 374–95.

Wheatley, Phillis. "To the University of Cambridge in New England." Lauter 576.

Whitman, Walt. *Leaves of Grass*. 1891-92. New York: Oxford UP, 1990.

———. *Song of Myself*. 1855. Lauter 1225–76.

Wilder, Burt. "Beast, Bird, and Fish." *Harper's New Monthly Magazine* 40.235 (1869): 21–32. 26 Mar. 2008. <http://cdl.library.cornell.edu/cgi-bin/moa/moa-cgi?notisid=ABK4014-0040-4>.

Williams, William Carlos. *The Collected Poems of William Carlos Williams*. 2 vols. Ed. A. Walton Litz, and Christopher MacGowan. New York: New Directions, 1986–88.

_____. *Selected Essays of William Carlos Williams*. New York: Random House, 1969.

Wright, James. *Above the River: The Complete Poems*. New York: Farrar, Straus, and Giroux, 1992.

Yagelski, Robert P. "English Education." McComisky 275–319.

———. *Literacy Matters: Writing and Reading the Social Self*. New York: Teachers College P, 2000.

———. "Stasis and Change: English Education and the Crisis of Sustainability." *English Education* 37.4 (2005): 262–71.

INDEX

AUTHOR

Photo by Randy Mascharka

John A. Staunton is assistant professor of English literature and language at Eastern Michigan University, where he teaches courses in English education and literary studies. Since 2000 he has worked with secondary and post-secondary teachers in local and national teacher-research networks in Indiana, Georgia, Pennsylvania, and Massachusetts, and from 2004 to 2007 he taught in the National Writing Project site at UNC Charlotte. His research on literature and the teaching of literature has appeared in *Journal of Adolescent and Adult Literacy*, *Journal of Teaching Writing*, *Studies in American Fiction*, and *Religion and Literature*. He lives in Ypsilanti, Michigan.

*This book was typeset in Sabon by Electronic Imaging.
Typefaces used on the cover include Trade Gothic Condensed Oblique
and Van Dijck Small Caps.
The book was printed on 50-lb. Williamsburg Offset paper
by Versa Press, Inc.*